The Human Vocal Tract

THE HUMAN VOCAL TRACT: ANATOMY, FUNCTION, DEVELOPMENT, AND EVOLUTION

by

Edmund S. Crelin, Ph.D., D. Sc.

Professor and Chief
Section of Human Anatomy and Development
Departments of Surgery and Orthopedics and Rehabilitation
Yale University School of Medicine
Chairman
Human Growth and Development Study Unit
Yale-New Haven Medical Center

VANTAGE PRESS
New York / Washington / Atlanta
Los Angeles / Chicago

TO THE MANY GRADUATE AND MEDICAL STUDENTS
FOR WHOM I SERVED AS A DISSERTATION OR THESIS ADVISER
AT YALE

In order to advise them, I was often compelled to broaden my scientific
horizons by going beyond my immediate areas of expertise.

Contents

Preface

In the 1950s my surgical colleagues in the section of otolaryngology (ear, nose, and throat) at Yale advised me to quit smoking because they were convinced it was the chief cause of the high rate of cancer of the larynx seen in their patients. It didn't take much for me to heed their advice because I was teaching the resident physicians in otolaryngology all of the detailed anatomy of the neck structures that are removed in what is known as a radical neck operation, when a cancerous larynx is excised. It was around this time that I also became aware that some of the people who had had their larynges removed were learning to talk by belching air they swallowed into their esophagus. This intrigued me because, up to that time, when I lectured to the medical students on the functions of the larynx, I had naively assumed that speech was not possible without a larynx. Although there were published studies that gave clues as to how speech could occur without a larynx, they were not then generally known, even to the otolaryngologists.

It was not until 1970 that I began to make a concerted effort to satisfy my curiosity about speech production in human beings. Even then it was a project peripheral to my main research interests of many years, which were concerned with the response of connective tissue cells to hormones and trauma. Since I undertook my first scientific research project in 1947, I have been prone to do the type of experiment that opens the door to the solution of particular problems. Rather than continue to try to narrowly investigate a problem in great detail for a long period of time, I have preferred to leave that to other researchers who have the necessary patience, tenacity, and ingenuity—attributes fundamental to Nobel laureates.

Over a fourteen-year period, I compiled sufficient data from a number of different, door-opening experiments in my research on the vocal tract to put them in the form of a videotape series in 1982. Publishing my research findings in this format was relatively expensive, and it required a videotape player and monitor to view the tapes. Therefore, to make my research findings more accessible to all interested people, especially students, I wrote this book. Much of the data is new. I trust they will inspire some budding investigators to delve more deeply and either extend some of my research findings, answering some of the many questions I have raised, or devise experiments that will corroborate or refute the hypotheses I have made based upon my findings. Hopefully, uninitiated readers will gain insight into how human beings are able to talk, why speech is unique to human beings, when the human ancestors were first able to talk, and the profound influence speech has had on the development of human intelligence. None of this would be possible without my devoted secretary, Mrs. June Connolly, who transformed my rough draft scribblings into a legible, typewritten form. I am indebted to my colleagues at Yale, Dr. Leon Kier, a neuroradiologist, and Dr. Daniel Snyder, a neuropsychologist, for allowing me to study the vocal tracts of the many diverse animals used for their research on the brain.

E. S. Crelin
New Haven, Connecticut

The Human Vocal Tract

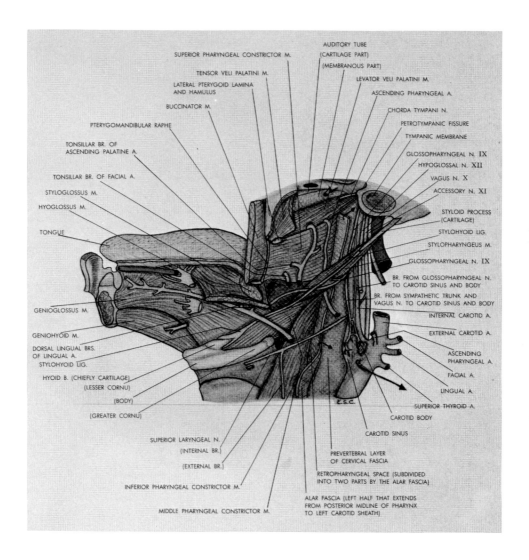

Figure 1. A lateral view of a drawing of a dissection of the left upper neck region of a human newborn infant. The removal of the left side of the mandible exposes the tongue located entirely within the oral cavity. The left lateral muscular wall of the pharynx is also exposed. *From Crelin (1969).*

Chapter 1

Introduction

After a period of six years, I completed the dissections and drawings of the anatomy of human newborn infants. Perfect reproductions of my pencil drawings were made in full color at the Polychrome Press of Princeton, New Jersey. Lea and Febiger of Philadelphia, Pennsylvania, published them in 1969 in the form of a beautiful book (Crelin 1969). Since the book was the first of its kind, every dissection was to me equivalent to original research experiments, and I made many personal discoveries. There were no courses offered at Yale on human newborn anatomy when I trained to be an anatomist. When I illustrated the structures related to the tongue and larynx in the newborn infant, I placed them high in the neck (Figure 1). I also placed the entire tongue within the oral cavity and the soft palate in a close relationship with the epiglottis, even when I pulled the tongue down from its position at rest (Figure 2). At that time I was quite unaware of the significance of the marked difference between the positions and relationships of the above newborn structures and those of an adult human being. It was not until a short time after the book was published that I first became aware of it.

Dr. Philip Lieberman, who was then a professor of linguistics and electrical engineering at the University of Connecticut, came to the medical school at Yale and asked if there was anyone who was familiar with the anatomy of the human newborn. He was directed to my laboratory. As I recall, Dr. Lieberman studied audiotapes of chimpanzee vocalizations from Rockefeller University and found that they were very similar to recorded vocalizations of human newborn babies he had acquired from the National Institutes of Health. He asked if I knew why. I admitted that I had no idea, but told him I would look into it. After he left, the first thing I did was take an adult chimpanzee skull I had in my laboratory and compare it with a number of human newborn skulls. Although the large chimp skull bore little resemblance to the little human newborn skulls when the top and sides were viewed, I immediately saw a striking and basic similarity when

1

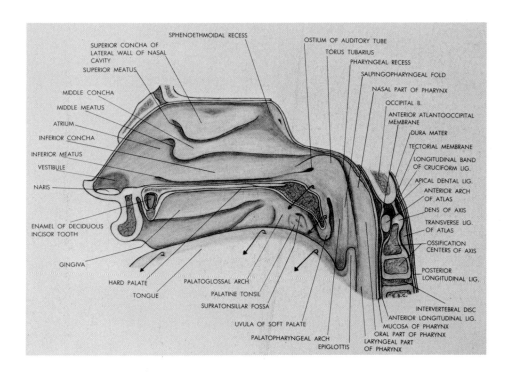

Figure 2. A drawing of a midsagittal section through the upper respiratory system of a human newborn infant. The nasal septum was removed exposing the right nasal cavity. Even though the entire tongue surface within the oral cavity is pulled down away from the palate, the epiglottis is still closely related to the soft palate. *From Crelin (1969).*

I looked at the skull bases. My next step was to compare these bases with the base of an adult human skull. I found the differences between the skull base of the adult human and those of the adult chimp and human newborn even more striking. I then realized that there was a direct correlation between the soft tissues of the neck and the base of the skull that made the spatial relationships of the neck structures of the human newborn and the adult chimp basically similar, in contrast to the very different spatial relationships of the neck structures in the adult human being.

About a week after his first visit, Dr. Lieberman returned to my laboratory, and I told him of my findings. On a third visit, he brought a plaster of paris cast of the reconstructed skull of the prehistoric La Chapelle Neanderthal man made at the Museum of the University of Pennsylvania. This was the first cast of a skull of a prehistoric man I had ever examined closely. Dr. Lieberman expressed a keen interest in the evolution of human speech and asked if I would examine the cast with that in mind. As I look back now, trying to deduce how speech evolved by examining the Neanderthal skull was like starting to read a mystery novel in the middle of the book. However, when I studied the Neanderthal skull, I came to a number of conclusions and made a number of assumptions, which appeared in two articles that I coauthored with Dr. Lieberman (Lieberman and Crelin 1971; Lieberman, Crelin, and Klatt 1972). Although I would rather have waited before publishing what I found, my findings fortunately have stood the test of time as well as the further research on the subject I have carried out since that time. This is all pointed out in detail in the chapter on the evolution of the vocal tract. Dr. Lieberman felt compelled to expound on the evolution of human speech. I felt I had to go to my laboratory and spend whatever time it took to investigate scientifically the development, anatomy, and function of the mammalian upper respiratory system, including the mammalian skull, before I was able to hypothesize about the evolution of the vocal tract. In order to prepare for the investigations, I had to wade through what was to me a lot of linguistic and anthropological jargon. It was necessary for me to reduce everything I had no direct experience with to its basic rudiments. This sometimes meant duplicating research done by others so I could feel secure that I had as firm a scientific basis as possible when I dared to make hypotheses based on the meager fossil data as to when the human ancestors were first able to speak. Thus, in 1975, Dr. Lieberman and I went our separate ways. I have not seen or talked to him since that time. He continued to publish on the origins of language, while I withdrew to the laboratory to devise and perform experiments that could serve as scientific bases for hypothesizing about the evolution of the human vocal tract. I emerged from the laboratory eight years later with the data presented in this book.

Along the way I was the adviser to two graduate students from the department of anthropology at Yale whose dissertation research was on the human vocal tract. One was Dr. Michael F. Gibbons, now an associate professor in the department of anthropology at the University of Massachusetts. The other was Dr. Jeffrey T. Laitman, now an associate professor in the department of anatomy at the Mount Sinai School of Medicine. Needless to say, working with them on the vocal tract greatly enhanced my own knowledge and insight.

I fully realize that time machines will probably always be in the realm of science fiction. Therefore, all of the hypotheses about exactly how and when the human vocal tract evolved will have to be nothing more than educated guesses. Even so, I am confident that, by applying the scientific method when evaluating all of the direct and indirect evidence pertaining to evolution, a scheme will ultimately be devised that will be quite close to what actually happened.

After an academic lifetime of over thirty years spent teaching and performing original research on vertebrate growth and development, I am convinced that the development of the human individual, or ontogeny, is a résumé, or synopsis, of human evolution, or phylogeny. I did not use the term "recapitulation," as in the often maligned phrase "ontogeny recapitulates phylogeny," in order to avoid the silly notion that ontogeny could possibly include all of the events that took place during the evolution of life on earth leading to human beings, beginning with the formation of the first living nucleated cell some fifteen hundred million years ago. The way the human body is formed is in many instances nonsensical unless it is viewed as a résumé of its evolutionary history. Much of the evolutionary story is missing or slurred over. In essence, what is retained is a brief résumé of the stem line forms that gave rise to the animals constituting the chordate phylum, especially those of the vertebrate lineage. This stem line gave rise to all vertebrates from fishes to mammals, most of which are now extinct. Embryos of fishes, amphibians, reptiles, and mammals all pass through similar stages of development. Embryos of the different groups of vertebrates resemble one another most closely in their early stages of development. As expected, this resemblance tends to diminish progressively as they advance to their final, specialized forms. Throughout development, the changes in form occur in a progressive sequence that fits into a logical scheme of evolution based on vertebrate comparative anatomy and the fossil record.

Comparative anatomy has been valuable in helping to piece together a woefully incomplete fossil record of vertebrate evolution. Developmental anatomy can also make valuable contributions in combination with comparative vertebrate anatomy and the fossil record, when speculating how life forms, both extant and extinct, evolved. Relating the development of the human vocal tract in the individual to its evolution in the species was greatly simplified by the uniqueness of the human vocal tract. There was no need to relate the later stages of development of the human vocal tract to any evolutionary forms except the human ancestors. Just as the development of the mature form of the human vocal tract occurs very late, actually long after birth, I found that the evolution of the tract also occurred very late, only during the last million years of a period of time consisting of many millions of years of human ancestral evolution.

I hope my research on the vocal tract, like that I have performed many times before, has opened some doors which will induce others to extend the findings in great depth and breadth. Already I have moved on to other interests. However, I will remain an atypical senior scientist and not be dismayed if further research on the anatomy and function of the vocal tract and/or the discovery of more ancestral human skulls cause my findings and hypotheses to become untenable. The sooner new data are discovered the better, because my time on this earth is growing short. I will continue to be fascinated until my dying breath as I meditate on how our ancestors became the human beings we are today.

Chapter 2

The Adult Human Vocal Tract

The human vocal tract is a part of the respiratory system. In clinical medicine, the respiratory system is artificially subdivided into upper and lower parts. The lower part consists of the trachea, bronchi, and lungs. The heart and great vessels are also included. Therefore, the medical specialty dealing with this part is known as cardiopulmonary or cardiothoracic. The specialty dealing with the upper part is known as otorhinolaryngology, otolaryngology, or simply ear, nose, and throat. The upper part of the system consists of the two nasal cavities, the nasopharynx, oral cavity, oropharynx, laryngopharynx, and larynx (Figure 3). Normally, the entire upper part of the respiratory system participates as a unit in the production of articulate speech. However, the nasal cavities and nasopharynx are not essential to produce speech. This is made obvious when the nostrils are completely blocked in a person with a severe head cold or when the two nostrils are squeezed closed with the fingers. All this does to alter the production of articulate speech is to modify certain sounds, especially the consonants "m" and "n." Although certain sounds are made to sound different, they can be clearly understood. Since the nasal cavities and nasopharynx are not essential for the production of articulate speech, I did not include them in my studies. Thus, the vocal tract part of the upper respiratory system consists of the oral cavity, or mouth; the oropharynx and laryngopharynx, or throat; and the larynx, or voice box (Figure 4).

Larynx (Voice Box)

The larynx has a cartilaginous skeleton (Figures 5, 8, 10, and 11). The individual cartilages articulate with each other at movable joints. Numerous small striated muscles attach to the cartilages (Figures 6, 7, 9, and 10). The larynx is attached by an extensive sheet of connective tissue to the hyoid bone above it. This connective tissue is the thyrohyoid membrane (Figures

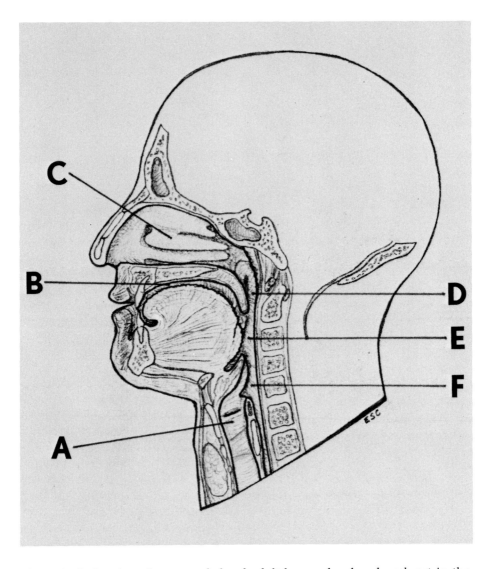

Figure 3. A drawing of an unembalmed adult human head and neck cut in the midsagittal plane. The nasal septum is removed. The right side of the entire upper respiratory system is exposed. A: larynx. B: oral cavity. C: right nasal cavity. D: nasopharynx. E: oropharynx. F: laryngopharynx.

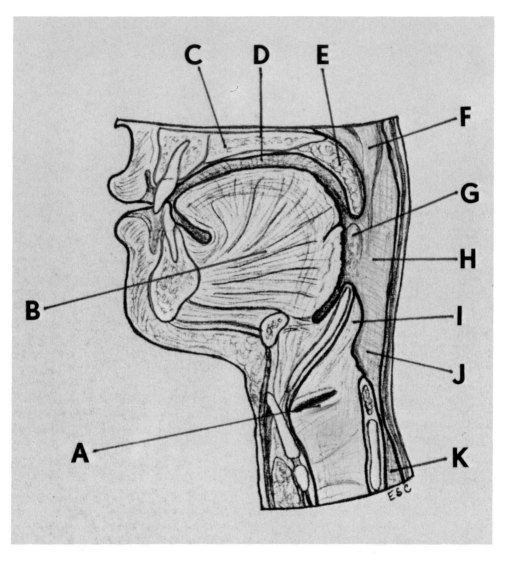

Figure 4. The vocal tract of the drawing shown in Figure 3. A: right vocal fold (cord) of larynx. B: tongue. C: hard palate. D: oral cavity. E: soft palate. F: nasopharynx. G: palatine tonsil. H: oropharynx. I: epiglottis. J: laryngopharynx. K: esophagus.

5, 7, and 14). The hyoid bone has been aptly called a "hitching post" because so many muscles attach to it (Figures 1, 12, 13, and 14).

Pharynx (Throat)

The oropharynx and laryngopharynx constitute the throat portion of the vocal tract (Figures 3, 4, 14, and 15). The roof of the throat is the elevated soft palate, which closes off the nasopharynx from the oropharynx during the production of speech sounds, known as phonation (Figure 14). During quiet respiration, when an adult breathes through the nose the soft palate is relaxed and pendulous, leaving a gap in the roof of the throat where the nasopharynx and oropharynx are in open communication (Figures 3, 4, and 15). The lateral (side) and posterior (back) walls of the throat consist almost entirely of a thin sheet of striated muscle made up of the superior, middle, and inferior pharyngeal constrictor muscles (Figures 1, 12, and 14). With the tongue at rest and the mouth closed, the laryngopharyngeal portion of the adult throat lacks an anterior (front) wall. This is because the vertical orientation of the epiglottis results in the lumen (cavity) of the laryngopharynx being directly continuous with the vestibule of the larynx (Figures 3, 4, and 14). With the tongue at rest and the mouth closed, except for a gap where the lumen of the oropharyngeal part of the throat is continuous with the narrow lumen of the oral cavity, the anterior (front) wall of the oropharynx consists almost entirely of the tongue in an adult (Figures 3, 4, 14, and 15). The surface of this part of the tongue is vertically oriented, roughly about a third of the total resting tongue surface, and known as the lingual tonsil because of an abundance of submucosal lymphatic tissue (Figure 14).

Oral Cavity (Mouth)

The roof of the oral cavity consists of the hard palate and a part of the elevated soft palate (Figures 3, 4, 14, and 15). The lateral walls of the oral cavity consist of the cheeks, each of which contains a buccinator striated muscle (Figure 12). The floor of the oral cavity consists almost entirely of the tongue (Figures 1, 2, 3, 4, 14, and 15).

Phonation

Normally, phonation begins with the larynx, which produces the fundamental frequency of a sound. The larynx functions as a sphincter to

9

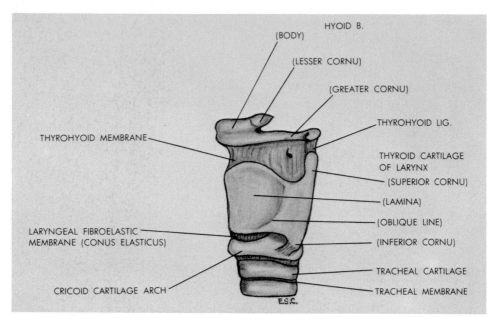

Figure 5. A drawing of a lateral view of the left side of the hyoid bone, larynx, and upper part of the trachea of a human newborn infant. *From Crelin (1969).*

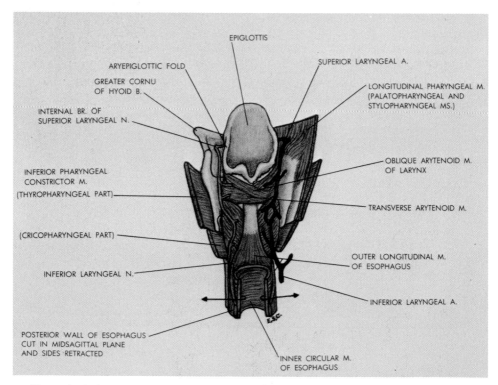

Figure 6. A drawing of a posterior view of the larynx of a human newborn infant. *From Crelin (1969).*

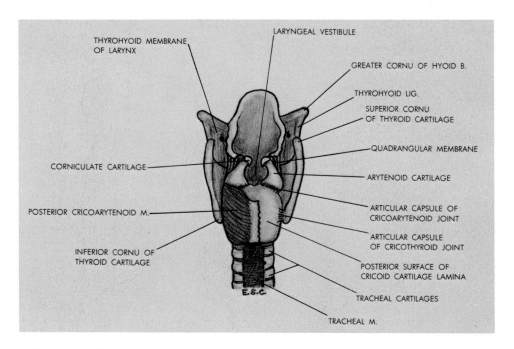

Figure 7. A drawing of a posterior view of the larynx of a human newborn infant. *From Crelin (1969).*

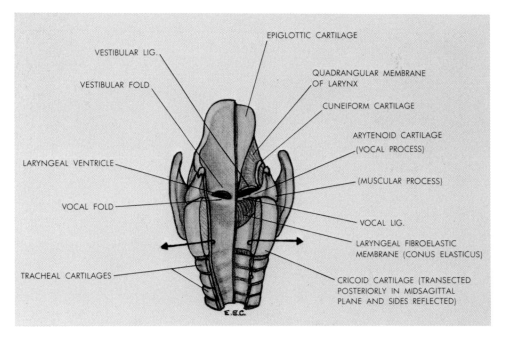

Figure 8. A drawing of a posterior view of the larynx of a human newborn infant. The cricoid cartilage lamina and upper trachea are cut in the midline and the halves reflected to expose the interior. *From Crelin (1969).*

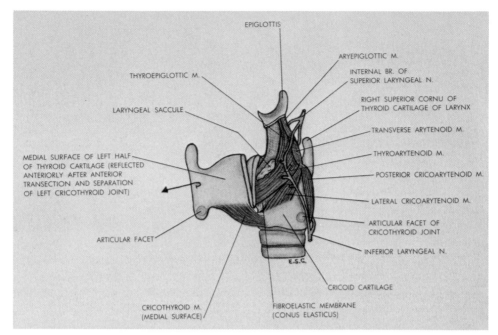

Figure 9. A drawing of a lateral view of the left side of the larynx of a human newborn infant. The thyroid cartilage is cut in the midline anteriorly and its left half reflected to expose underlying muscles. *From Crelin (1969).*

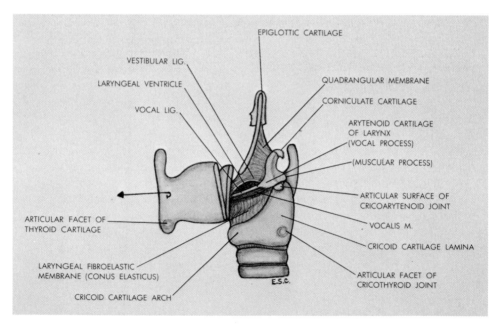

Figure 10. A drawing of a lateral view of the left side of the larynx of a human newborn infant. The thyroid cartilage is cut in the midline anteriorly and its left half reflected to expose the left half of the fibroelastic membrane *(conus elasticus).* *From Crelin (1969).*

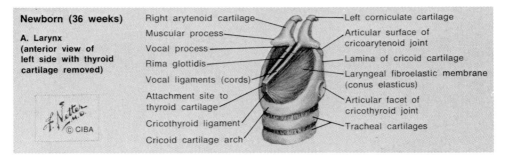

Figure 11. A drawing of an exposure of the entire laryngeal fibroelastic membrane *(conus elasticus)* of a human newborn infant. *From Crelin (1976). ©Copyright 1976, CIBA Pharmaceutical Company, Division of CIBA-GEIGY Corporation. Reprinted with permission from CLINICAL SYMPOSIA, illustrated by Frank H. Netter, M.D. All rights reserved.*

regulate the air flow into and out of the trachea and to protect the lower respiratory system from the entrance of fumes, liquids, or solid objects that could cause damage. The regulated opening of the larynx is known as the rima glottidis. It is actually a slitlike gap in a dense sheet of fibroelastic tissue known as the laryngeal fibroelastic membrane or conus elasticus (Figure 11). The free edges of the fibroelastic membrane are known as the vocal ligaments (Figures 8, 10, and 11). The mucosa, or covering, of the vocal ligaments is subjected to abrasive activity. It is stratified squamous epithelium, similar to the epidermis of skin. The mucosa of the interior of the larynx, which is not subjected to abrasion, resembles the ciliated, glandular mucosa of the trachea. The vocal ligaments and their epithelial covering are known as the vocal folds or cords (Figure 8). The free edges of the fibroelastic membrane, the vocal ligaments, are attached anteriorly to the thyroid cartilage; posteriorly, each is attached to the vocal process of an arytenoid cartilage (Figures 8, 10, and 11). The arytenoid cartilage articulations with the cricoid cartilage are typical synovial joints that allow a wide range of sliding and rotatory movements. Thus, the numerous intrinsic muscles that act directly or indirectly upon the thyroid and arytenoid cartilages cause the vocal folds to be separated and loose or taut, or approximated and loose or taut, to variable degrees. As air rushes from the lungs and respiratory tubes to pass between the approximated vocal folds, it forces the folds to separate and then slam together at rapid intervals. This releases puffs, packets, or waves of compressed air that create sound waves. These, in turn, cause the eardrum of a person to vibrate.

The scientific bases of human speech are only beginning to be established. Many of the analyses are highly theoretical and in a state of flux. This is because human speech is so complex. To make matters more complicated, linguists have created an extensive language of their own. At-

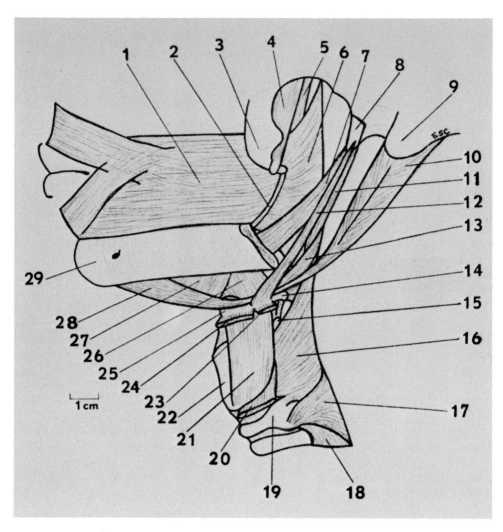

Figure 12. A drawing of the left side of the musculature of the vocal tract of a human adult. The ramus of the mandible is removed to expose the underlying muscles. 1: buccinator m. 2: pterygomandibular raphe. 3: pterygoid process. 4: tensor veli palatini m. 5: levator veli palatini m. 6: superior pharyngeal constrictor m. 7: styloglossus m. 8: base of styloid process. 9: mastoid process. 10: posterior belly of digastric m. 11: stylopharyngeus m. 12: stylohyoid m. 13: middle pharyngeal constrictor m. 14: greater cornu of hyoid bone. 15: superior cornu of thyroid cartilage. 16: inferior pharyngeal constrictor m. 17: cricopharyngeus m. 18: esophagus. 19: cricoid cartilage. 20: sternothyroid m. (cut). 21: thyrohyoid m. 22: thyroid cartilage. 23: omohyoid m. (cut). 24: sternohyoid m. (cut). 25: body of hyoid bone. 26: hyoglossus m. 27: mylohyoid m. 28: anterior belly of digastric m. 29: mandible.

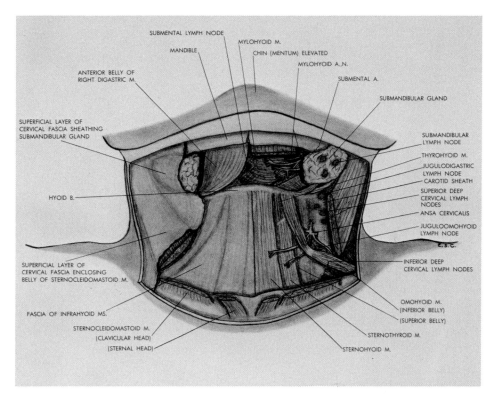

Figure 13. A drawing of an anterior view of the neck of a human newborn infant showing the supra and infrahyoid (strap) muscles. *From Crelin (1969)*

tempts to simplify what is known about the production of speech for the nonlinguist cannot help but contain some minor inaccuracies. I am sure my attempt is no exception.

Human speech sounds exhibit two kinds of acoustically measurable phenomena. One of these is called the fundamental frequency; the other is called the formant frequency. The fundamental frequency is a property of the complex sound generated by the movements or vibrations of the vocal folds in the larynx. In order for the fundamental frequency and its harmonic overtones to become an articulate speech sound, they must be modified. This modification is produced by the specific shape assumed by the remainder of the vocal tract. Modified thus, the glottic waves' frequency spectrum shows peaks, called formant frequencies, which are one of the bases of human speech. Voiced human speech sounds generally show a fundamental frequency and a set of formant frequencies.

Beyond the larynx, the vocal tract consists of the pharynx and oral cavity. Since this part is above the larynx, it is referred to as the supra-

15

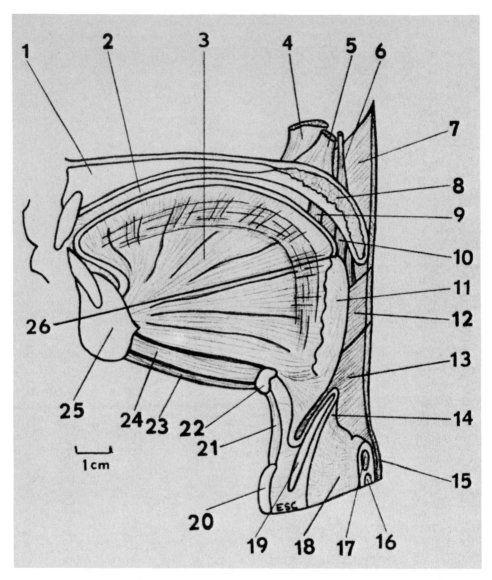

Figure 14. A drawing of the musculature of the right half of the vocal tract of a human adult cut in the midsagittal plane. 1: hard palate. 2: oral cavity. 3: genioglossus m. of tongue. 4: tensor veli palatini m. 5: levator veli palatini m. 6: salpingopharyngeus m. 7: superior pharyngeal constrictor m. 8: soft palate (musculus uvulae). 9: palatoglossus m. 10: palatopharyngeus m. 11: lingual tonsil part of tongue. 12: middle pharyngeal constrictor m. 13: inferior pharyngeal constrictor m. 14: epiglottis. 15: cricopharyngeus m. 16: cricoid cartilage lamina. 17: transverse arytenoid m. 18: vestibule of larynx. 19: epiglottic cartilage. 20: thyroid cartilage. 21: thyrohyoid membrane. 22: body of hyoid bone. 23: mylohyoid m. 24: geniohyoid m. 25: mandible. 26: foramen cecum of tongue. (Tongue also contains the chondroglossus m. and the superior longitudinal, inferior longitudinal, transverse, and vertical intrinsic muscles)

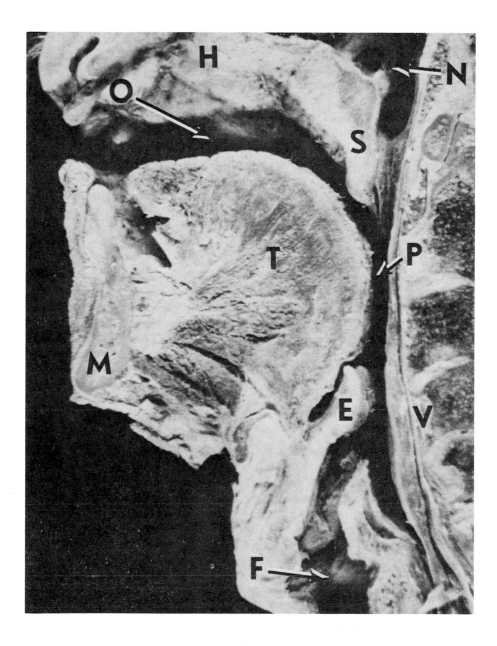

Figure 15. Right side of the vocal tract of a human adult embalmed cadaver cut in the midsagittal plane. O: oral cavity. H: hard palate. S: soft palate. N: nasopharynx. T: tongue. P: oropharynx. M: mandible. E: epiglottis. V: vertebral column. F: right vocal fold (cord).

Rubber Vocal Tract Construction

I have been in charge of the human anatomy and development course at Yale for many years. The final dissection of the cadaver by the students is a midsagittal cut made through the head and neck to expose the interior of the upper part of the respiratory system (Figure 15). Thus, I am quite familiar with the anatomy of the human adult vocal tract. I made a solid silicone rubber cast of the entire upper part of the respiratory system of an unembalmed adult male human cadaver with a full set of teeth, after the head and neck had been cut in the midsagittal plane. The silicone rubber had the consistency of toothpaste when it was used to fill the airway of each side of the head and neck completely. When the rubber had set, it had the consistency of a rubber eraser. The casts of the two halves of the airway were then sealed together with a thin layer of unset rubber to represent the exact size and shape of the space of the upper part of the respiratory system (Figure 16). I then filled the vocal tract of the same cadaver with Plasteline nonhardening modeling clay. Each half of the cadaver's mouth was placed in the closed position, and the palate was elevated to close off the nasopharynx. The clay was removed from each side of the vocal tract and the two casts fused together to represent the entire space of the vocal tract, from the front teeth to the vocal folds. Then the clay was coated with a thin layer of latex rubber having the consistency of mayonnaise and allowed to air dry. This process of coating the specimen with a thin layer of rubber and letting it air dry was repeated until the desired thickness and flexibility of the rubber was attained. Two slits were made in the rubber tract to make an oral and a laryngeal opening. I then firmly squeezed the specimen to free the flexible clay from its rubber coating. The clay was then removed through the two openings, leaving a hollow, latex rubber tract, representing the mucosal lining of the entire vocal tract of an adult male human being (Figure 17). A latex rubber copy of the hard palate of the cadaver was made and fused to its proper position on the rubber vocal tract using a thin layer of unset latex rubber (Figure 17).

Plastic Larynx

After testing every device I could find that would produce sound by having air pass through it, I chose a toy noisemaker to serve as the larynx for the rubber vocal tract (Figure 18). This is a plastic tube that produces sound when air from an attached, deflating rubber balloon passes through it. A flexible plastic reed located in a narrow section of the tube vibrates as air passes through the section and produces a sound (Figure 19). Thus,

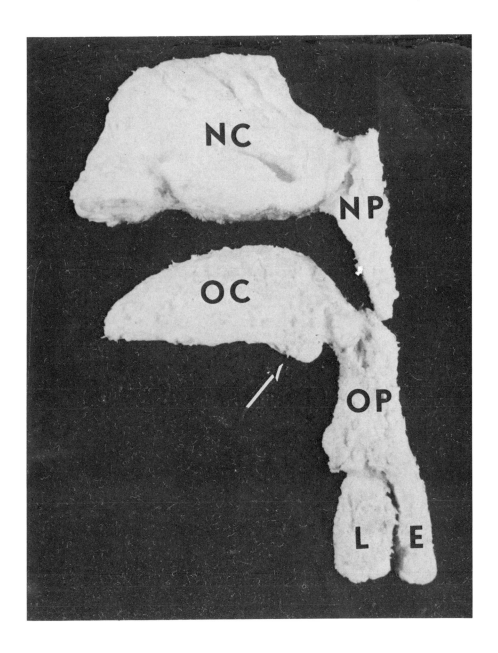

Figure 16. A left lateral view of a solid silicone rubber cast that represents the space of the upper part of the respiratory system of an adult human male. NC: left nasal cavity. NP: nasopharynx. OC: oral cavity. OP: oropharynx. L: larynx. E: esophagus.

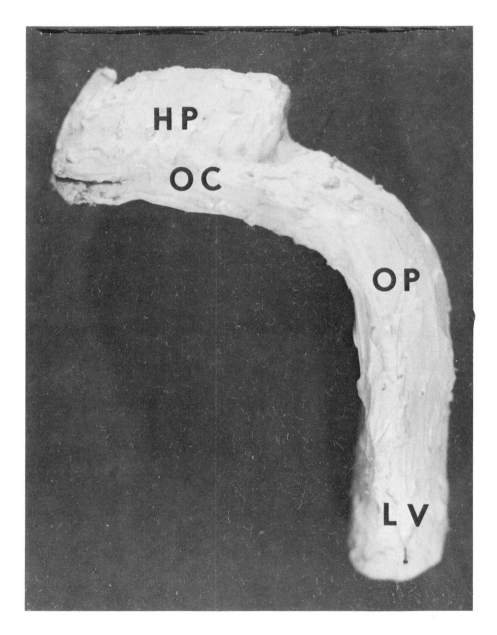

Figure 17. Left side of a hollow latex rubber duplicate of a human adult male vocal tract. A solid rubber hard palate duplicate (HP) is fused in its proper position to the top of the oral cavity (OC) part of the tract. OP: oropharynx. LV: laryngeal vestibule.

the narrow section of tube serves as the rima glottidis of a larynx and the reed acts much like the single functioning vocal cord in a person with one cord paralyzed.

Rubber Vocal Tract Function

The plastic larynx is placed in a clamp within the confines of a rubber-coated wire basket, and a plastic hose with a three-quarter–inch inside diameter conveys air under pressure to it from a wall outlet in my laboratory (Figures 20 and 21). The rubber vocal tract is suspended within the wire basket by a rod inserted into a hole drilled in the solid rubber hard palate of the tract. The laryngeal end of the tract is placed over the larynx by passing the tubular extension of the larynx through the laryngeal opening of the tract. Numerous small fishhooks are attached at strategic points to the wall of the tract. Each fishhook is attached to transparent plastic fishline. Several small metal washers are also attached to the wall of the vocal tract with fishlines. The shape of the vocal tract is altered by attaching the fishlines from the hooks under tension with metal clamps to various positions on the wire basket. The same thing is done with the fishlines from the metal washers to reduce the size of the lumen of the tract anywhere along its length.

The sound produced by the plastic larynx when air under three pounds of pressure is passed through it serves as the source acoustic wave for the production of vowel sounds by the rubber vocal tract (Figure 22). This is about three times the air pressure used for ordinary phonation. Thus, the fundamental frequency is above that of my baritone voice during normal conversation and a little louder. I decided to produce six of the basic vowels of the English language—"ä" as in father, "ā" as in day, "ē" as in easy, "ī" as in side, "ō" as in know, and "ü" as in you,—with my own voice and then duplicate them with the rubber vocal tract. (I have used the vowel symbols found in an ordinary English dictionary rather than the IPA symbols, which are confusing to the nonlinguist.) I kept the pitch at a constant monotone. Ordinarily, when a person alters the pitch of his voice during speech, the larynx is raised and lowered automatically. This lengthens and shortens the pharynx chiefly in an indirect manner. Numerous muscles arising from the skull and mandible, including the tongue, attach to the hyoid bone and elevate it (Figures 1, 12, and 13). The larynx, attached to the hyoid bone, is also elevated, and the pharynx is shortened. A number of muscles, known as the infrahyoid or strap muscles, arise from the sternum, clavicle, first rib, and scapula and attach to the hyoid bone and larynx (Figures 12 and 13). Although the pitch of the voice is generally raised or

Figure 18. The tubular plastic larynx used with the latex rubber duplicate of the adult human male vocal tract to produce vowel sounds.

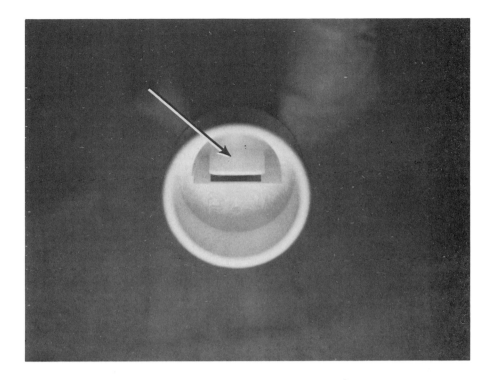

Figure 19. A view of the interior of the plastic larynx shown in Figure 18. A plastic reed (arrow) is set into motion when air is made to pass through the narrow opening within the tube.

lowered by activity of the vocal folds themselves, the whole larynx is usually elevated as the pitch is raised and lowered when the pitch is lowered. To avoid any complications caused by lengthening and shortening the rubber vocal tract, it was kept the same length as it produced all of the vowel sounds.

The shape changes were kept within the anatomical limits of a living human being. No change was made in the surface of the roof of the oral cavity where it borders the unyielding, bony, hard palate in a living person. Likewise, no change was made where the posterior wall of the vocal tract directly borders the unyielding cervical vertebral column. Raising the soft palate to close off the nasopharynx eliminated a shape change along the surface of the tract formed by the soft palate. Only limited expansion can occur in the lateral walls of the oropharynx, and even less occurs in the lateral walls of the oral cavity. This leaves the tongue surface, forming the

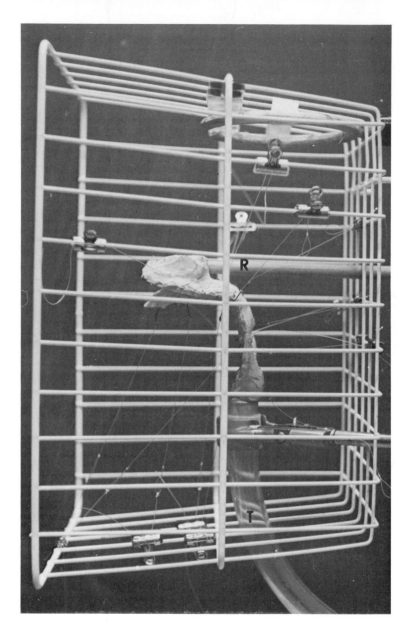

Figure 20. Lateral view of the hollow latex rubber duplicate of a human adult male vocal tract. It is suspended within a rubber coated wire basket by a rod (R) inserted into a hole within the solid rubber hard palate fused to the top of the oral cavity part of the tract. The opening of the laryngeal end of the tract is placed over a tubular plastic larynx that is held by a clamp. Air under pressure is brought to the larynx via the clear plastic tubing (T). Fishhooks and small metal washers attached to the tract at various points are pulled into tension by clear plastic fishlines clamped to the wire basket in order to alter the shape of the vocal tract so that it produces the "ä" vowel sound.

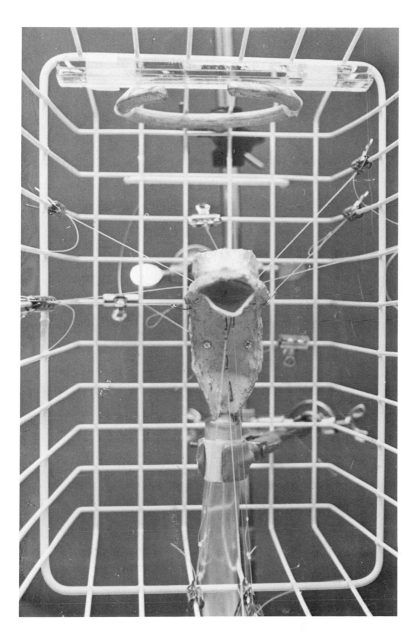

Figure 21. Anterior view of the rubber vocal tract shown in Figure 20 producing the "ä" vowel sound.

floor of the oral cavity and the anterior wall of the oropharynx, to undergo the greatest range of changes in position and shape to alter the configuration of the vocal tract significantly for the production of vowel sounds.

In order not to be fooled by mimicry as I listened and altered the shape of the rubber vocal tract to duplicate the vowel sounds I uttered, I was assisted by Mr. Donald Summers, a mechanical engineer in the surgery department of the Biomechanical Research Laboratory at Yale, in using an oscilloscope. A single sweep of the wave pattern of the sounds that I and the rubber tract produced were photographed by a polaroid camera attached to the oscilloscope. The photograph of the pressure waveform is known as an oscillogram (Figure 22).

The procedure of matching the rubber-tract–produced vowels to those produced by my own tract began with my uttering a vowel sound at a pitch level comparable to that of the rubber tract. I would then make an oscillogram of the wave pattern of my vowel sound, slowly and carefully adjusting the shape of the phonating tract by clamping the fishlines from the attached hooks and washers to various positions on the wire basket under variable tension. I listened and viewed the wave pattern on the oscilloscope fluorescent screen as I adjusted the shape of the vocal tract, until what I saw and heard of a specific vowel sound being produced coincided with the wave pattern and perceptual quality produced when I uttered the vowel sound. I then made an oscillogram of the wave pattern produced by the tract (Figure 23 and 24). This procedure could take many hours to complete. Since the altered shape of the tract was maintained by the clamped fishlines, I could take all the time I needed to measure the rubber tract, especially its cross-sectional size and shape throughout its length. I then made exact, to-scale drawings of the tract in the midsagittal plane and in cross sections.

The vowels produced by the rubber tract duplicated the acoustic quality of those I uttered, and the formant frequency alterations of the wave patterns of each vowel appeared to be very similar to mine. Dr. Vijay Goel of the Biomechanical Research Laboratory critically examined the oscillograms to assure me that the tract was indeed producing vowel sounds. As a double check, the vowel sounds produced by the rubber tract were recorded on TDK SA audiotape, using a Tandberg TCD 330 cassette deck for spectral analysis.

The frequencies of the first and second formants (F1 and F2) of the taped vowel sounds were then ascertained by Dr. Michael Gibbons of the University of Massachusetts. F1 and F2 are the formants most clearly and regularly dependent on the anatomy of the vocal tract, whether it is the human tract or a rubber copy. The analysis revealed that the rubber tract is capable of producing vowel sounds very close to human vowel sounds (Figure 25). The rubber tract was also videotaped in color, so it can be seen as well as heard as it produces vocalic sounds.

Even though the lack of a warm, moist mucosal lining causes the vowel

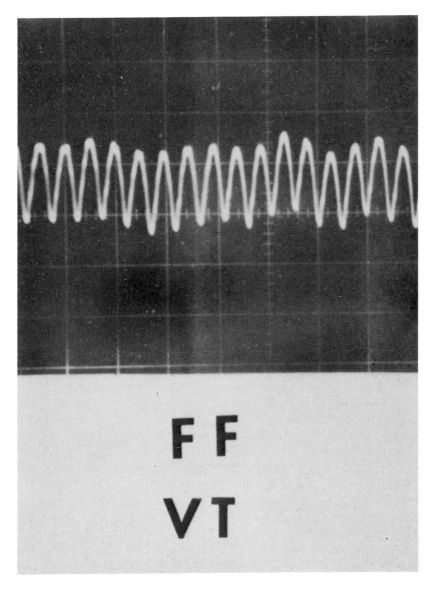

Figure 22. An oscillogram of a single sweep of the wave pattern created by the fundamental sound produced by the plastic larynx at 3 pounds of air pressure. FF: fundamental frequency. VT: rubber vocal tract.

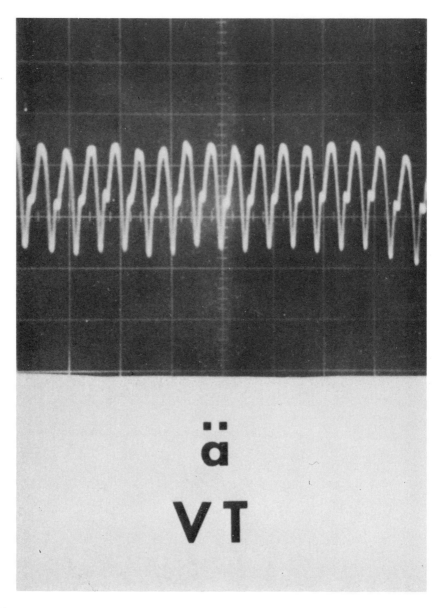

Figure 23. An oscillogram of a single sweep of the wave pattern created by the rubber human adult male vocal tract producing the "ä" vowel sound. VT: rubber vocal tract.

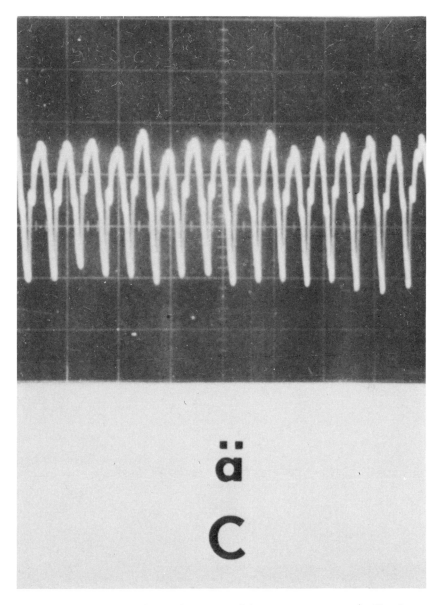

Figure 24. An oscillogram of a single sweep of the wave pattern created by the vocal tract of the author when he produced the "ä" vowel sound. C: Crelin's vocal tract.

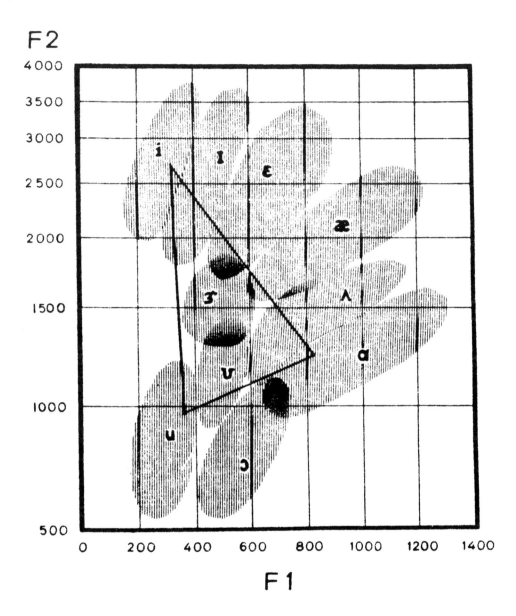

Figure 25. This is a chart showing the human vowel triangle. The apices of the triangle are connected to represent the formant frequency range of the extreme vowels for adult human beings. The coordinates for this triangle were derived from the arithmetic mean of seventy-six men, women and children compiled by Peterson and Barney (1952). The ovals on the chart represent the range of the first, or F1, and the second, or F2, formant frequencies in cycles per second of vowel sounds produced by the seventy-six subjects.

sounds produced by the rubber tract to have a raspy quality, they are quite distinct. The higher-than-ordinary phonation air pressure used probably contributes to the raspy quality of the sounds. Although the rubber tract is a very crude duplicate of the living tract, I deduce that an adult human vocal tract assumes a configuration basically similar to that of the rubber tract in order to produce the same vowel sounds that the rubber tract does. I observed and palpated a number of adult human subjects, including myself, as we produced vowel sounds. I compared these findings with those derived from the rubber vocal tract as it produced the same vowel sounds and arrived at the following conclusions. For example, in order to produce "ä," as in the word "father," the opening of the mouth is fairly wide (Figure 26). Even though the sides of the tongue are raised, the central portion of the tongue throughout the oral cavity is lowered. This results in a fairly spacious oral cavity and is chiefly the result of intrinsic tongue muscle action. The vertical part of the tongue forming the anterior wall of the oropharynx is drawn back, causing the entire oropharynx to assume a wide, flattened shape. This also causes the oral cavity to resemble a flared tube. In fact, the whole vocal tract is essentially a flared tube from the larynx to the oral opening, flattened in its pharyngeal portion and bent at a right angle at its oropharyngeal junction. The high elevation of the tongue at the back of the oral cavity is why a physician using a bent mirror to view the larynx uses a tongue depressor. With this, he pushes the elevated part of the tongue down and forward as he has the patient say "ah." The posterior displacement and elevation of the back of the tongue is due chiefly to the action of the muscles arising from the skull and attaching to the hyoid bone along with the styloglossus muscle that inserts directly into the tongue (Figures 1 and 12).

To produce the vowel "ā," as in the word "day," the mouth is opened fairly wide, though less wide than when producing "ä" (Figure 27). The sides of the tongue are raised against the upper premolar and molar teeth. The tongue is depressed centrally in the anterior half of the oral cavity but elevated in the posterior half. The posterior displacement and elevation of the tongue causes the oropharyngeal junction of the vocal tract to be flat and wide. However, the lower part of the vertical part of the tongue is drawn forward, resulting in a gradually widened oropharynx from the oropharyngeal junction to the larynx.

To produce the "ē" vowel, as in the word "easy," nearly all of the oral cavity is reduced to a small slit (Figure 28). The sides of the tongue are elevated to make contact with the hard palate from the upper canine to the last molar teeth. The tip of the tongue is placed against the lower incisor teeth and the mandible is elevated to such a high position that the mouth is opened only slightly. However, the posterior vertical surface of

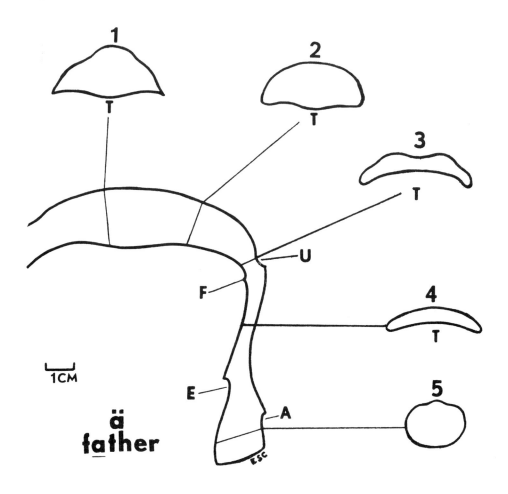

Figure 26. A drawing of the shape of the rubber human male adult vocal tract in the midsagittal and cross-sectional planes when it produced the "ä" vowel sound. The cross sections are through the anterior part of the oral cavity (1), posterior part of the oral cavity (2), upper part of the oropharynx (3), lower part of oropharynx (4), and vestibule of the larynx (5). U: uvula of soft palate. F: foramen cecum of tongue. E: epiglottis. A: arytenoid muscle. T: tongue surface.

the tongue is drawn forward, away from the soft palate and the posterior wall of the entire oropharynx. Thus, the whole throat is a spacious, though slightly flattened, tube.

To produce the "ī" vowel, as in the word "side," the mouth is opened fairly wide (Figure 29). Even though the sides of the tongue touch the upper premolar and molar teeth, the surface of the tongue is flattened to cause the oral cavity to be rather spacious throughout. The uppermost part

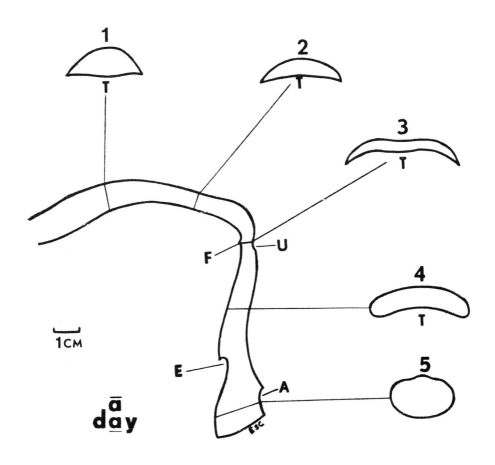

Figure 27. A drawing of the shape of the rubber human adult male vocal tract in the midsagittal and cross-sectional planes when it produced the long "ā" vowel sound. U: uvula of soft palate. F: foramen cecum of tongue. E: epiglottis. A: arytenoid muscle. T: tongue surface.

of the tongue at the oropharyngeal junction is elevated and drawn back toward the posterior wall of a widened pharynx. In fact, it is so close that the lumen of the pharynx is only a wide slit. Immediately beyond this narrowed interval, the remainder of the vertical surface is drawn forward to cause the rest of the pharynx to be spacious. The "ī" sound was the most difficult to produce, probably because it is a diphthong. A diphthong is a gliding syllabic nucleus that starts at or near the articulatory position for one vowel and then moves to or toward the position of another. The "ī" sound is actually "ä" plus the "i" in "bit."

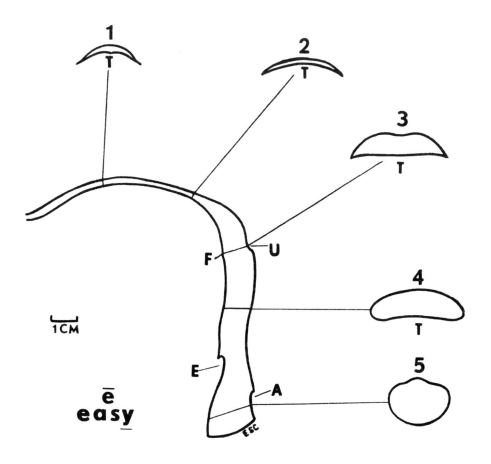

Figure 28. A drawing of the shape of the rubber human adult male vocal tract in the midsagittal and cross-sectional planes when it produced the long "ē" vowel sound. U: uvula of soft palate. F: foramen cecum of tongue. E: epiglottis. A: arytenoid muscle. T: tongue surface.

To produce the vowel "ō," as in the word "know," the mouth is opened quite wide and the lips are shaped to form a large circle (Figure 30). The tongue is lowered throughout the oral cavity, especially its central portion. This results in the oral cavity forming somewhat of a spacious tube. The lowering of the bulk of the tongue shortens the length of the vertical part. The surface of the vertical part protrudes backward at its midpoint to cause the lumen of the pharynx to be flat and narrow for a short interval.

To produce the "ü" vowel, as in the word "you," the mouth is opened only a little, and the lips are shaped to form a small circle (Figure 31). The sides of the tongue touch the upper teeth from the canines to the last

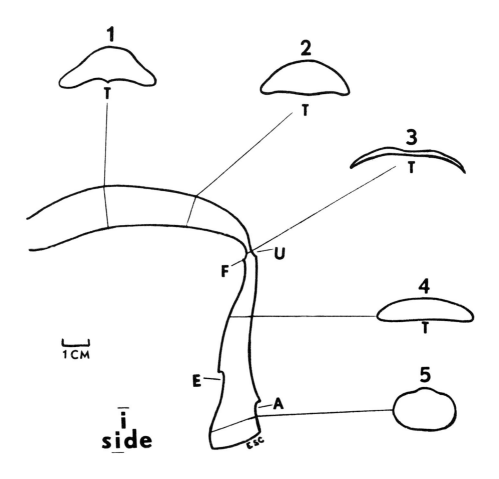

Figure 29. A drawing of the shape of the rubber human adult male vocal tract in the midsagittal and cross-sectional planes when it produced the long "ī" vowel sound. U: uvula of soft palate. F: foramen cecum of tongue. E: epiglottis. A: arytenoid muscle. T: tongue surface.

molars. All of the tongue, except for its posterior quarter in the oral cavity, has its surface in the midline depressed to produce a small tube. The posterior part of the surface is drawn up and back so that it is close to the surface of the soft palate. Thus, this part of the lumen is narrowed and flattened. The surface of the vertical part of the tongue is drawn forward, creating a spacious pharynx between the oropharyngeal junction and the larynx.

The functioning of the rubber vocal tract indicates that, of all the muscles that can affect the shape of the human vocal tract to produce the vowel sounds, the group of muscles constituting the tongue is the most important. The tongue surface is what moves and changes the shape of

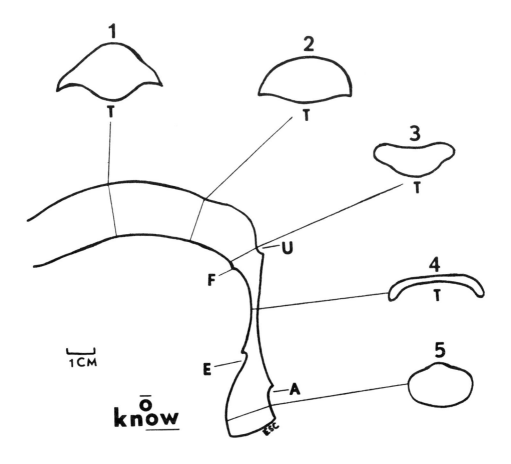

Figure 30. A drawing of the shape of the rubber human adult male vocal tract in the midsagittal and cross-sectional plane when it produced the long "ō" vowel sound. U: uvula of soft palate. F: foramen cecum of tongue. E: epiglottis. A: arytenoid muscle. T: tongue surface.

the oral cavity and pharynx to produce the vowel sounds. The whole tongue moves up and down and back and forth to affect the size of the lumen of the oral cavity and pharynx of the vocal tract. These positional changes of the tongue are chiefly the result of contractions of its principal extrinsic muscles—the genioglossus, styloglossus, and hyoglossus—with assistance from muscles that cause the mandible and hyoid bone to shift position. Localized changes in the shape of the surface of the tongue that affect the size and shape of segments of the lumen of the vocal tract are chiefly the result of contractions of the superior longitudinal, inferior longitudinal, transverse and vertical intrinsic muscles of the tongue, with assistance from its extrinsic muscles.

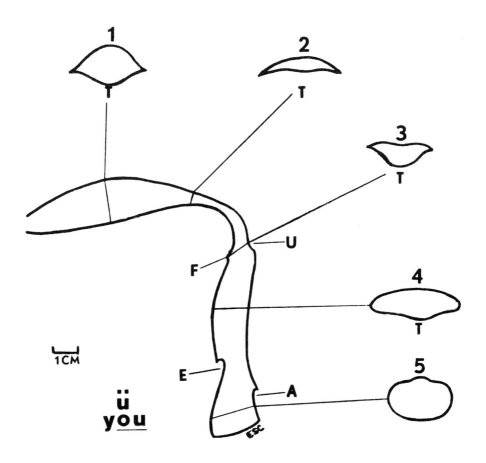

Figure 31. A drawing of the shape of the rubber human adult male vocal tract in the midsagittal and cross-sectional planes when it produced the long "ü" vowel sound. U: uvula of soft palate. F: foramen cecum of tongue. E: epiglottis. A: arytenoid muscle. T: tongue surface.

The motor innervation of the extrinsic and intrinsic muscles of the tongue is via the twelfth cranial, or hypoglossal, nerves. The muscles which move the mandible and the hyoid bone, directly or indirectly, receive motor innervation from the fifth cranial, or trigeminal; the seventh cranial, or facial; the ninth cranial, or glossopharyngeal; the tenth cranial, or vagus; the eleventh cranial, or accessory; and the first, second, and third cervical spinal nerves. Thus, the changes in shape of the vocal tract to produce vowel sounds are the result of a complex interaction of a number of different muscles and nerves. All of the intrinsic muscles of the larynx that affect the vocal folds to produce the fundamental frequency of a vowel sound receive their motor innervation from the cranial portion of the eleventh

39

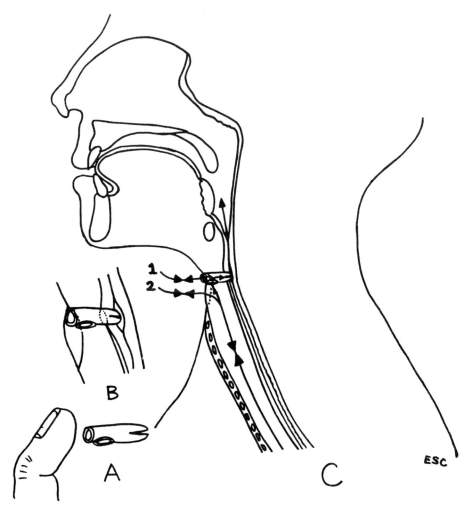

Figure 32. A drawing showing how a person can have speech following the removal of the larynx. In (A) a finger is shown in position so it can be placed over an opening in the end of a plastic tube. Another hole, at the bottom of the tube allows air to enter from the trachea when the finger blocks the hole at the end. The air from the trachea would then pass into the tube and out through a slit in the opposite end into the lumen of the junction of the pharynx and esophagus, from which the larynx was removed. In (B) the tube is shown in position in the upper part of the opening of the trachea to the outside of the neck. When the finger is placed against the opening in the tube, it is also made to cover the opening of the trachea. In (C) arrows (1) and (2) indicate how air passes up from the lungs and out of the tracheal and plastic tube openings to the outside of the neck. If these openings on the neck are blocked with a finger, the air from the trachea passes into the plastic tube and then out of it through the slit into the lumen of the junction of the pharynx and esophagus. As the air passes up into the vocal tract, the approximated walls of the lower pharynx are made to vibrate in the same manner as when air passes from the esophagus during a belch. The vibrating pharyngeal walls act as vocal folds (cords) to produce a fundamental sound frequency. The remaining part of the pharynx and the oral cavity then change shape to add formant frequencies to the fundamental sound to produce the vowel sounds. The tongue within the oral cavity, especially its tip, along with the lips produce the consonant sounds.

cranial nerves, which reaches the muscles via branches of the tenth cranial nerves (Crelin 1981).

Larynx Removal and Speech

The functioning rubber vocal tract reveals how a person who has had his larynx removed can still have articulate speech. Such a person can learn to swallow air into the esophagus. This air is then belched through the approximated walls of the junction of the pharynx and esophagus. The air causes the walls to separate and then slam together repeatedly, so that the air is released in puffs or waves of compressed molecules in a manner similar to the normal action of the vocal folds when producing the fundamental frequency of a speech sound. Formant frequencies are produced by the supralaryngeal vocal tract configuration, which modifies the source wave of the belched air to result in the vowel sounds. These people may combine consonants with the vowel sounds to form syllables in the same manner as a person with a larynx. However, the speech produced by belching is low pitched, monotone, and halting, because only a few words at a time can be spoken with the air swallowed into the esophagus. The duration of continuous speaking, or phonation time, can be greatly extended in people lacking a larynx by using a plastic tube as a shunt (Figure 32). This plastic tube is often erroneously called an artificial larynx. The approximated walls of the pharynx at its junction with the esophagus in the region where the larynx was removed are what substitute for the vocal folds.

The plastic tube is placed at the top of the opening of the trachea to the outside of the person's neck. It extends back to project into the collapsed lumen of the lowest part of the pharynx or the upper part of the esophagus (Figure 32). When the person with the tube in position places a finger over the opening of both the tube and the trachea at the surface of the neck and exhales, the air from the lungs comes up the trachea and into an opening in the bottom of the plastic tube. The tube then shunts the air from the trachea into the esophagus or pharynx through a slit at its inner end where the air causes the approximated mucosal walls to vibrate, or produce a fundamental sound frequency. The person then modifies the source wave with the supralaryngeal vocal tract in the usual manner to produce speech for as long a period of time as there is air left in the lungs to exhale.

Chapter 3

Development of the Vocal Tract

Embryology and Comparative Anatomy

The development of the human vocal tract is actually the development of the upper respiratory system. There are three separate parts: the nasal cavities, the oral cavity, and the pharynx and larynx. These parts begin to develop in a four-week embryo that is only 3.9 millimeters (a little less than 3/16 of an inch) long (Figure 33). The future nasal cavities are two thickenings of the body surface lining, or ectoderm, known as the nasal plac-

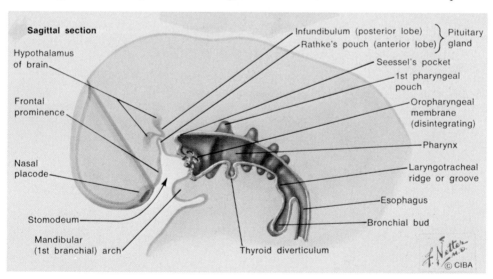

Figure 33. Diagram of a human embryo at four to five weeks of development. The pharynx is cut in the midline to expose the openings into its right pouches. The bronchial bud that gives rise to the lining of the larynx and the entire lower respiratory system is an outgrowth of the pharynx. *From Crelin (1976). ©Copyright 1976, CIBA Pharmaceutical Company, Division of CIBA-GEIGY Corporation. Reprinted with permission from CLINICAL SYMPOSIA, illustrated by Frank H. Netter, M.D. All rights reserved.*

odes. The future oral cavity is an inpocketing of the body surface lined with ectoderm, known as the stomodeum. A tube lined with endoderm, known as the foregut, gives rise to the pharynx and larynx. Between the fourth and fifth week, the oropharyngeal membrane begins to disintegrate (Figure 33). This results in a permanent open communication between the oral cavity and pharynx. In an embryo at five to six weeks, each future nasal cavity is a blind nasal sac (Figure 34). A primitive tongue lacking muscle is present in the floor of the future oral cavity, and outpocketings of the pharynx, the pharyngeal pouches, represent what become the gills in fishes. A ventral midline outgrowth of the pharynx, the lung or bronchial bud, gives rise to the respiratory tubes, including the larynx (Figures 33 and 34). Thus, the respiratory system of the human embryo at four to five

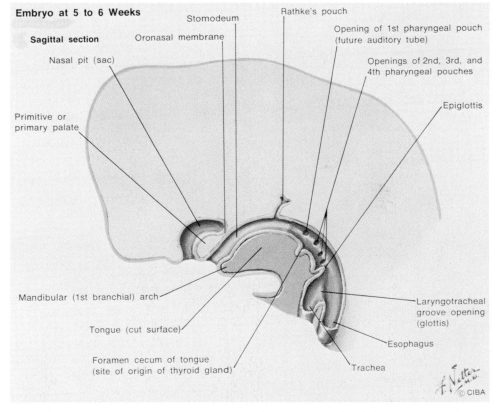

Figure 34. Diagram of a human embryo at four to six weeks of development. The upper respiratory system is cut in the midline. At this stage the nasal sacs do not yet open into the oral cavity, and the tongue is only beginning to acquire its musculature. *From Crelin (1976). ©Copyright 1976, CIBA Pharmaceutical Company, Division of CIBA-GEIGY Corporation. Reprinted with permission from CLINICAL SYMPOSIA, illustrated by Frank H. Netter, M.D. All rights reserved.*

weeks of development is similar to that of adult fishes. The two nasal cavities of fishes are blind sacs (Figure 35). The fish tongue is a sac of connective tissue lacking muscle. Living fishes are representative of the ancestral forms of the early, water-breathing, fishlike vertebrates. The respiratory tubes of the air-breathing vertebrates evolved from the air or swim bladders of these ancestral forms (Hyman 1946; von Frisch 1964). In a living perch, the air bladder loses it developmental connection with the pharynx. It is filled with gases and serves as a hydrostatic organ to adjust the specific gravity of the fish to that of the water at different depths (Storer 1943). Von Frisch (1964) notes that, in a living trout, the bladder retains an opening into the pharynx (Figure 36). In those fish that emit sounds, the air bladder contains extrinsic striated muscles that force the gases out of the bladder through the sphincterlike connection with the pharynx, producing sound vibrations (Goodrich 1958).

The transition stage in the development of a water-breathing respiratory system of gills into an air-breathing lung system in the four to five week human embryo is what occurs during metamorphosis in living amphibians such as the frog. The air-respiratory system of the human embryo arises from the pharyngeal wall of the water-respiratory system (Figure 33). Likewise, its blood supply, the pulmonary artery, arises as a branch of the sixth aortic arch of the water-respiratory system blood supply (Figure 37). Von Frisch shows that, in the living lung fish, the paired air bladders, which can also function as lungs, receive their blood supply through a side

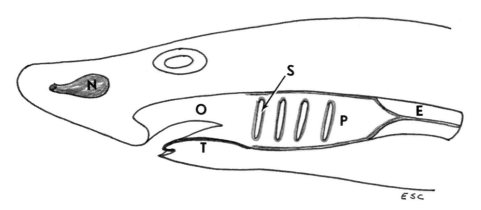

Figure 35. Diagram of the head of an adult shark showing how the oral cavity (O) is directly continuous with the pharynx (P). Water enters the mouth and passes out through the gill slits (S). The exchange of carbon dioxide and oxygen occurs between the water and the blood in the capillaries of the aortic arches of the gills. There are two nasal sacs (N) that do not communicate with the oral cavity (O). The tongue (T) is merely a sac of connective tissue located entirely within the oral cavity (O). The pharynx (P) is directly continuous with the esophagus (E).

44

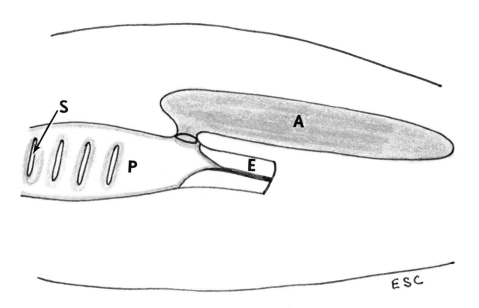

Figure 36. Diagram of an adult trout showing its air or swim bladder (A) opening into the pharynx (P). Gill slits (S) and the esophagus (E) are also shown.

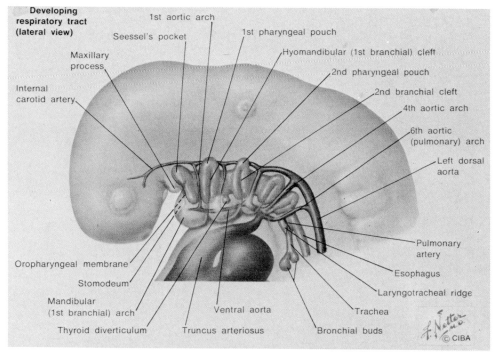

Figure 37. Diagram of a human embryo at four to five weeks of development showing the pulmonary artery arising as a branch of the left sixth aortic arch. *From Crelin (1976). ©Copyright 1976, CIBA Pharmaceutical Company, Division of CIBA-GEIGY Corporation. Reprinted with permission from CLINICAL SYMPOSIA, illustrated by Frank H. Netter, M.D. All rights reserved.*

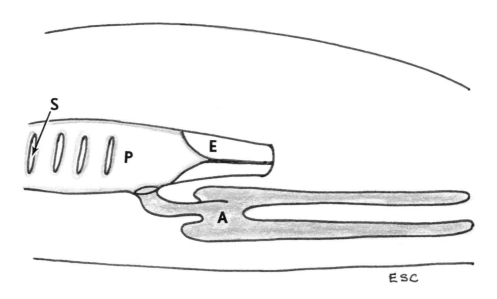

Figure 38. Diagram of an adult lung fish showing its paired air or swim bladders (A) opening into the pharynx (P). The gill slits (S) and esophagus (E) are also shown.

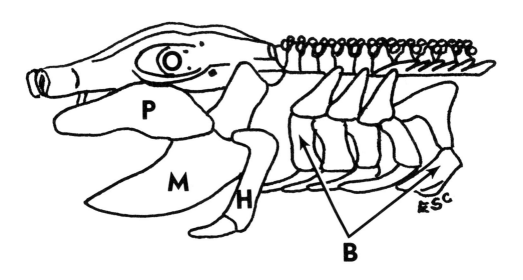

Figure 39. A drawing of a left lateral view of the cartilaginous skull, anterior part of the spinal column, and gill arch skeleton of an adult dogfish shark (Hemiscyllium). O: orbit. P: palatoquadrate or upper jaw. M: Meckel's cartilage or lower jaw. H: hyoid arch. B: branchial arch cartilages. *After Parker and Haswell (1921)*.

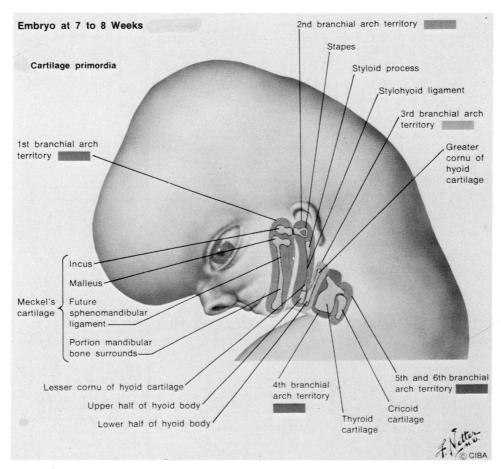

Embryo at 7 to 8 Weeks

Cartilage primordia

2nd branchial arch territory

Stapes

Styloid process

Stylohyoid ligament

3rd branchial arch territory

1st branchial arch territory

Greater cornu of hyoid cartilage

Incus

Malleus

Meckel's cartilage

Future sphenomandibular ligament

Portion mandibular bone surrounds

Lesser cornu of hyoid cartilage

Upper half of hyoid body

Lower half of hyoid body

4th branchial arch territory

5th and 6th branchial arch territory

Cricoid cartilage

Thyroid cartilage

© CIBA

Figure 40. Diagram of a human embryo at seven to eight weeks of development. The structures of the ear and neck that arise from the tissues which give rise to the gill arch skeleton of the fishes are indicated. *From Crelin (1976). ©Copyright 1976, CIBA Pharmaceutical Company, Division of CIBA-GEIGY Corporation. Reprinted with permission from CLINICAL SYMPOSIA, illustrated by Frank H. Netter, M.D. All rights reserved.*

branch of the last gill arch artery (Figure 38). The living lung fish exemplifies the stem line, ancestral lung fish from which the amphibians arose.

The skeleton of the branchial arches supporting the gills of fishes transformed into the skeleton of the upper part of the air-respiratory system and the bones of the middle ear during vertebrate evolution (Figure 39). This is recapitulated in the seven- to eight-week human embryo (Figure 40). Also in the seven- to eight-week embryo, the nasal cavities open into the oral cavity with only a primitive or primary palate forming an anterior shelf (Figure 41). The tongue is a muscular structure at this amphibian stage, in which the basic structure of the upper respiratory system resembles that of a living adult frog (Figure 42). The frog larynx opens into the pharynx and contains vocal cords that vibrate to produce croaking sounds. Only the primitive or primary palate, which forms the anterior-most part of the human hard palate, is present in the frog. In the eight- to ten-week human fetus, the two lateral palatine shelves, which appeared during evolution in the reptiles, have joined the primary palate to form a structure equivalent to the hard palate of living alligators (Figures 43 and 44). Only a short soft palate forms in reptiles (Hyman 1946). Therefore, the nasal cavities cannot be completely walled off from the pharynx. The alligator larynx opens into the pharynx directly behind the tongue and contains vocal cords, which, in adults, can produce loud sounds (Storer 1943).

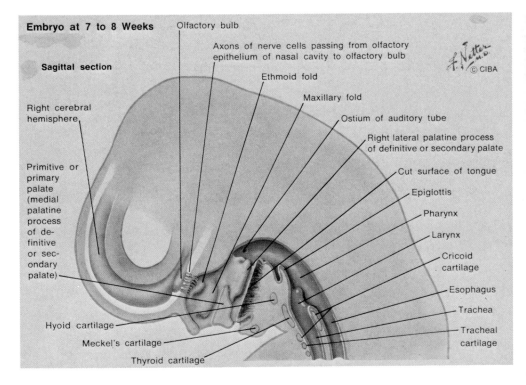

Figure 41. Diagram of the upper respiratory system of a human embryo at seven to eight weeks of development. Only the primitive or primary palate forms the floor of the nasal cavities, resulting in a wide communication between the nasal and oral cavities. *From Crelin (1976). ©Copyright 1976, CIBA Pharmaceutical Company, Division of CIBA-GEIGY Corporation. Reprinted with permission from CLINICAL SYMPOSIA, illustrated by Frank H. Netter, M.D. All rights reserved.*

Although birds evolved from reptiles just as the mammals did, their vocal cords are not located in their larynx but rather in their syrinx at the lower end of the trachea (Storer 1943). Otherwise, their upper respiratory system is essentially the same as that of the living reptiles (Figure 45). When the mammals evolved from the reptiles, they acquired two unique upper respiratory system structures: a soft palate and an epiglottis. Even though the rudiments of the mammalian soft palate and epiglottis are present in reptiles, they did not become vital functional structures of the respiratory system until long after the mammals evolved. This was un-doubtedly associated with the evolution of the ability of newborn mammals to suckle the teat of the mammary gland efficiently. Evidence for this is the lack of a functional soft palate and epiglottis in the living, nonsuckling, primitive, egg-laying mammals (Goodrich 1958; Hyman 1946).

The egg-laying mammals—the duckbilled platypus and the spiny ant-eater—are living indicators that the first mammals to evolve retained certain reptilian features in their skeletal structure, reproductive system, and egg-

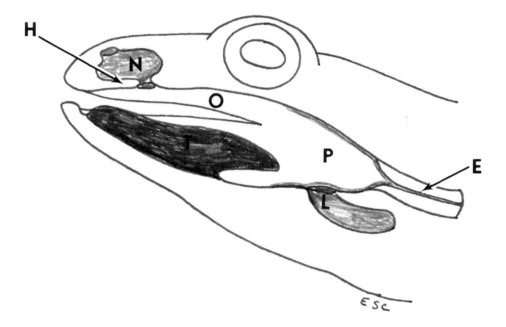

Figure 42. Diagram of the head of an adult frog showing one of the two nasal sacs or cavities (N) communicating with the oral cavity (O). The primitive or primary palate (H) forms the floor of the nasal cavities. The muscular tongue (T) is located entirely within the oral cavity (O). P: pharynx. E: esophagus. L: larynx.

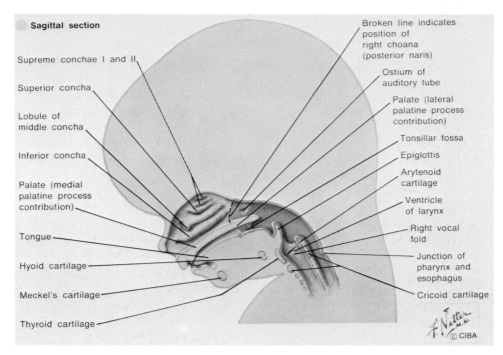

Figure 43. Diagram of the upper respiratory system of an eight to ten week human fetus. The palate forms the roof of the oral cavity. The soft palate portion has not yet formed, leaving the nasal cavities and nasopharynx in open communication. *From Crelin (1976). ©Copyright 1976, CIBA Pharmaceutical Company, Division of CIBA-GEIGY Corporation. Reprinted with permission from CLINICAL SYMPOSIA, illustrated by Frank H. Netter, M.D. All rights reserved.*

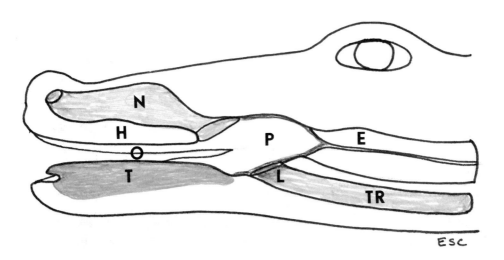

Figure 44. Diagram of the head of an adult alligator showing a hard palate (H) forming the roof of the oral cavity (O). A soft palate is only a short flap or velum in reptiles. Therefore, the nasal cavities (N) are in open communication with the pharynx (P). The tongue (T) is located entirely within the oral cavity (O). E: esophagus. L: larynx. TR: trachea.

laying ability, even as they developed a warm blood system, mammary glands (from modified sweat glands), and hair. The upper respiratory system acquired the suckling function later, because the mammary glands of the first egg-layers must have lacked teats, just as the present-day ones do. The infants of the living egg-layers lick up the milk that is secreted onto the fur from the openings of the mammary glands (Hyman 1946; Parker and Haswell 1921; Storer 1943). The epiglottis evolved from tissue independent of the original branchial arch skeletal tissue from which all of the other cartilages of the larynx evolved (Hyman 1946; Parker and Haswell 1921). Its appearance during human development is earlier than its appearance during evolution, relative to the other structures of the respiratory system (Figure 34). This is probably the result of heterochrony (Gould 1977).

In all of the suckling mammals, the epiglottis serves to guide the larynx into the nasopharynx. Simultaneously, the soft palate evolved as a flexible extension of the hard palate. The soft palate became a flap, or velum, of striated muscle, which can either close off the nasopharynx, resulting in a complete separation of the nasal cavities and the oral cavity and pharynx, or fit tightly against the front and sides of the larynx when it is inserted into the nasopharynx (Figure 46). The elevation and lockup of the larynx into the nasopharynx allows newborn mammals, including marsupials, to

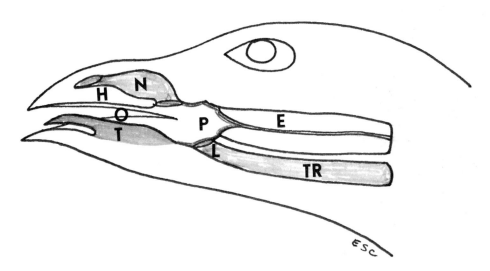

Figure 45. Diagram of the head of an adult song sparrow showing a hard palate (H) forming the roof of the oral cavity (O). A soft palate is lacking in birds. Therefore, the nasal cavities (N) are in open communication with the pharynx (P). The tongue (T) is located entirely within the oral cavity (O). E: esophagus. L: larynx. TR: trachea.

51

swallow milk and breathe air simultaneously. This ability in the newborn mammal is a reflex known as obligate nose breathing. Once solid food is ingested, it is imperative that the larynx retract or unlock from the naso-pharynx and descend to allow the bolus of food to pass freely from the oral cavity into the pharynx through the relatively wide communication between the two structures, the isthmus faucium, as it is swallowed. With one exception besides the egg-layers, all mammals, including the cetaceans (whales, dolphins, and porpoises), retain the ability to lock the larynx into the nasopharynx throughout their lives (Goodrich 1958). The one exception is human beings. Otherwise, besides the egg-layers, all other adult mam-mals are essentially obligate nose-breathers during quiet respiration, be-cause they shut their mouth, lock their larynx into the nasopharynx, and breathe through their nose. This is illustrated in Figure 46, which shows the status of the upper respiratory system of an adult horse during quiet respiration. The lockup of the larynx into the nasopharynx of another adult herbivore, a sheep, is shown in Figure 47. The lockup is shown in two

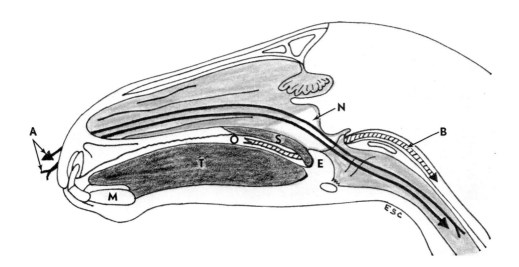

Figure 46. Diagram of the head of an adult horse during quiet respiration. The soft palate (S) is in snug contact with the epiglottis (E) because the larynx is locked into the nasopharynx (N). Arrows (A) indicate the free flow of air passing from the nasal cavities, through the larynx and down the trachea to the lungs and back again; all the while liquid can be swallowed from the oral cavity (O), on either side of the larynx into the pharynx and esophagus as indicated by the hatched arrow (B). The tongue (T) is located entirely within the oral cavity (O). Original symphysis of the mandible (M). *After Figure 339 (E), E. Pernkopf, 1980. Atlas of topographical and applied human anatomy. Vol. 1,* Head and Neck. *Baltimore-Munich: Urban and Schwarzberg.*

adult carnivores—a dog (Figure 48) and cat (Figure 49)—two adult monkeys (Figures 50 and 51), and an adult chimpanzee (Figure 52).

Rubber Chimpanzee Vocal Tract

I made a solid silicone rubber cast of the upper respiratory system of an adult male chimpanzee using a cadaver head cut in the midplane in the same manner described for that of an adult male human being in Chapter 2 and shown in Figure 16. The configuration of the silicone rubber cast of the chimpanzee upper respiratory system is that found in an adult during quiet respiration, breathing through the nose with the mouth closed (Figures 53 and 54). The larynx is locked into the nasopharynx and the entire tongue is in the oral cavity. This, of course, resulted in it being quite different in configuration from the silicone rubber cast of the adult human male upper respiratory system during quiet respiration (Figure 16). The chimpanzee vocal tract is gently curved, whereas the adult human tract is bent at a right angle.

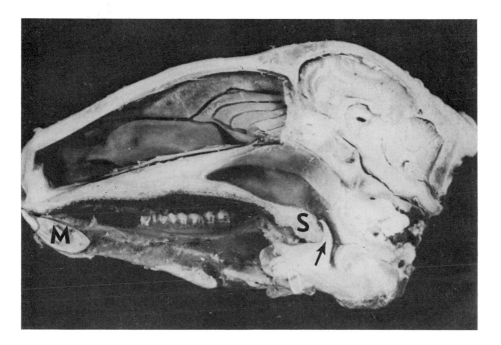

Figure 47. Right half of the head of an adult female sheep cut in the midplane. The epiglottis (arrow) is in direct contact with the soft palate (S) because the larynx is locked into the nasopharynx. The excised tongue was located entirely within the oral cavity. Original symphysis of the mandible (M).

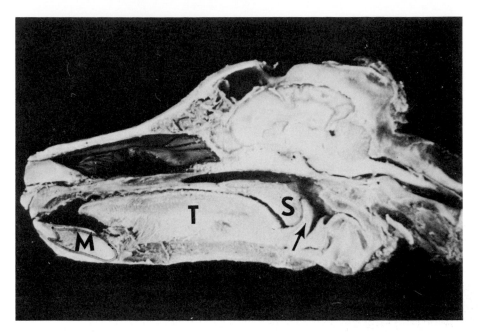

Figure 48. Right half of the head of an adult male dog, *Canis familiaris*, cut in the midplane. The epiglottis (arrow) is in direct contact with the soft palate (S) because the larynx is locked into the nasopharynx. The tongue (T) is located entirely within the oral cavity. Original symphysis of the mandible (M).

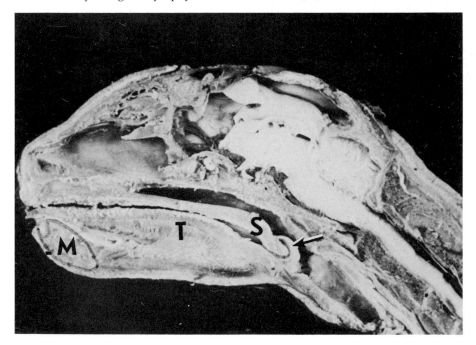

Figure 49. Right half of the head of an adult female cat, *Felis domestica*, cut in the midplane. The epiglottis (arrow) is in direct contact with the soft palate (S) because the larynx is locked into the nasopharynx. The tongue (T) is located entirely within the oral cavity. Original symphysis of the mandible (M).

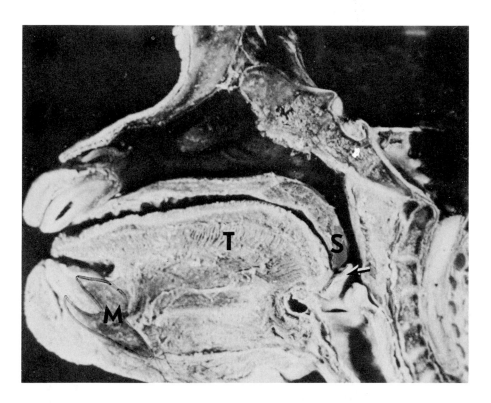

Figure 50. Right half of the head of an adult female stumptail macaque, *Macaca arctoides*, cut in the midplane. The epiglottis (arrow) is in direct contact with the soft palate (S) because the larynx is locked into the nasopharynx. The tongue (T) is located entirely within the oral cavity. Original symphysis of the mandible or simian shelf (M).

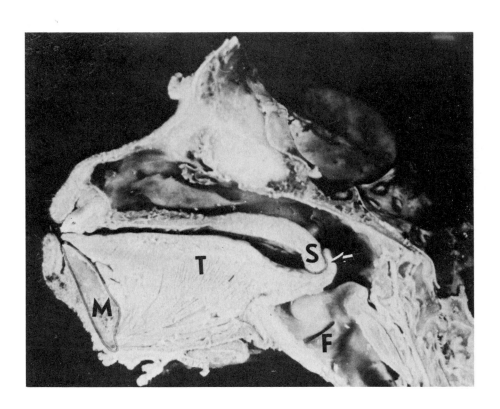

Figure 51. Right half of the head of an adult male spider monkey, *Ateles paniscus,* cut in the midplane. The epiglottis (arrow) is in direct contact with the soft palate (S) because the larynx is locked into the nasopharynx. The tongue (T) is located entirely within the oral cavity. Original symphysis of the mandible or simian shelf (M).

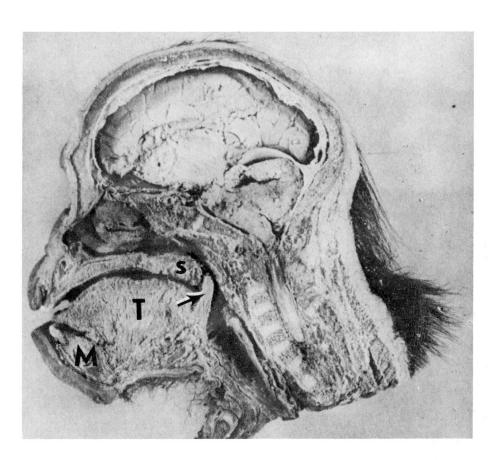

Figure 52. Right half of the head of an adult male chimpanzee, *Pan troglodytes,* cut in the midplane. The epiglottis (arrow) is in direct contact with the soft palate (S) because the larynx is locked into the nasopharynx. The tongue (T) is located entirely within the oral cavity. Original symphysis of the mandible or simian shelf (M).

Obligate Nose Breathing

In 1973 I published a book on the functional anatomy of the human newborn infant (Crelin 1973). By that time, through my own research I had become aware of the fact that the upper respiratory system of the human infant differed markedly from that of a human adult. The fact that all adult nonhuman mammals above the egg-laying ones could lock their larynges into their nasopharynges was generally stated in zoology textbooks used before I was born (Parker and Haswell 1921). However, a description of this ability is conspicuously absent from the current biology textbooks. The fact that the human newborn infant is an obligate nose breather is also conspicuously absent from the current biology and medical textbooks, including those on human embryology. This is surprising because there have

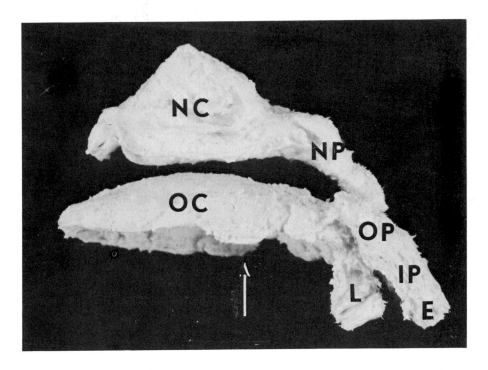

Figure 53. A solid silicone rubber cast of the space of the upper respiratory system of an adult male chimpanzee, *Pan troglodytes.* The arrow points toward the location of the foramen cecum of the tongue, which indicates the junction of the anterior two-thirds and the posterior one-third of the tongue within the oral cavity (OC). NC: nasal cavities. NP: nasopharynx. OP: oropharynx. IP: infralaryngeal pharynx. E: esophagus. L: larynx.

Figure 54. An adult female chimpanzee, *Pan troglodytes,* during quiet respiration. The larynx is locked into the nasopharynx. *From Yerkes and Yerkes (1929).*

been a number of technical studies published in the last twenty years in the research journals on the functional development of the human respiratory system (Polgar and Weng 1979).

In my book on the functional anatomy of the human newborn infant, I describe the newborn infant as an obligate nose breather (Crelin 1973). The infant locks its larynx into the pharynx in the same manner as the adult nonhuman mammals, except the egg-laying ones, do (Figure 55). Since the airway resistance contributed by the nasal passages of human newborn infants is slightly less than half that contributed by the adult human passages, obligate nose breathing is a most efficient form of respiration (Polgar and Kong 1965). I assume this is also true in all of the adult nonhuman mammals that have essentially the same anatomical configu-

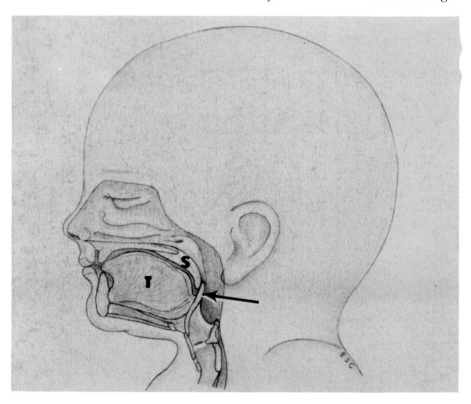

Figure 55. A drawing of the head and neck of a full-term human newborn infant during quiet respiration. The right half of the upper respiratory system is exposed with a midline cut. The epiglottis (arrow) is in direct contact with the soft palate (S) because the larynx is locked into the nasopharynx. The tongue (T) is located entirely within the oral cavity.

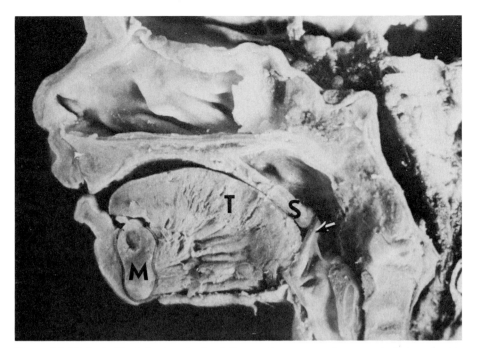

Figure 56. Right half of the head of a full-term human newborn male infant cut in the midplane. The epiglottis (arrow) is in direct contact with the soft palate (S) because the larynx is locked into the nasopharynx. The tongue (T) is located entirely within the oral cavity. Original symphysis of the mandible (M).

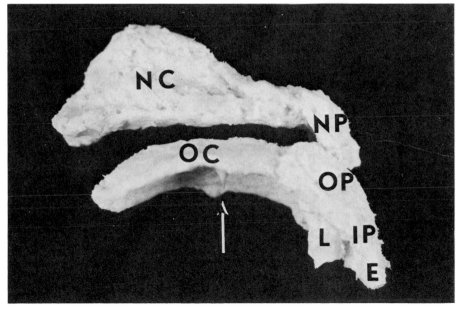

Figure 57. A solid silicone rubber cast of the space of the upper respiratory system of a full-term human male infant. The arrow points to the location of the foramen cecum of the tongue. NC: nasal cavities. NP: nasopharynx. OC: oral cavity. OP: oropharynx. IP: infralaryngeal pharynx. E: esophagus. L: larynx.

ration as a human newborn infant and are, in essence, obligate nose breathers. I used the head of a full-term, human, male, newborn infant cadaver cut in the midplane to make a silicone rubber cast of the upper respiratory system (Figures 56 and 57). I found that the cast closely resembled that of an adult chimpanzee rather than that of an adult male human (Figures 16 and 53). My former medical student, Dr. Howard W. Smith, who is presently a professor of otolaryngology at Yale, allowed me to view his collection of many thousands of radiographs of patients ranging in age from birth to puberty. I found that, during quiet respiration, breathing through the nose with the mouth closed, the human newborn infant has the larynx locked into the nasopharynx (Figure 58).

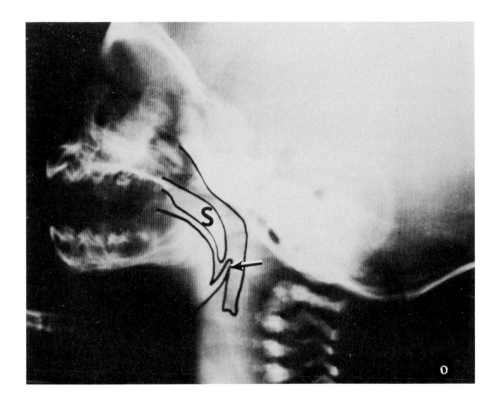

Figure 58. A radiograph of a living full-term newborn male infant. The neck is rotated so that a lateral view of the head is obtained. The pharynx, soft palate, posterior tongue and epiglottis are outlined with ink. The epiglottis (arrow) is in direct contact with the soft palate (S) because the larynx is locked into the nasopharynx as the infant breathes through his nose with his mouth closed.

To confirm the notion that human newborn infants can breathe air and swallow liquid simultaneously, I examined cineradiographic films of twelve infants less than one week old taken by pediatric radiologists at Yale for various diagnostic purposes. Each child swallowed a barium-milk mixture. Although it appeared that the larynx remained locked into the nasopharynx when the infants swallowed the mixture, the views could be questioned due to the lack of clarity of the tiny soft tissues of the upper respiratory system on the films. To obtain supportive evidence, I suggested to Dr. Laitman, when he was my graduate student, that he should attempt to place a small tantalum hemoclip on the tip of the uvula of the soft palate and on the tip of the epiglottis of a young monkey. When cineradiographic and still radiographs were made of the monkey swallowing a barium-milk mixture, the clearly visible metal clips would show the exact location of the tips of the soft palate and epiglottis. As reported in Laitman, Crelin, and Conlogue (1977), with the able assistance of X-ray technician G. J. Conlogue, he was successful in performing this procedure (Figures 59 and 60). When the monkey swallowed the mixture, the metal clips showed that

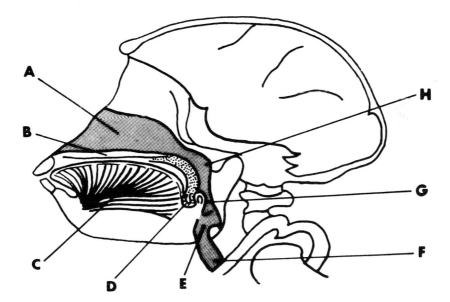

Figure 59. A drawing of the juvenile male stumptail macaque Macaca arctoides, shown in Figure 60. The epiglottis (G), with a tantalum clip attached to it, is in direct contact with the uvula of the soft palate (D) that also has a tantalum clip attached to it. The larynx (E) is locked into the nasopharynx (H) while the monkey breathes quietly with his mouth closed. A: nasal cavities. B: hard palate. C: tongue. F: trachea.

the larynx remained locked into the nasopharynx (Figure 61). The cine-radiographic films of the monkey were compared frame by frame with those of the human infants, confirming that the human newborn infant can swallow milk and breathe air simultaneously. I found this to be a difficult concept to teach to the resident physicians in otolaryngology, who had only been taught adult anatomy and function. Therefore, I made exact, latex rubber copies of the tongue, larynx, pharynx, and soft palate and attached them to the skull of a human newborn infant (Figures 62 and 63). With the tongue and larynx attached to the separate mandible, I could slide the epiglottis up behind the soft palate, which was shaped so that it embraced the front and sides of the larynx when it was locked into the nasopharynx (Figure 64). When the larynx was locked into the nasopharynx, it divided the wide continuation of the oral cavity with the oropharynx, the isthmus faucium, into two channels or clefts, one on each side of the

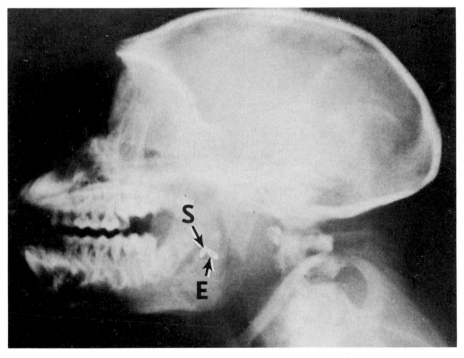

Figure 60. Lateral radiograph of the living juvenile male stumptail monkey depicted in Figure 59. A tantalum metal clip (S) is attached to the tip of the uvula of the soft palate. A tantalum clip (E) is also attached to the tip of the epiglottis. The position of each clip shows that the larynx is locked into the nasopharynx as the monkey quietly breathes through his nose with his mouth closed.

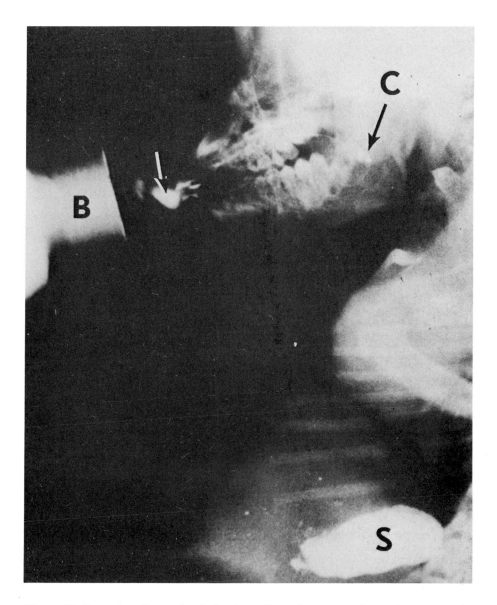

Figure 61. Lateral radiograph of the juvenile male stumptail monkey shown in Figure 60, taken while he was ingesting a bottle of barium-milk mixture. The mixture is seen in the neck of the bottle (B), in the nipple (arrow) of the bottle held between the monkey's lips, and in his stomach (S). A cineradiographic film was also taken during the swallowing. The metal clips (C) attached to the tips of the closely approximated uvula and epiglottis did not change their position, showing that the monkey breathed air and swallowed liquid simultaneously.

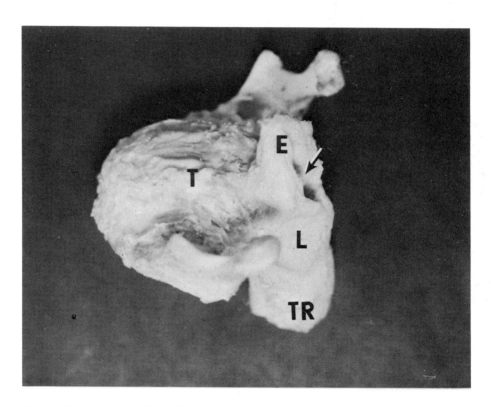

Figure 62. A view looking down on the left side of the mandible of a full-term newborn male infant to which is attached a latex rubber tongue (T), epiglottis (E), larynx (L), and uppermost part of the trachea (TR). The arrow points to the opening into the vestibule of the hollow rubber larynx.

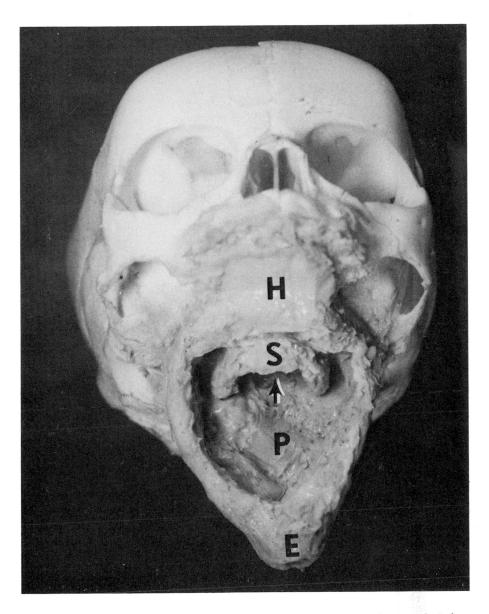

Figure 63. A view of the under surface of a full-term human newborn male infant skull to which is attached a latex rubber mucosa of the hard palate (H), soft palate (S), pharynx (P), and uppermost part of the esophagus (E). The lateral walls of the pharynx end where they would be continuous with the lateral walls of the oral cavity. With the tongue and larynx missing, the interior of the rubber pharynx (P) is exposed. This allows the shape of rubber soft palate (S) when it wraps around the front and sides of the larynx that is locked into the nasopharynx to be seen. Thus, the tubular opening (arrow) through which the larynx, led by the epiglottis, slides upward to lock into the nasopharynx is formed in front and on each side by the soft palate, and posteriorly by the posterior wall of the pharynx.

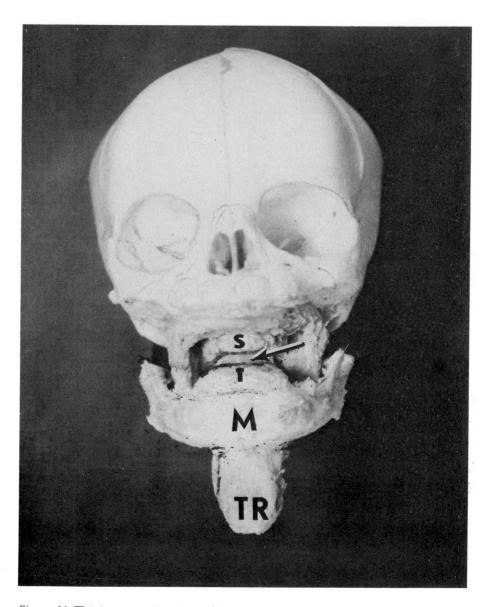

Figure 64. This is an anterior view of the skull shown in Figure 63 and the mandible shown in Figure 62. The rubber epiglottis and larynx attached to the mandible (M) have been slid up behind the rubber soft palate (S) to lock into the nasopharyngeal portion of the rubber pharynx attached to the skull. The lockup is not complete. This results in a wide space between the mandibular condyles and the articular fossae of the skull. It also allows some of the epiglottis (arrow) to be seen. T: rubber tongue. TR: rubber uppermost part of the trachea.

larynx (Figure 65). When I passed plastic coated wires into each of these channels, they converged in the rubber pharynx and then passed out through the uppermost part of the esophagus (Figure 66). This is the route taken by swallowed milk in the human newborn infant when the larynx is locked into the nasopharynx. When I passed plastic coated wires into each nasal cavity of the skull, they converged in the rubber larynx and then passed out of the uppermost part of the trachea (Figure 66). This is the route respired air takes during the swallowing of milk by the human newborn infant when the larynx is locked into the nasopharynx. The air and liquid routes are completely walled off from each other.

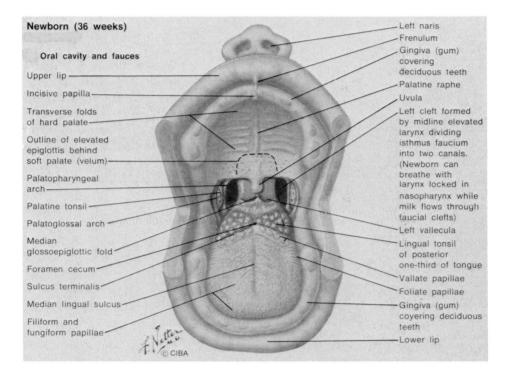

Figure 65. A drawing looking into the oral cavity of a full-term human newborn infant to show the larynx locked into the nasopharynx. The mouth is opened abnormally wide for a better view by slitting the cheek wall on each side. The elevated larynx locked into the nasopharynx divides the direct continuation of the oral cavity with the pharynx, the isthmus faucium, into two channels or clefts through which liquid can pass and be completely walled off from the airway. *From Crelin (1976). ©Copyright 1976, CIBA Pharmaceutical Company, Division of CIBA-GEIGY Corporation. Reprinted with permission from CLINICAL SYMPOSIA, illustrated by Frank H. Netter, M.D. All rights reserved.*

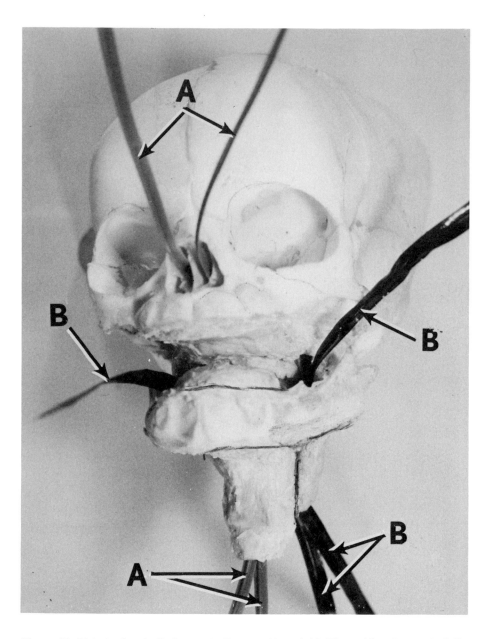

Figure 66. This is the skull shown in Figures 63 and 64. The rubber larynx is fully locked into the rubber nasopharynx. Two plastic coated wires (A) are inserted, one each through a nasal cavity. They converge in the rubber nasopharynx to enter the rubber larynx and then pass out through the rubber uppermost part of the trachea. Two wires (B) are inserted, one each through the divided isthmus faucium. They converge in the rubber infralaryngeal part of the rubber pharynx to pass out through the rubber uppermost part of the esophagus. The rubber larynx is snugly encircled by the rubber pharyngeal wall posteriorly and by the rubber soft palate anteriorly and laterally.

Descent of Human Larynx

The heads and necks of human cadavers of both sexes, differing in age from about six months after birth to ten years of age, were cut in the midplane. Silicone rubber casts of the upper respiratory system of these cadavers were also made to compare differences in size and form. Up to two years of age, the upper respiratory system is essentially the same as that of a newborn infant (Figures 67 and 68). The larynx can be locked into the nasopharynx, and the entire tongue is located within the oral cavity. It also has a close resemblance to the upper respiratory system of an adult chimpanzee (Figures 52 and 53). Between two and six years of age, there is a gradual descent of the larynx to a lower position in the neck. The larynx cannot be locked into the nasopharynx of the cadaver of a five-year–old child. Along with the descent of the larynx, there is a descent of the

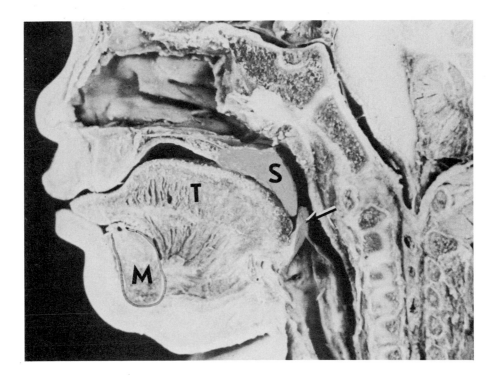

Figure 67. Right half of the head of a two-year–old human female cut in the mid-plane. The epiglottis (arrow) is in direct contact with the soft palate (S) because the larynx is locked into the nasopharynx. The tongue (T) is located entirely within the oral cavity. Original symphysis of the mandible (M).

71

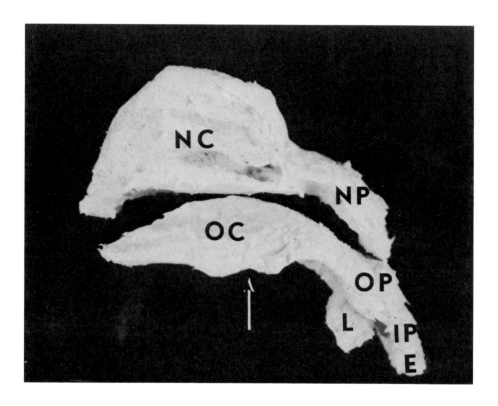

Figure 68. A solid silicone rubber cast of the space of the upper respiratory system of a two-year–old human female. The arrow points to the location of the foramen cecum of the tongue. NC: nasal cavities. OC: oral cavity. NP: nasopharynx. OP: oropharynx. IP: infralaryngeal pharynx. E: esophagus. L: larynx.

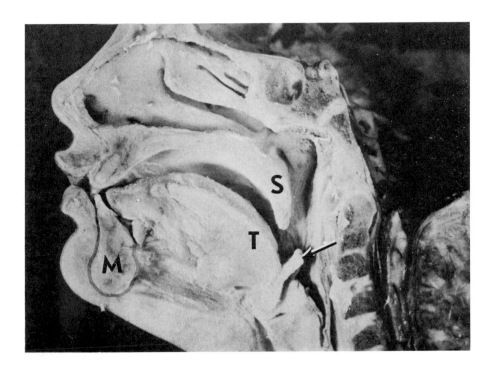

Figure 69. Right half of the head of a six-year–old human male cut in the midplane. The epiglottis (arrow) of a maximally elevated larynx is not in contact with a pendulous soft palate (S). The posterior third of the tongue (T) is vertically oriented to form the anterior wall of the oropharynx. Original symphysis of the mandible (M).

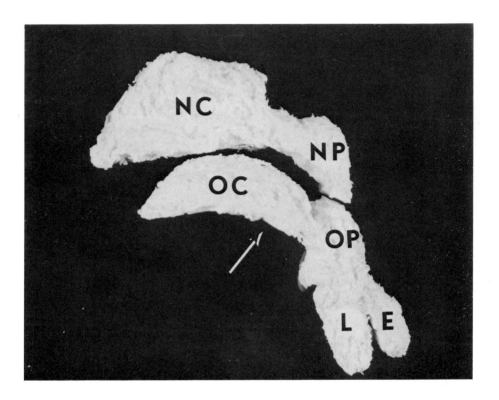

Figure 70. A solid silicone rubber cast of the space of the upper respiratory system of a six-year–old human male. The arrow points to the location of the foramen cecum of the tongue. NC: nasal cavities. OC: oral cavity. NP: nasopharynx. OP: oropharynx. E: esophagus. L: larynx.

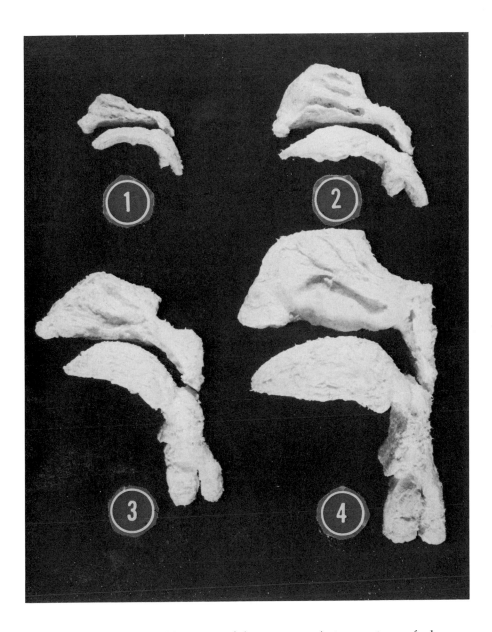

Figure 71. Solid silicone rubber casts of the upper respiratory systems of a human newborn male infant (1), a two-year–old female child (2), a six-year–old male child (3), and a male adult (4), showing the actual differences in size and shape.

posterior part of the tongue, which gradually forms more and more of the anterior wall of the oropharynx. By six years of age, the upper respiratory system has essentially the adult configuration (Figures 69, 70, 71, and 72). The tip of the epiglottis cannot be made to touch the uvula of a pendulous soft palate, and the posterior third of the tongue is vertically oriented to form the anterior wall of the oropharynx. It is not possible to forcibly return the posterior third of the tongue in the cadaver of a six-year–old child to its original position in the oral cavity. The separation of the soft palate and epiglottis becomes greater as the upper respiratory system grows to its adult size (Figure 73). When the larynx is elevated in a living adult, the soft palate is simultaneously elevated (Figure 74). Therefore, there is always a wide separation between the uvula of the soft palate and the tip of the epiglottis in human adults.

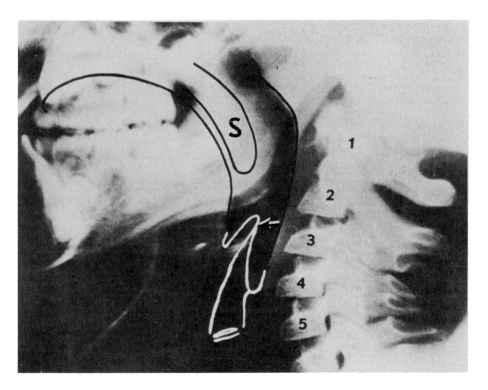

Figure 72. Lateral radiograph of a living six-year–old human male. The pharynx, larynx, soft palate (S), and tongue are outlined in ink. The vocal folds are at the low level of the articular disc between the fifth and sixth cervical vertebrae. The posterior third of the tongue is vertically oriented to form the anterior wall of the oropharynx. The epiglottis (arrow) is not in contact with the pendulous soft palate (S) as the child breathes through his nose with his mouth closed.

When an adult human being swallows, the epiglottis may remain in a vertical position. When the epiglottis is destroyed, there are no untoward effects, even when the person swallows (Williams and Warwick 1980). Thus, the epiglottis can, but does not of necessity, serve as a trap door to cover the opening into the larynx. Its function in nonadult human beings is to guide the larynx up behind the soft palate so it can lock into the nasopharynx. This ability is retained in all adult mammals above the egg-layers except human beings, who lose the ability between the third and fifth year after birth. As the larynx and posterior third of the tongue descend into the neck, the supralaryngeal pharynx increases in length. This results in a considerable extent of the pharynx serving as a common passageway for both inspired air and ingested food (Figures 3, 4, 73, and 74). Such an arrangement causes many thousands of people in the world each year to

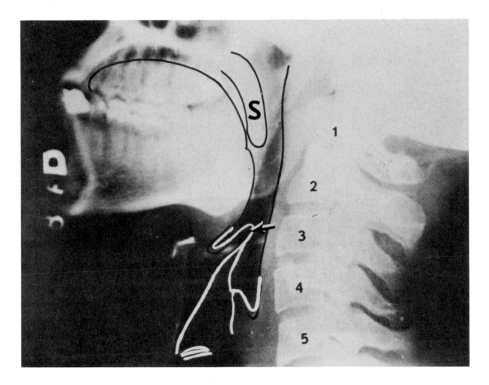

Figure 73. Lateral radiograph of a living human male adult. The pharynx, larynx, soft palate (S), and tongue are outlined in ink. The vocal folds are at the normal level of the articular disc between the fifth and sixth cervical vertebrae. The posterior third of the tongue is vertically oriented to form the anterior wall of the oropharynx. The epiglottis (arrow) is widely separated from the pendulous soft palate (S) as the man breathes through his nose with his mouth closed.

choke to death from suffocation due to something being stuck in their throat. Since it is usually a large bolus of food that is frequently eaten at a restaurant, the cause of death is referred to as a "café coronary." Another common cause of death directly related to the adult pharyngeal morphology is the aspiration of vomitus into the respiratory tubes. The "Heimlich maneuver" is used to free a bolus of food stuck in a person's throat (Day, Crelin, and Dubois 1982). The person is grabbed from behind around the waist and abruptly squeezed to force air from the lungs and hopefully dislodge the bolus. The selective pressures during evolution resulting in the attainment of the unique arrangement of the upper respiratory system in the human adult must have been very positive when one considers how detrimental the arrangement is in regards to the susceptibility for choking

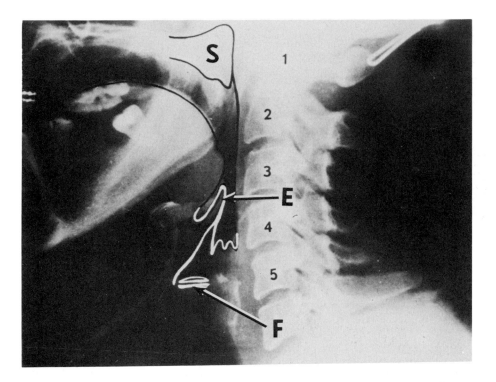

Figure 74. Lateral radiograph of a living human female adult. The pharynx, larynx, soft palate (S), and tongue are outlined in ink. The vocal folds (F) are at a high level of the middle of the fifth cervical vertebra. The posterior third of the tongue is vertically oriented to form the anterior wall of the oropharynx. The epiglottis is widely separated from the soft palate (S), which is elevated to close off the nasopharynx as the woman produces a high pitched "ō" vowel sound, as in the word kn**ow**.

to death. The use of the unique rearrangement of the vocal tract to produce speech sounds, which led to the unique human characteristic of a spoken language, must have been an important selective pressure.

It was with this in mind that I experimented on the functional development of the human vocal tract, hoping to find clues to what might have occurred during the functional evolution of the tract. I first decided to test a nonhuman vocal tract to see just how unique the adult human tract was in producing the sounds of speech. I chose that of an adult male chimpanzee, because its vocal tract has the basic configuration of all of the nonhuman vocal tracts and yet the primate is in so many other ways very similar to human beings. Using the head and neck of an adult male chimpanzee cadaver cut in the midplane, I made a hollow latex rubber vocal tract in the same manner described for that of the adult human male in Chapter 2 (Figure 75). The rubber tract closely resembled those of human infants up to two years of age. It differed in that the hard palate and oral cavity were relatively much longer. Also, a solid rubber "simian" shelf was

Figure 75. A hollow latex rubber vocal tract of an adult male chimpanzee. H: hard palate. O: oral cavity. S: simian shelf. OP: oropharynx. IP: infralaryngeal pharynx. L: larynx.

attached to the chimpanzee tract to serve as an unmodifiable region of the tract in the same manner that the attached solid rubber hard palate does (Figure 75). The so-called simian (meaning monkey or ape) shelf is located at the anterior-inferior part of the mandible (Figure 76). Actually, the shelf is a general characteristic of the mandibles of all nonhuman mammals (Figure 77). Its presence is reflected in the absence of a chin, because it is merely a slanted part of the mandible containing the roots of the lower incisor teeth, which are arranged more in the horizontal plane than in the vertical. This is evident when the anterior arch of the mandibular body is cut in cross section at the site of what was the separation of the two halves of the newborn mandible by fibrous tissue, the symphysis. The two bony

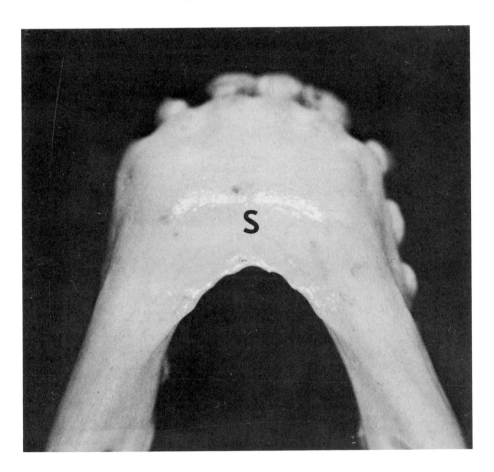

Figure 76. A view of the bottom of the front of the mandible of an adult male chimpanzee. The so-called simian shelf (S) is at the site of the original symphysis.

halves of the human mandible are joined at the symphysis when this is obliterated during the first year after birth (Williams and Warwick 1980).

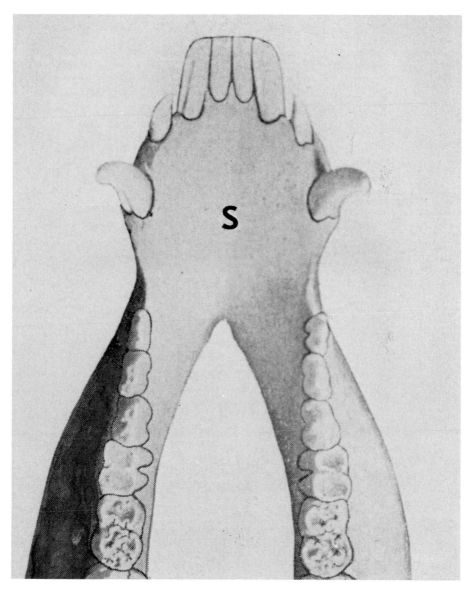

Figure 77. A view of the top of the front of the mandible of an adult male pig. (S) indicates the site of the original symphysis. From S. Sisson and J. D. Grossman. 1947. *Anatomy of the domestic animals.* Philadelphia: W. B. Saunders Co.

81

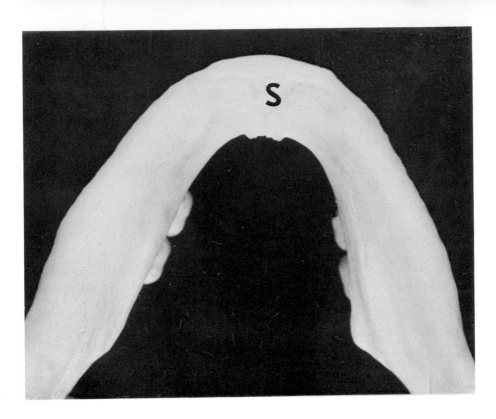

Figure 78. A view of the bottom of the front of the mandible of a human adult male. (S) indicates the site of the original symphysis.

The human mandible is quite different, because a shelf is totally lacking in a normal-sized mandible from birth to adulthood (Figure 78). An exception is the shorter-than-normal human mandible that results in the person lacking a chin and having lower incisor teeth oriented more horizontally than vertically. The lack of a shelf in the human mandible is evident when the site of the symphysis is viewed in cross section (Figures 3, 4, 14, 15, 32, 55, 56, 67, 69, 104, and 110). It is interesting that the shelf is lacking in the mandible of a newborn chimpanzee (Figure 114). However, by the time of the eruption of the full set of deciduous teeth, the shelf is present (Figure 119).

Chimpanzee Vocalizations

I have only been a casual observer of chimpanzees vocalizing. However, their vocalizations have been recorded and studied extensively (Andrew 1963; Bauer 1984). The sounds are low-pitched grunts and pants or the "ah" cry and its variations. The cry varies from a long, loud scream to short ones, which may be whimpers or barks. The "ah" is produced with the least effort on the part of the chimpanzee vocal tract. It is logical that this vowel-like sound and slight variations of it are the most common vocalizations chimpanzees make. Chimpanzees communicate with each other by making vocal sounds just as most mammals do, but they don't have the capacity for true language, either verbally or by using signs and symbols.

A detailed investigation by Terrace, Petitto, Saunders and Bever (1979) shows that apes can learn many isolated symbols (as can dogs, horses, and other nonhuman species), but they show no unequivocal evidence of mastering the conversational, semantic, or syntactic organization of language. Although chimpanzees make a wide range of what may be called vowel sounds, they don't clearly enunciate the vowel sounds "ā," "ē," "ī," "ō," "ü" as mature human beings do. The formant frequencies of adult human speech are very difficult to identify in chimpanzee sounds (Bauer 1984). I was always curious if the chimpanzee vocal tract could be shaped to produce the necessary formant frequencies for the vowel sounds, even though the tract differs markedly in its configuration from that of the adult human. Therefore, I attached the latex rubber chimpanzee vocal tract to the plastic larynx used for the rubber adult human vocal tract and tested its ability to produce the vowels in the same manner described for the rubber adult human tract in Chapter 2. Again, I used three pounds of air pressure. After the experience I had of making the rubber human adult vocal tract produce vowel sounds, I relied on my hearing alone to judge the vowel-producing ability of the chimpanzee rubber tract. Once I could shape the tract to produce a desired vowel sound, I made exact drawings to scale of the tract in the midsagittal and cross-sectional planes (Figures 79–84).

The chimpanzee "ah" sound is more like the shorter "ah" sound at the beginning and end of the word "America" and is the most common sound the chimpanzee makes. It was a simple process to get the rubber chimpanzee tract to produce the "ä" vowel sound. The chimpanzee opens its mouth wide and forms the whole oral cavity into a gradually flared tube by depressing its tongue (Figure 79). Air passes freely out of the larynx into the anterior end of a wide pharynx then directly into and out of the oral cavity. The infralaryngeal part of the pharynx is also wide. To produce the "ā," the vocal tract was made to assume the shape needed to produce the "ä" vowel, except that the posterior part of the oral cavity was reduced slightly in size by elevating the entire posterior third of the tongue. The whole pharynx was also reduced in size (Figure 80). Apparently, the chimpanzee avoids any narrowing of the tract when vocalizing, including the slight narrowing of the tract to produce the "ā" vowel. Therefore, it prefers to make the "ä" rather than the "ā" vowel.

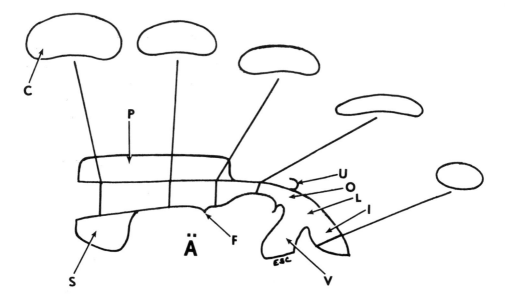

Figure 79. A drawing of the shape of the latex rubber adult male chimpanzee vocal tract in the midsagittal and cross-sectional planes when it produced the "ä" vowel sound. The cross sections (C) are through the anterior, middle, and posterior parts of the oral cavity; the junction of the oral cavity and the pharynx; and the infralaryngeal part of the pharynx. P: hard palate. S: simian shelf of mandible. F: foramen cecum of tongue. U: uvula of soft palate. O: oropharynx. I: infralaryngeal part of pharynx. V: vestibule of larynx.

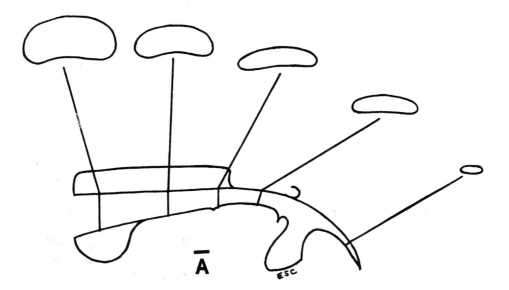

Figure 80. A drawing of the shape of the rubber adult male chimpanzee vocal tract in the midsagittal and cross-sectional planes when it produced the "ā" vowel sound.

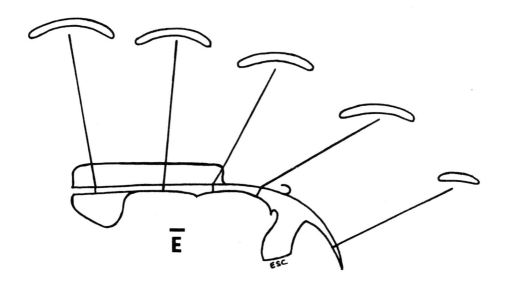

Figure 81. A drawing of the shape of the rubber adult male chimpanzee vocal tract in the midsagittal and cross-sectional planes when it produced the "ē" vowel sound.

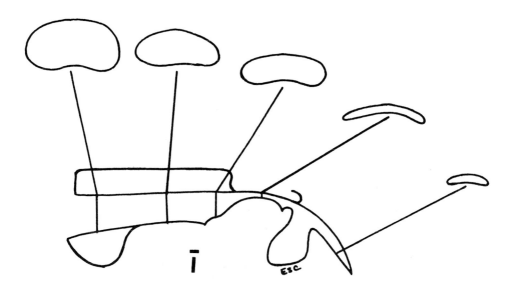

Figure 82. A drawing of the shape of the rubber adult male chimpanzee vocal tract in the midsagittal and cross-sectional planes when it produced the "ī" vowel sound.

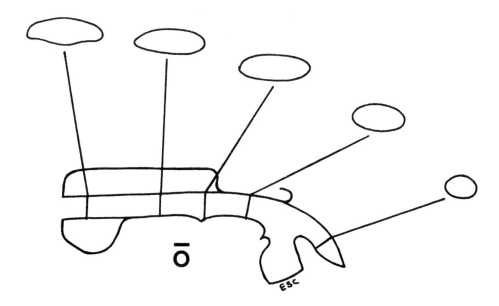

Figure 83. A drawing of the shape of the rubber adult male chimpanzee vocal tract in the midsagittal and cross-sectional planes when it produced the "ō" vowel sound.

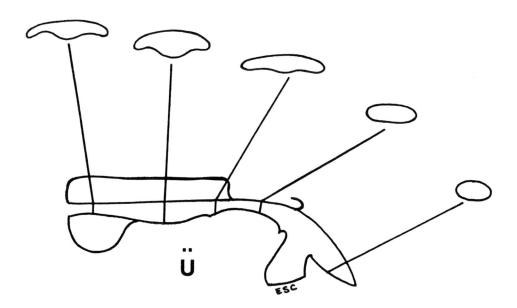

Figure 84. A drawing of the shape of the rubber adult male chimpanzee vocal tract in the midsagittal and cross-sectional planes when it produced the "ü" vowel sound.

To produce the "ē" vowel, the chimpanzee has to reduce its entire vocal tract to a flattened slit (Figure 81). The restriction in the air flow was so great it caused the "ē" vowel sound to have a very raspy quality and be of a very low volume using three pounds of air pressure. The diphthong "ī" was never produced to my satisfaction (Figure 82). The extreme narrowing of the back-most part of the oral cavity and the whole pharynx caused the "ī" vowel sound to be very raspy in quality and low in volume with three pounds of air pressure. Raising the air pressure to five pounds made the sound so raspy that it was difficult to recognize what the vowel was supposed to be.

To produce the vowel "ō," the rubber chimpanzee vocal tract was made to assume the form of a long, round tube that would be extended by the rounding of the lips (Figure 83). The anterior part of the tongue could only with difficulty be depressed centrally in order to have that part of the oral cavity form a round tube, due to the presence of the simian shelf. Opening the mouth wider in order to lower the anterior part of the tongue centrally caused the vowel sound to shift from the "ō" to the "ä" vowel. The "ü" vowel was even more difficult for the rubber chimpanzee tract than the "ō" sound because the mouth had to be opened only slightly (Figure 84). Again, the simian shelf interfered with making the anterior part of the tongue form a small round tube. The fact that the whole vocal tract had to be made to assume the form of a flattened small tube produced a lot of air turbulence. Thus, the "ü" vowel sound was quite raspy.

The experiments with the rubber chimpanzee vocal tract assure me that I could force a rubber tract of many nonhuman mammals to produce a set of vowel-like sounds, including those of mammals with even longer snouts, such as a horse. It is obvious that the chimpanzee vocal tract's lack of a right angle bend and of a long pharynx with the posterior third of the tongue forming its anterior wall and the larynx opening into the bottom of it make it less well adapted to producing vowel sounds than the human adult tract. It appears that the back and forth activity of the posterior third of the tongue to alter the shape of the vowel tract in the human adult is much more efficient in producing vowel sounds than the up and down movement of the comparable part of the tongue in all of the adult nonhuman mammals. The presence of an anterior mandibular shelf and the fact that the tongue is arranged horizontally and located entirely within the oral cavity in all of the adult nonhuman mammals must greatly interfere with the rapid activity of the tongue required to produce consonant sounds. At least 60 percent of the repertoire of American English speech sounds are consonants (Bauer 1984). Therefore, the speech sound production ability of a chimpanzee vocal tract is extremely limited, because it lacks the ability to produce the segmental contrast of consonants and vowels in a series. Chimpanzees avoid making the vowel sounds that require a restriction in the air flow of the vocal tract, especially the "ē," "ī," and "ü" vowel sounds. This greatly restricts their repertoire of speech sounds. For example, if the chimpanzee doesn't make the "ē" vowel, it eliminates it as a syllable nucleus and, consequently, eliminates a number of simple words formed by combining "ē" with consonants, for example, "bee," "fee," "gee," "he," "key," "lea," "me," "knee," "pea," "see," "tea," "wee," "ye," as well as a myriad of complex words consisting of a combination of many vowels and consonants that include the "ē" vowel one or more times. I conclude that all of the foregoing basic structural and functional deficiencies of the chimpanzee vocal tract, which interfere or limit the production of speech sounds, also pertain to all of the other nonhuman primates.

Human Infant Vocal Tract

I made a latex rubber vocal tract of a human male newborn infant and a two-year–old human female cadaver in the same manner described for that of an adult human male in Chapter 2 (Figures 85 and 86). Since the

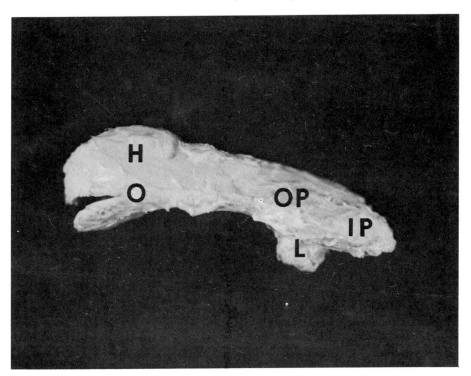

Figure 85. A hollow latex rubber vocal tract of a full-term human male infant. H: hard palate. O: oral cavity. OP: oropharynx. IP: infralaryngeal pharynx. L: larynx.

newborn and two-year–old tracts were identical except in size, I only tested the two-year–old tract, because it was much easier to handle. I used the same plastic larynx that produced the fundamental frequency for the adult human and chimpanzee tracts. Before I tested the two-year–old tract, I examined Dr. Howard Smith's radiographs of infants between birth and two years of age. Many lateral views of the infants were made when they were crying (Figure 87). When the infant cries, the larynx is withdrawn from its locked position in the nasopharynx. This allows the crying sounds to be emitted through both the nose and the mouth. As soon as the very young infant stops vocalizing, the larynx is returned as a neuromuscular reflex to its locked position within the nasopharynx. Thus, the newborn human infant is an obligate nose breather. This means that the newborn infant is a reflex organism that will attempt to breathe only through the nose even if it is impossible. Infants born with a membranous wall across the posterior openings of the nasal cavities into the nasopharynx, a condition known as choanal atresia, usually suffocate if the condition is not immediately recognized and treated (Winther 1978). Any nasal obstruction

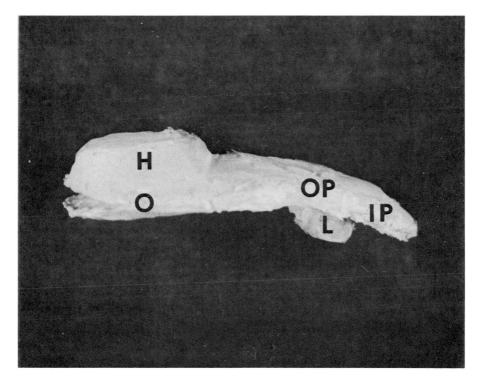

Figure 86. A hollow latex rubber vocal tract of a two-year–old human female. H: hard palate. O: oral cavity. OP: oropharynx. IP: infralaryngeal pharynx. L: larynx.

in the newborn infant caused by trauma, infection, or a tumor involves imminent risk of suffocation, because the infant will not breathe through the mouth. Breathing through the mouth when crying at intervals merely prolongs the period of suffocation. It was obvious to me that the child becomes a mouth breather long before the posterior part of the tongue and the larynx begin their permanent descent into the neck during the third year after birth. However, the exact time was not determined until a study, headed by my former medical student, Dr. Clarence Sasaki, who is now the chief of the section of otolaryngology at Yale, was made (Sasaki, Levine, Laitman, and Crelin 1977). Cineradiography and direct physical examinations revealed that human infants begin to cease being obligate nose breathers between four and six months of age. This period of time coincides with the peak incidence of sudden infant death syndrome (SIDS), commonly known as crib death.

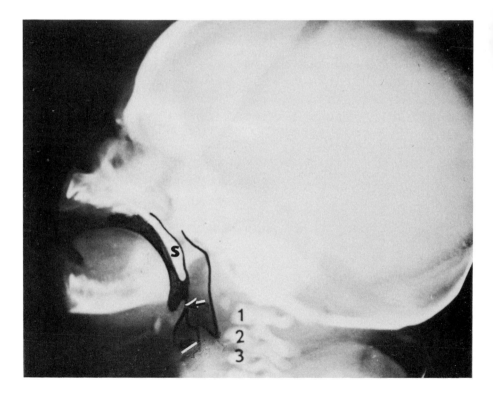

Figure 87. Lateral radiograph of a living human full-term female infant. The pharynx, larynx, soft palate (S), and tongue are outlined in ink. The epiglottis (arrow) is not in contact with the pendulous soft palate because the posterior part of the tongue and the larynx are pulled down into the neck as the infant emits crying sounds through the mouth and nose.

Sudden Infant Death Syndrome (SIDS)

SIDS is the cause of death of as many as 10,000 ostensibly healthy infants a year in the United States alone (Beckwith, Drage, and Naeye 1978). There are undoubtedly a number of causes of SIDS. One is surely neurological. Another could well be related to the switch from obligate nose breathing to volitional mouth breathing. In 1964 the late Dr. Harvey Kravitz, an Illinois pediatrician, observed from the medical literature that SIDS victims were usually found in a horizontal position, either face up or face down. Dr. Kravitz instructed each new mother in his practice to elevate the head of the baby's bed and encouraged her to keep the infant in a semireclining seat when out of the crib. Over twelve years, not one death from SIDS occurred among 1,800 infants Dr. Kravitz followed, whereas five SIDS deaths might be expected in that population. He contacted me and asked me what I thought about his findings. I told him that it made sense to me because, if a baby was in a transitional period of obligate nose breathing to volitional mouth breathing and was sleeping in a horizontal position with the larynx not locked into the nasopharynx, the tip of the soft palate could be in such a position that it would slip into the larynx if the baby suddenly awoke (Figure 88). Still having the reflexes of an obligate nose breather, the more tightly the soft palate became jammed into the larynx, the more vigorously the baby would try to breathe through its nose with it there, until it suffocated. Once the baby died, all would appear normal at autopsy, because the relaxed uvula of the soft palate would slip out of the retracted larynx. Such a cause of death would present the typical autopsy findings occurring in a SIDS death, which generally point to a cessation of breathing. Tiny hemorrhages in the lungs suggest a sufficiently high negative intrathoracic pressure was present to cause capillary blood vessel rupture during a desperate struggle to breathe. As stated in Crelin and Scherz (1978), if a baby in the transitional stage of breathing sleeps with its head inclined upward twenty to thirty degrees and awakes suddenly the larynx can unlock from the nasopharynx with the soft palate in a position that allows the epiglottis to slide up behind the soft palate as the larynx relocked by reflex into the nasopharynx (Figure 89). All human beings go through the transitional stage of obligate nose breathing to volitional mouth breathing as part of the functional development of the vocal tract. Therefore, all human beings are exposed to the hazards of the sudden infant death syndrome because of it. Again, the selective pressures during evolution that resulted in the unique structure and function of the upper respiratory system in the human adult must have been quite positive when one considers that human beings are exposed to the hazards of both an early SIDS death and a later choking death because of this structure and function.

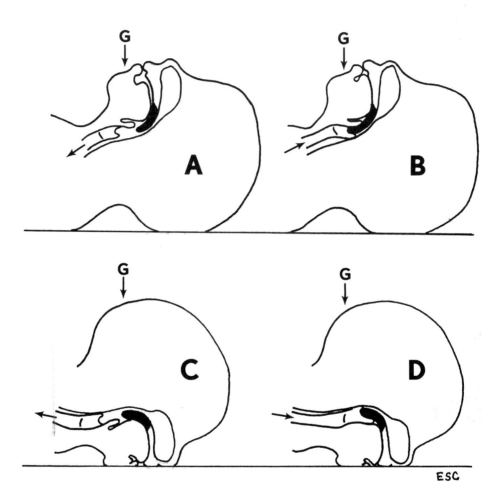

Figure 88. Diagrams of the head of a young human infant cut in the midplane showing how the head on the same horizontal plane as the reclining body could result in sudden death if the infant unlocks its larynx from the nasopharynx when sleeping. In A and C the larynx is unlocked from the nasopharynx. The affect of gravity (G) on the mobile neck structures results in the soft palate (solid black) being more posterior than the epiglottis. In B and D the larynx is drawn toward the nasopharynx with the soft palate jammed into it. *After Crelin and Scherz (1978).*

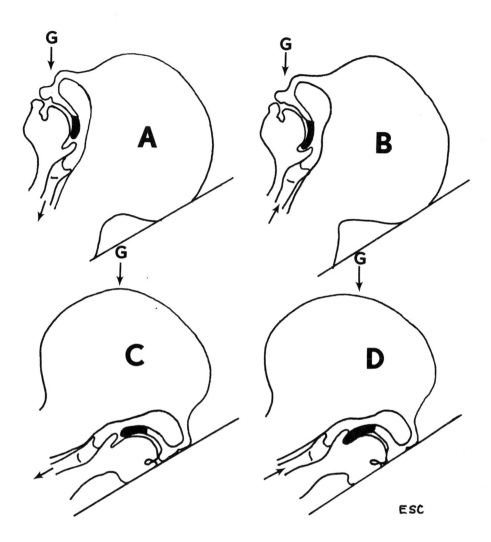

Figure 89. Diagrams of the head of a young human infant cut in the midplane showing how the elevation of the head end of a reclining infant reduces the possibility of sudden infant death if the infant unlocks its larynx from the nasopharynx when sleeping. In A and C, the larynx is unlocked from the nasopharynx. Gravity (G) does not cause the soft palate (solid black) to be posterior to the epiglottis with the head elevated. In B and D the larynx is locked into the nasopharynx with the soft palate anterior to the epiglottis. *After Crelin and Scherz (1978).*

Human Infant Vocalizations

Before I tested the ability of the two-year–old rubber human vocal tract to produce vowel sounds, I closely examined a number of infants as I listened to them vocalize. At that time, my grandson, Waynie Ross, Jr., was two years and one month old. In regard to speaking, he was precocious, having a large vocabulary for his age. He was able to produce the vowels "ä," "ā," "ē," "ī," "ō," "ü" distinctly. I videotaped Waynie as he made the vowel sounds and attempted to speak English words with a complex combination of consonant sounds (Figure 90). Knowing that his vocal tract was anatomically similar to that of a chimpanzee and essentially the same as when he was born, it at first disturbed me when I found he could produce the vowel sounds so well. The fact that all of his deciduous teeth had erupted probably enhanced his ability to make speech sounds, and, of course, he lacked a simian shelf. Also, since the time he first produced vocal sounds, the acoustic input to his own nervous system induced the establishment of neuronal connections, fulfilling his genetic

Figure 90. Two-year–old Wayne T. Ross, Jr., being videotaped by his grandfather as he clearly enunciates vowel sounds.

potential to have human speech. The examination of the radiographs of two-year–old living children showed that their larynx and the posterior part of their tongue shifted to a low position in the neck when vocalizing (Figure 91). This shift resulted in an elongated supralaryngeal pharynx, with the tongue forming its anterior wall, which could change its shape and enhance formant frequencies in the spectrum of the glottic wave produced by the vocal folds in the larynx. The vocal tract thus attempts to take on temporarily the shape it ultimately achieves by permanent structural modifications occurring from the second to the sixth year of age. I found by testing the rubber two-year–old tract that it does this quite well in producing vowel sounds. However, the bulk of the tongue remains in the oral cavity at two years of age, making it difficult to produce consonant sounds.

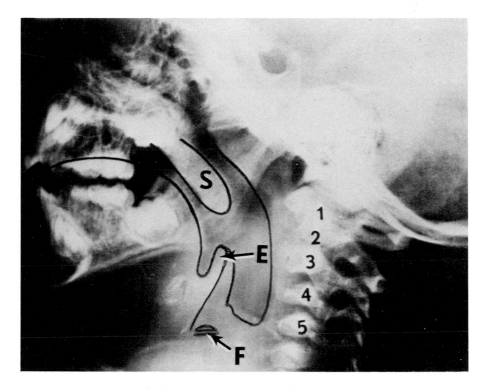

Figure 91. Lateral radiograph of a living human two-year–old male. The pharynx, larynx, soft palate (S), and tongue are outlined in ink. The epiglottis (E) is not in contact with the pendulous soft palate (S) because the larynx and posterior part of the tongue are pulled down to a low level in the neck as the child emits crying sounds through the mouth and nose. The posterior part of the tongue is vertically oriented to form the anterior wall of the oropharynx.

When the larynx and posterior part of the tongue are pulled down into the neck of a vocalizing two-year–old child, the elongated pharynx abuts the vertebral column, which is vertically oriented by the time a child first begins to stand erect and walk bipedally, around one year of age. This produces a flexure of the vocal tract at the junction of the oral cavity and pharynx similar to the permanent flexure of the adult vocal tract. This undoubtedly makes the tract more efficient in producing vowel sounds other than the "ä" sound. In the nonhuman mammal, including the ape, the cervical vertebral column is more horizontally than vertically oriented, due to the way the first cervical vertebra articulates with the occipital condyles of the skull (Figures 121 and 123). This is why a retraction of the pharynx to a lower position in the neck of an adult chimpanzee to elongate it results in a sloping curve as it abuts the inclined vertebral column, rather than a right angle flexure. I asked my grandson Waynie to sing out the vowel sounds as I videotaped him. He opened his mouth wide, raised his chin, projected his head forward, and extended his neck when he produced the "ä" vowel sound. This resulted in a vocal tract resembling a gradually flared tube, similar to the shape of the rubber, two-year–old human tract when I got it to produce the "ah" sound (Figure 92). The extended head and neck position Waynie used to produce the "ä" sound was similar to

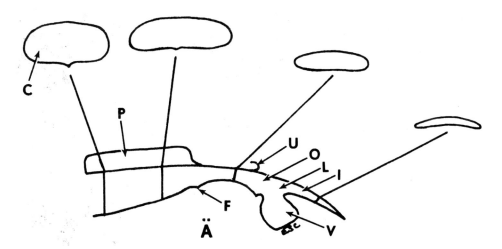

Figure 92. A drawing of the shape of the rubber two-year–old human male vocal tract in the midsagittal and cross-sectional planes when it produced the "ä" vowel sound. The cross sections (C) are through the anterior and middle parts of the oral cavity, the junction of the oral cavity and oropharynx, and the infralaryngeal part of the pharynx. P: hard palate. F: foramen cecum of tongue. U: uvula of soft palate. O: oropharynx. L: laryngopharynx. I: infralaryngeal part of pharynx. V: vestibule of larynx.

that adopted by a wolf when it howls or a cow when it lows. However, as the videotape clearly shows, Waynie flexed his cervical vertebral column and drew back his chin to produce the other vowel sounds. This enhanced the right angle bend in his vocal tract when he lowered his larynx in his neck in order to vocalize. I simulated this configuration of his vocal tract with the rubber two-year–old tract when it produced all of the vowel sounds other than the "ä" (figure 93–97). The shorter hard palate, the lack of a simian shelf, the elongation of the pharynx, and the bending of the junction of the oral cavity and pharynx of the two-year–old rubber tract allowed it to produce the vowel sounds with greater ease and distinctness than the rubber adult chimpanzee tract.

Formant frequencies are very difficult to identify in human infant sounds, just as they are in chimpanzee sounds (Bauer 1984). Buhr (1980), made recordings of the vocal production of a single infant between sixteen and sixty-four weeks of age. These recordings were subjected to perceptual and acoustic analysis. Sounds resembling the vowel sounds of English were identified, and formant frequency measurements were made from spectrograms. Until more children are studied and more critical analyses of their vocal sounds are made, one can make only certain generalizations. The cry of the human newborn infant is essentially an "ä" vowel. For the

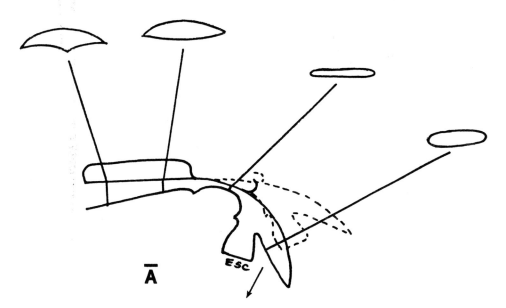

Figure 93. A drawing of the shape of the rubber two-year–old human male vocal tract in the midsagittal and cross-sectional planes when it produced the "ä" vowel sound. The arrow and broken lines indicate the displacement of the pharynx and larynx from the non-phonating position.

97

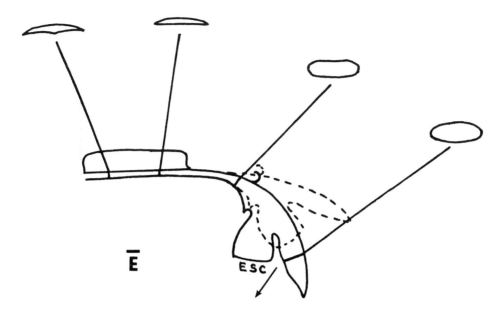

Figure 94. A drawing of the shape of the rubber two-year–old human male vocal tract in the midsagittal and cross-sectional planes when it produced the "ē" vowel sound. The arrow and broken lines indicate the displacement of the pharynx and larynx from the nonphonating position.

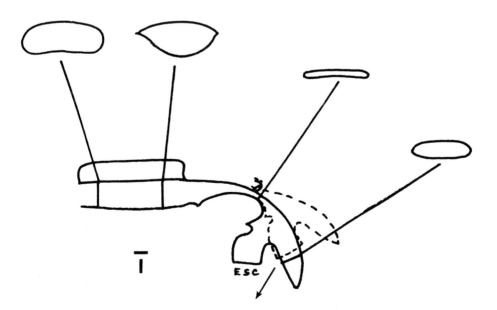

Figure 95. A drawing of the shape of the rubber two-year–old human male vocal tract in the midsagittal and cross-sectional planes when it produced the "ī" vowel sound. The arrow and broken lines indicate the displacement of the pharynx and larynx from the nonphonating position.

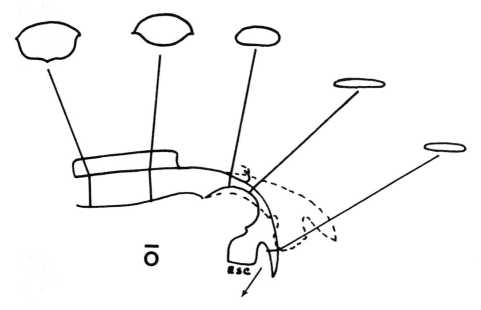

Figure 96. A drawing of the shape of the rubber two-year–old human male vocal tract in the midsagittal and cross-sectional planes when it produced the "ō" vowel sound. The arrow and broken lines indicate the displacement of the pharynx and larynx from the nonphonating position.

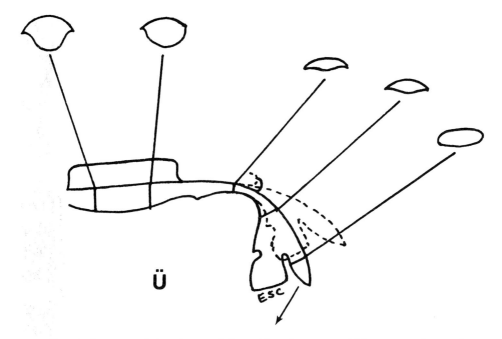

Figure 97. A drawing of the shape of the rubber two-year–old human male vocal tract in the midsagittal and cross-sectional planes when it produced the "ü" vowel sound. The arrow and broken lines indicate the displacement of the pharynx and larynx from the nonphonating position.

first four months after birth, the sounds a baby makes are "ah" vowel sounds during crying and what are referred to as cooing sounds. By the sixth month after birth, an infant can make the "ā" vowel fairly distinctly and quite consistently along with what are known as babbling sounds. Infants don't make the "ī" vowel until near the end of the first year after birth. This coincides with the ability of the infant between the ninth and fourteenth month after birth to include the first words with the babbling sounds (Brown, John, Owrid, and Taylor 1974).

Speech Defects

My studies of the development of the human vocal tract lead me to conclude that the tract anatomy involved in vowel sound production is rarely, if ever, the cause of a speech defect. Vocal tract abnormalities that would prevent the production of recognizable vowel sounds would have to be so extreme that the ability to produce consonant sounds would also be impaired. Extreme birth defects that interfere with speech production in general, such as a cleft palate or a combination of small tongue and mandible (hypoplasia), may be compatible with life. Others may not be, such as an almost complete absence of the mandible and tongue and/or a tiny oral opening (Potter and Craig 1976). Tongue abnormalities that would prevent the production of vowel sounds, including defective innervation, would probably be so severe that the condition would be lethal, causing an inability to swallow. Therefore, I have never come across a description of an adult human in whom the normal descent of the larynx and posterior part of the tongue into the neck failed to occur. The only condition that I believe could allow this failure to occur would be if the base of the skull between the hard palate and the foramen magnum grew abnormally long, so that the base of the skull took on the relative dimensions of a chimpanzee skull base. This would be a form of platybasia. If it were severe enough to prevent the normal descent of the larynx into the neck, it would result in an early death from detrimental effects on the brainstem (Potter and Craig 1976). On the other hand, a speech defect that involves the inability to produce a specific consonant sound but does not interfere with sound production, may or may not be due to a structural abnormality of the vocal tract. The problem could be within the neural circuitry of the brain that normally controls a specific activity of the lips and/or the tongue. The abnormal circuitry could be at the microscopic level in the brainstem or in the cerebral cortex, or both.

Nearly all normal human infants have the reflex ability to temporarily alter the shape of their vocal tract so that it can produce vowel sounds long before the mature form of the vocal tract is attained. Even though the pharynx can be flexed and elongated by the descent of the larynx and the posterior part of the tongue into the neck, the remainder of the tongue continues to form a bulky mass within a relatively small oral cavity. Coupled with a lagging maturation of the neuronal circuitry controlling the

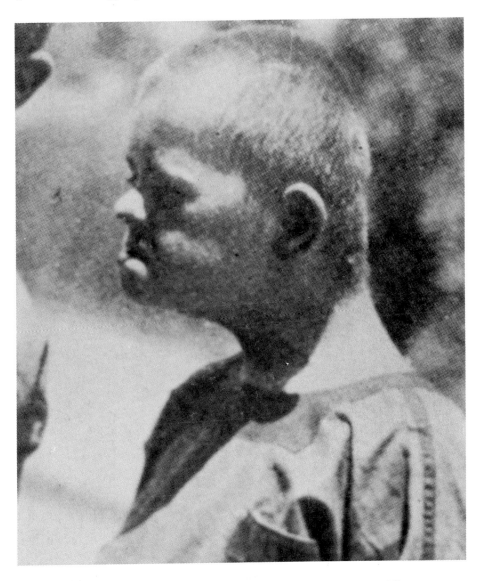

Figure 98. A young adult male with Down's Syndrome (Trisomy 21).

tongue activity that produces consonant sounds, many children under the age of four have great trouble articulating certain consonant sounds.

Although my two-year–old grandson Waynie distinctly produced vowel sounds with ease, he had great difficulty moving his tongue around his oral cavity to articulate consonant sounds. This difficulty of a young, normal child in manipulating his relatively bulky tongue to produce consonant sounds could be similar to the difficulty many Down's Syndrome individuals have throughout their lives. Although the Down's Syndrome, or mongolism, includes various structural abnormalities, it is characterized by a small, round head (Figure 98). The shortness of the base of the skull

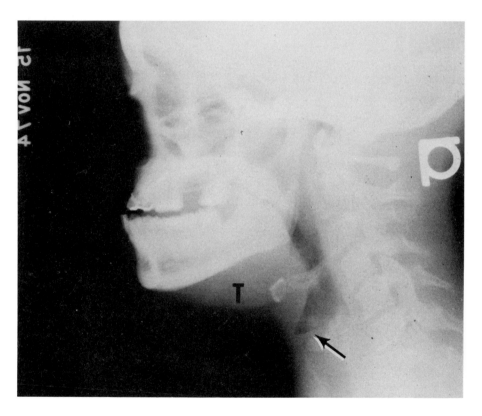

Figure 99. Lateral radiograph of a living adult male with Down's Syndrome (Trisomy 21). The vocal folds (arrow) are at the usual low level in the neck opposite the articular disc between the fifth and sixth cervical vertebrae during quiet breathing through the nose. An abnormally short hard palate results in the lower incisor teeth being positioned in front of the upper incisor teeth. A smaller-than-normal oral cavity causes the normal-sized tongue to project below the mandible (T) with the mouth closed.

is related to a short hard palate and a smaller-than-normal oral cavity. The tongue and lower jaw are of normal size. This causes the chin to protrude and the upper incisor teeth to be behind, rather than in front of, the lower incisor teeth (Figure 99). The normal-sized tongue in a smaller-than-normal oral cavity produces a tendency to keep the mouth open and the tongue protruding. When the mouth is closed, the tongue is forced downward to form a bulge below the lower level of the mandible. Dr. Eric Effmann, a pediatric radiologist who was a student in my human growth and development study unit at Yale, made radiographs of a number of Down's Syndrome individuals of both sexes and of all ages. They revealed that each subject's tongue was of normal size. I once watched and listened to a Down's Syndrome young man with an intelligence level sufficient for him to realize that he suffered from Down's Syndrome. He stumbled over a long word containing difficult consonants. He apologized for doing this by making the common mistake of saying that, since he had Down's Syndrome, his abnormally large tongue made it difficult for him to say certain words.

Human Vocal Tract Maturity

Menyuk (1972) states that, between three and four years of age, children use all of the basic syntactical structures and, between four and six years of age, the correct articulation of all of the speech sounds in context. This period, when a child is between three and six years old, coincides with the time when I found the human vocal tract becomes anatomically mature. Thus, the development of a mature human vocal tract that can articulate all of the sounds of speech consists merely of modifications of the configuration of the immature, or typical nonhuman mammalian, vocal tract. No new vocal tract structures develop. The modifications allow changes in function so that the articulate sounds of speech can be produced with rapidity and ease. Obviously, new neuronal connections appear within the central nervous system during human development that allow a unique control of the functioning of the rearranged vocal tract structures, especially the tongue.

Related Developmental Changes of Vocal Tract and Skull

Since I already knew that the base of the skull of an adult chimpanzee and a newborn human infant were more similar to each other than either was to that of an adult human, I made a study of the skull bases of children

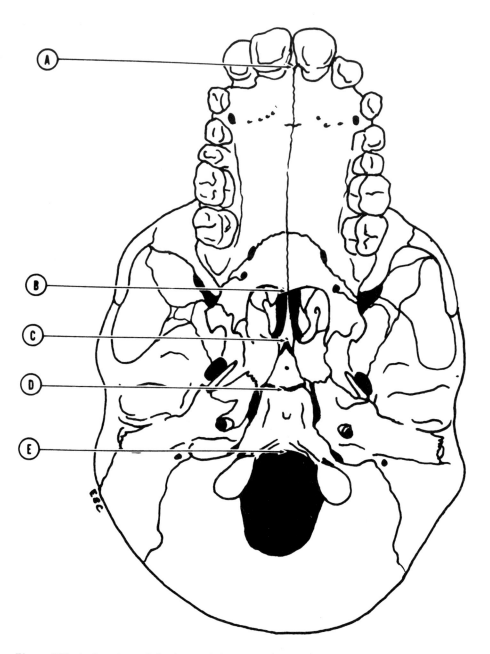

Figure 100. A drawing of the base of the skull of an adult female chimpanzee. The midline craniometric points of the basicranial line are indicated. A: anterior margin of the bony palate *(prosthion)*. B: posterior margin of the hard palate *(staphylion)*. C: posterior extent of the vomer bone *(hormion)*. D: spheno-occipital synostosis *(sphenobasion)*. E: anterior margin of the foramen magnum *(basion)*. *From Laitman, Heimbuch, and Crelin (1978).*

who died between birth and puberty. Recognizing that the roof of the oral cavity and nasopharynx are directly related to the base of the skull, I analyzed the changes simultaneously occurring in the vocal tract and skull base during development. Dr. Laitman and another former graduate student of mine, Raymond Heimbuch, made a study of the relationship between alterations in the basicranial line and changes in the upper respiratory system of a number of nonhuman primates and human beings (Laitman, Heimbuch, and Crelin 1978). The basicranial line runs along the midline of the base of the skull. The craniometric points along this line are shown in Figure 100. The line is horizontal and straight along the length of the bony palate. It is curved or arched to a greater or lesser degree between the bony palate and the foramen magnum, reflecting the contour of this part of the skull base. In a chimpanzee this part of the skull base is relatively long and only slightly arched (Figure 101). This is directly related to the anatomy of the typical nonhuman upper respiratory system, where the larynx is located high in the neck and the tongue is entirely within the oral cavity.

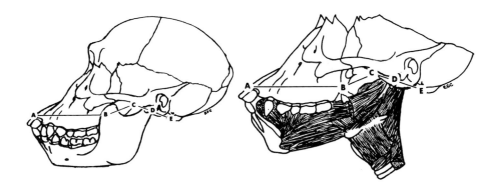

Figure 101. Drawings of left lateral views of the skull of an adult female chimpanzee. On the right the view lacks the upper part of the skull. The left half of the mandible was excluded to expose the muscles of the tongue, the extrinsic laryngeal muscles, and the pharyngeal constrictor muscles. A topographic projection of the basicranial line was made on each view. *From Laitman, Heimbuch, and Crelin (1978).*

The skull base of the adult chimpanzee between the bony palate and foramen magnum is typical of the adult, nonhuman mammalian skull (Figures 102 and 103). There is a relatively wide interval between the vomer bone, which forms the posterior part of the nasal septum, and the syn-

105

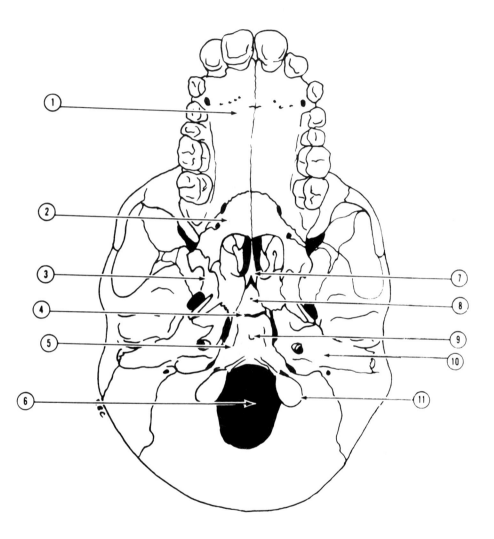

Figure 102. A drawing of the base of the skull of an adult female chimpanzee. 1: maxillary bone of bony palate. 2: palatine bone of bony palate. 3: right pterygoid process of sphenoid bone. 4: spheno-occipital synostosis. 5: basilar part of occipital bone. 6: foramen magnum. 7: vomer bone. 8: basilar part of sphenoid bone. 9: pharyngeal tubercle. 10: petrous part of temporal bone. 11: left occipital condyle.

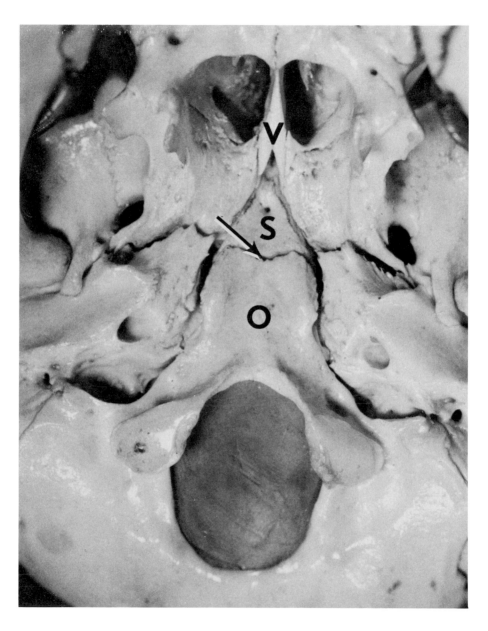

Figure 103. A view of the base of the skull of an adult male chimpanzee skull from the bony palate to the occipital bone bordering the back of the foramen magnum. V: vomer bone. S: basilar part of sphenoid bone. O: basilar part of occipital bone. Arrow points to spheno-occipital synostosis.

ostosis of what was the spheno-occipital synchondrosis. During the development of the skull base, the synchondrosis consists of growth cartilage that participates in most of the growth in length of the skull base. When growth ceases, the cartilage is replaced by bone, and the site is then known as the spheno-occipital synostosis. The synostosis joins the sphenoid and occipital bones together. The wide interval between the vomer bone and synostosis in the adult chimpanzee skull allows the inferior surface of the body of the sphenoid bone to be seen when the base of the skull is viewed. The part of the occipital bone articulating with the body of the sphenoid bone is known as the basilar part and is inclined only slightly in the adult, nonhuman, mammalian skull.

Since the human newborn upper respiratory system is so similar to that of nonhuman mammalian adults, the basicranial line is also similar (Figure 104). The base of the newborn's skull between the bony palate and the foramen magnum is relatively long and only slightly arched. As might be expected, this part of the skull base is essentially the same as that of the chimpanzee (Figures 105 and 106). The wide interval between the vomer bone and the spheno-occipital synchondrosis of the human newborn skull allows the body of the sphenoid bone to be seen. Also, the basilar part of the occipital bone is inclined only slightly.

By one year of age, the skull is much larger than it was at birth, but the anatomy of the skull base is virtually unchanged (Figure 107). This fact

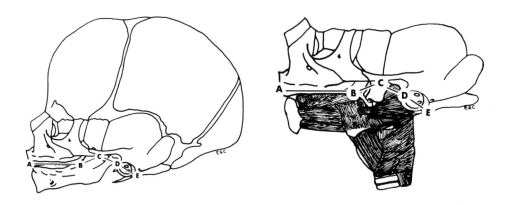

Figure 104. Drawings of left lateral views of the skull of a human full-term newborn infant. On the right, the view lacks the upper part of the skull. The left half of the mandible was excluded to expose the muscles of the tongue, the extrinsic laryngeal muscles, and the pharyngeal constrictor muscles. A topographic projection of the basicranial line was made on each view. *From Laitman, Heimbuch, and Crelin (1978).*

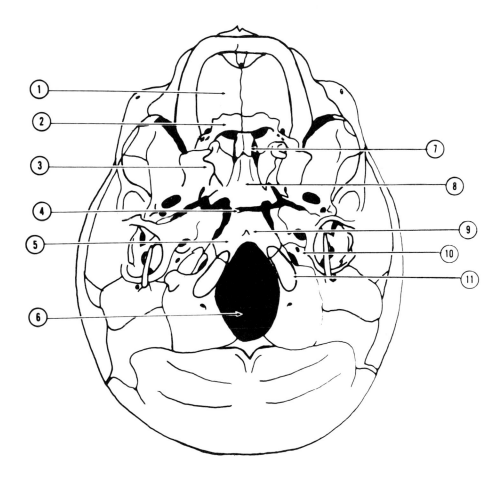

Figure 105. A drawing of the base of the skull of a human newborn infant. 1: maxillary bone of bony palate. 2: palatine bone of bony palate. 3: right pterygoid process of sphenoid bone. 4: spheno-occipital synchondrosis. 5: basilar part of occipital bone. 6: foramen magnum. 7: vomer bone. 8: basilar part of sphenoid bone. 9: pharyngeal tubercle. 10: petrous part of temporal bone. 11: left occipital condyle.

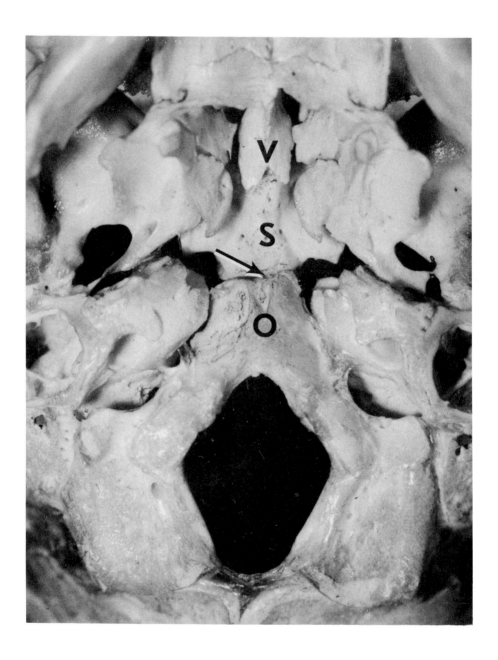

Figure 106. A view of the base of the skull of a human full-term newborn infant from the bony palate to the occipital bone bordering the back of the foramen magnum. V: vomer bone. S: basilar part of sphenoid bone. O: basilar part of occipital bone. Arrow points to spheno-occipital synchondrosis.

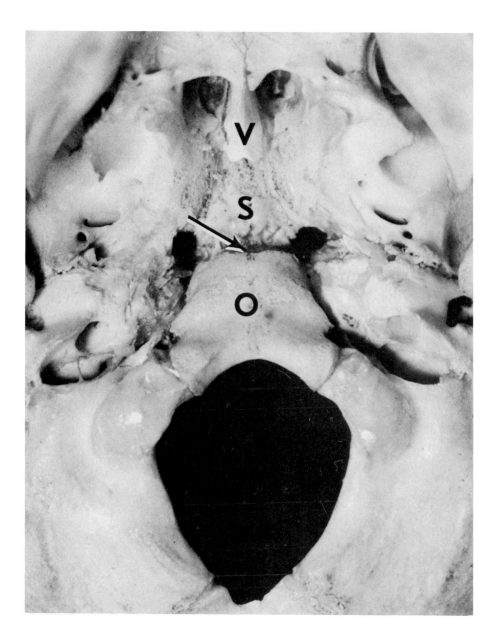

Figure 107. A view of the base of the skull of a one-year–old human male from the bony palate to the posterior border of the foramen magnum. V: vomer bone. S: basilar part of sphenoid bone. O: basilar part of occipital bone. Arrow points to spheno-occipital synchondrosis.

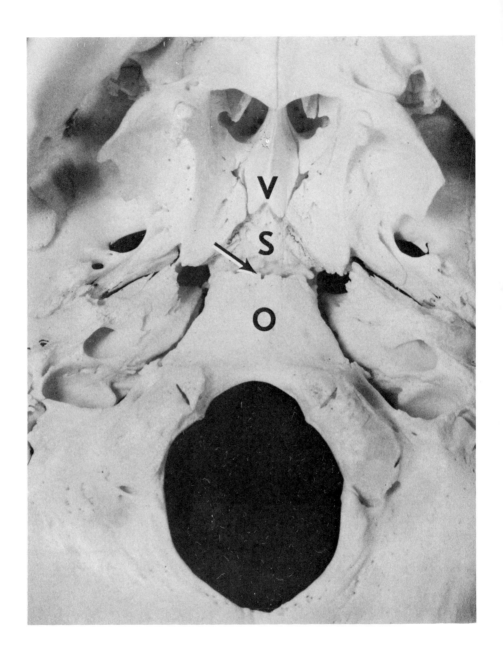

Figure 108. A view of the base of the skull of a three-year–old human female from the bony palate to the posterior border of the foramen magnum. V: vomer bone. S: basilar part of sphenoid bone. O: basilar part of occipital bone. Arrow points to spheno-occipital synchondrosis.

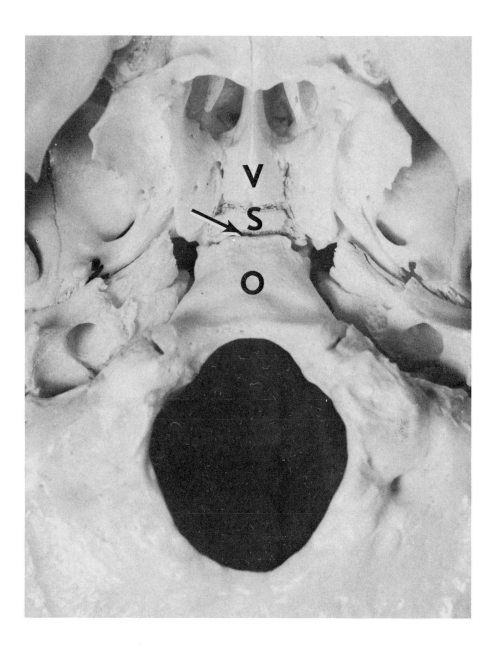

Figure 109. A view of the base of the skull of a six-year–old human male from the bony palate to the occipital bone bordering the back of the foramen magnum. V: vomer bone. S: basilar part of sphenoid bone. O: basilar part of occipital bone. Arrow points to spheno-occipital synchondrosis.

is directly related to the unchanged anatomy of the vocal tract. By the third year after birth, the distance between the hard palate and the foramen magnum starts to become relatively shorter, and the base of the skull of this region starts to become a deeper concavity (Figure 108). The relative distance between the vomer bone and the spheno-occipital synchondrosis starts to diminish, so that less of the body of the sphenoid bone is visible when the skull base is viewed. The basilar part of the occipital bone becomes more inclined toward the vertical plane. These changes found in the skull of a three-year–old child are directly related to the ongoing descent of the larynx and posterior part of the tongue to a low position in the neck. In the skull of a six-year–old child, the distance between the bony palate and the foramen magnum is relatively further reduced, and this part of the skull base forms a deep concavity (Figure 109). The distance between the vomer bone and spheno-occipital synchondrosis is very short, allowing little or none of the body of the sphenoid bone to be seen when the skull base is viewed. The basilar part of the occipital bone is inclined more toward the vertical plane. These findings are directly related to the attainment of the configuration of the human adult vocal tract by six years of age. The basicranial line is the same as that of the human adult (Figure 110). Beyond

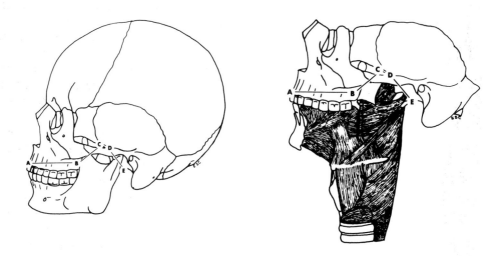

Figure 110. Drawings of left lateral views of the skull of a human adult male. On the right, the view of the skull lacks the upper part. The left half of the mandible has been excluded to expose the muscles of the tongue, extrinsic laryngeal muscles and the pharyngeal constrictor muscles. A topographic projection of the basicranial line was made on each view. *From Laitman, Heimbuch and Crelin (1978).*

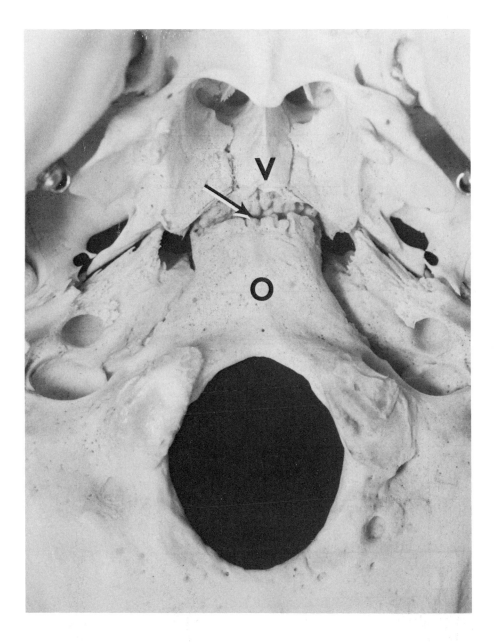

Figure 111. A view of the base of the skull of a ten-year–old human male from the bony palate to the occipital bone bordering the back of the foramen magnum. V: vomer bone. O: basilar part of occipital bone. Arrow points to spheno-occipital synchondrosis.

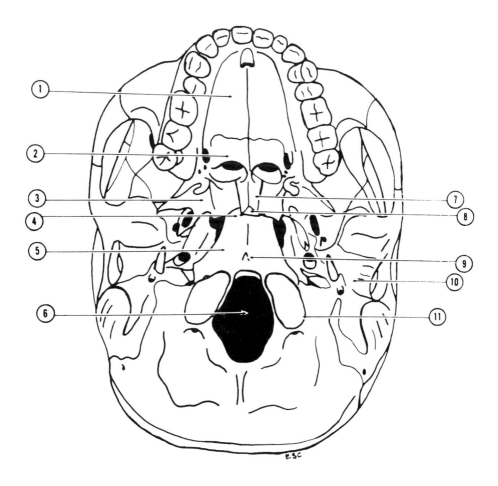

Figure 112. A drawing of the base of the skull of a human adult male. 1: maxillary bone of bony palate. 2: palatine bone of bony palate. 3: right pterygoid process of sphenoid bone. 4: spheno-occipital synostosis. 5: basilar part of occipital bone. 6. foramen magnum. 7: vomer bone. 8: basilar part of sphenoid bone. 9: pharyngeal tubercle. 10: petrous portion of temporal bone. 11: left occipital condyle.

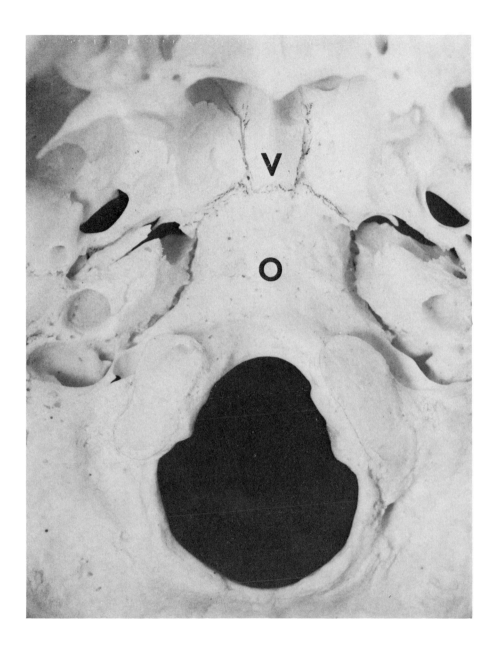

Figure 113. A view of the base of the skull of a human adult female from the bony palate to the posterior border of the foramen magnum. V: vomer bone. O: basilar part of occipital bone.

the sixth year, the body of the sphenoid has completely shifted to a position behind the vomer bone and, therefore, cannot be seen when the base of the skull is viewed (Figures 111–113). The cartilaginous spheno-occipital synchondrosis starts to become a bony synostosis shortly after puberty (Crelin 1973a).

I compared the entire skulls of human beings and chimpanzees during the developmental period. Besides having the same skull base at birth, human and chimpanzee skulls resemble each other in their entirety (Figures 114–116). Related to this, their vocal tracts are essentially the same. In

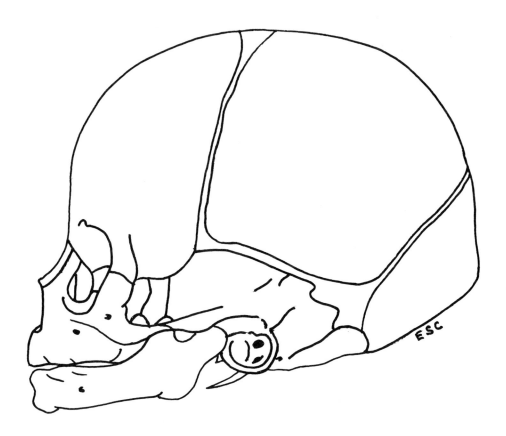

Figure 114. A drawing of a skull of a full-term newborn infant chimpanzee *(Pan troglodytes).*

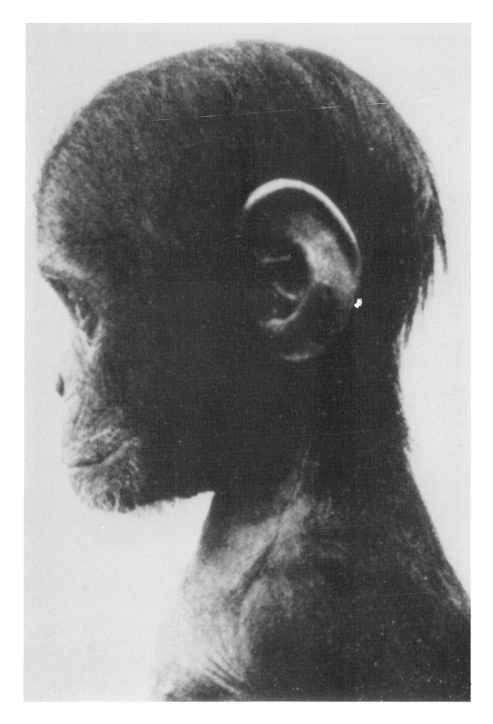

Figure 115. An infant male chimpanzee *(Pan troglodytes). From Yerkes and Yerkes (1929).*

many respects the skull of a six-year–old child viewed from the side appears to have changed little from that of a human newborn, except for the presence of fully erupted deciduous teeth (Figure 117). However, as has already been described, the skull base has changed markedly as the vocal tract attained the adult configuration. The six-year–old child is able to articulate correctly all of the sounds of his or her language in context (Figure 118). At a comparable stage of development, the skull of a prepubertal chimpanzee with a full set of erupted deciduous teeth shows marked changes in skull morphology when viewed from the side (Figure 119). The changes

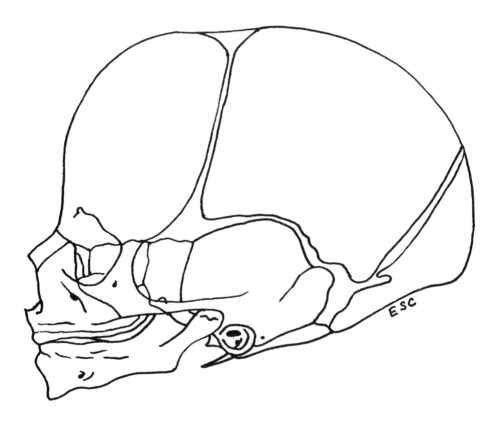

Figure 116. A drawing of a skull of a full-term human newborn infant.

are basically related to the acquisition of a robust masticatory, or chewing, apparatus. The mandible is structurally strong, the chewing muscles are massive, and a snout, or muzzle, that contains large deciduous teeth, especially large canines, is forming. Supraorbital brow ridges are beginning to appear, and the forehead has become low and flat. The frontal lobes of the brain are greatly reduced in size relative to the overall size of the brain. In contrast, the skull base is essentially the same as that of a newborn chimpanzee. The configuration of the vocal tract is also unchanged, as well as the ability to produce a variety of vocal sounds (Figure 120).

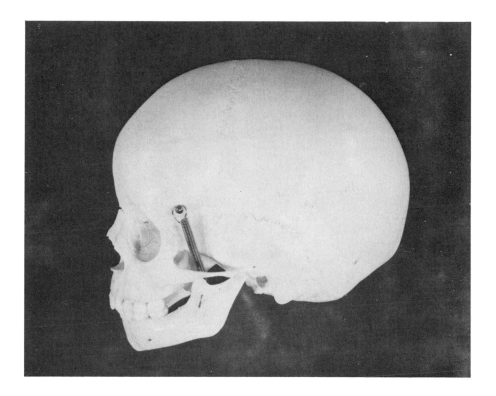

Figure 117. A skull of a six-year–old human male with a full set of deciduous teeth.

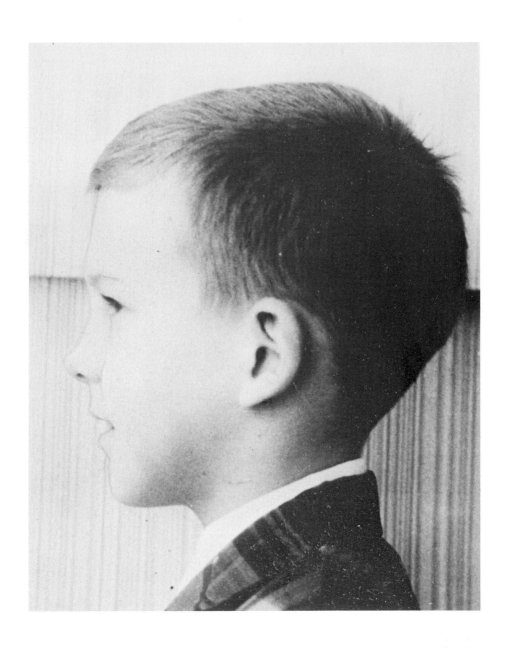

Figure 118. Robert M. Crelin when he was six years old in 1965.

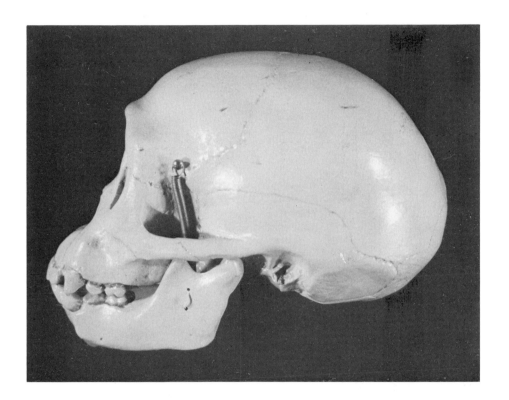

Figure 119. A skull of an immature male chimpanzee *(Pan troglodytes)* with a full set of deciduous teeth.

Figure 120. An immature male chimpanzee *(Pan troglodytes)* with some remaining deciduous teeth and newly erupting central incisor teeth. *From Yerkes and Yerkes (1929).*

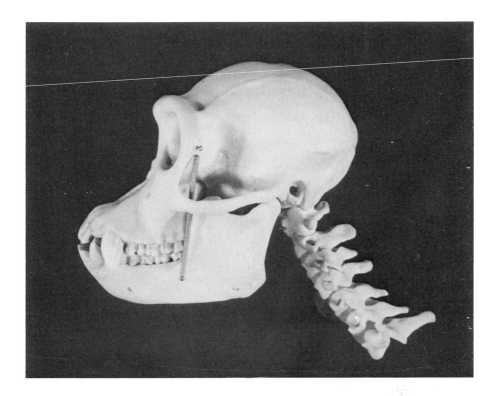

Figure 121. A skull of an adult male chimpanzee *(Pan troglodytes)* to which a human adult male cervical vertebral column is articulated.

When the male chimpanzee reaches adulthood, his masticatory apparatus is well developed (Figure 121). His mandible is massive, and his teeth are large, especially the canines. A long muzzle is present. Large supraorbital brow ridges are present, and a forehead is lacking. He has a small brain compared to a human adult, especially in regard to the frontal lobes. The early man-ape had a skull almost identical in size and shape to that of a living chimpanzee (Figure 122). In time the skull of human ancestors stopped developing robust masticatory apparatuses as they matured. Modern adult human beings have relatively small teeth (Figure 123). Their canines may even lack points. They lack snouts and supraorbital ridges and have vertical foreheads (Figure 124). They also have large brains with well-developed frontal lobes. Thus, the overall appearance of the head of a newborn changes very little from birth to adulthood compared to the

Figure 122. An adult male chimpanzee *(Pan troglodytes). From Yerkes and Yerkes (1929).*

living chimpanzee and the man-ape ancestors. This "remaining young" is the result of an evolutionary process known as neoteny. However, the skull base and vocal tract anatomy of a human adult deviate markedly from

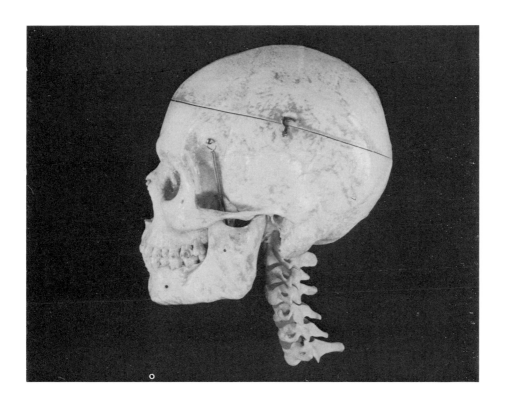

Figure 123. A skull and cervical vertebral column of an adult human male.

their immature state. These changes are a unique human phenomenon. They are a résumé of the changes that occurred in the skull base and vocal tract during the last million years of human evolution.

Figure 124. The outstanding pioneer neurosurgeon, Harvey W. Cushing, M.D., when he was fifty-one years of age in 1920.

Chapter 4

Evolution of the Vocal Tract

Hominid Fossil Skulls

Armed with the knowledge gained from my own research on the direct relationship of developmental skull base changes to the development of the vocal tract, I set out to discover what the fossil skulls of our human ancestors could reveal about how the vocal tract evolved. In contrast with previous researching, I would concentrate on the skull base rather than the front and top of the skull. I naively thought this would be a monumental task because of all of the fossil skulls I would have to study. To my surprise and dismay, I found that there are so few human ancestral fossil skulls, or parts of them, that Howell (1972) is quite correct in describing them as "very precious." There are less than forty incomplete skulls that are useful in tracing the evolution of the human ancestral vocal tract, from the oldest known human ancestral fossil skull part, dated to 5 million years ago, to the known parts dating to about 20,000 years ago. I was very fortunate to be able to acquire every fossil skull copy or cast produced by the casting programs of the Wenner-Gren (W-G) Foundation and the University of Pennsylvania (PA) Museum before these were terminated. I also acquired a number of postcranial fossil bone casts from these two programs. The W-G Foundation made extremely accurate casts of the original fossil specimens using epoxy resin plastic under the direction of Dr. F. Clark Howell, curator of the casting program. Permission to use photographs of the W-G Foundation casts was obtained from the Foundation and the owners of the original specimens. The excellent plaster of paris casts of the PA Museum program were from duplicate molds made by the late F. O. Barlow directly from the original fossil material. Only a few casts made by the two programs are duplicates.

129

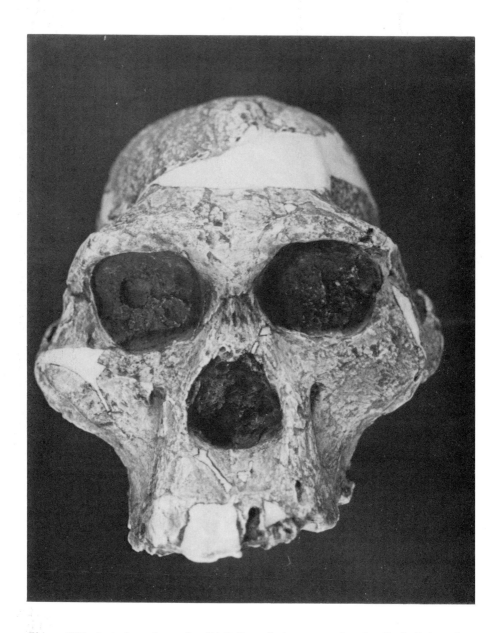

Figure 125. Anterior view of a W-G Foundation cast of a fossil skull found at Sterkfontein, Africa. It is known as "Mrs. Ples" and is classified as an adult *Australopithecus africanus*. It is dated at around two million years old and lacks a mandible and teeth. *Photographs of casts used courtesy of the Wenner-Gren Foundation for Anthropological Research, Inc., New York, and with permission of the owners of the original specimens. Permission granted by the Transvaal Museum.*

Australopithecine (Man-Ape) Skulls

If the development of the human vocal tract is a résumé of the evolution of the tract, the unique alterations occurring late in development, long after birth, should have occurred relatively recently during human evolution. That is precisely what I found. There was no need to go back very much beyond the last one million years of human evolution. This eliminated any concern about the human ancestral evolution prior to the hominids. The hominids comprise the family of bipedal primate mammals that includes the man-apes and all of the forms evolving from them down to present-day human beings. The earliest hominid skeleton ever found that could be determined to have been definitely bipedal, or to have walked erect, is nearly four million years old and is classified as an australopithecine, or man-ape (Johanson and Maitland 1981). The australopithecine fossils were all found in Africa. Although they are all basically similar to one another, there are indications that there were different species. There were larger, more robust types and smaller, gracile types, although in some instances the differences may merely reflect the sexual dimorphism of one species. The best-preserved fossil skull of a gracile type is that classified as an *Australopithecus africanus,* affectionately known as Mrs. Ples because she was originally named *Plesianthropus* (Figures 125, 127, 129, 131). She is dated as around two million years old. Although the australopithecines walked bipedally, they were quite apelike (Figure 133). The cranial capacity of Mrs. Ples's skull, which indicates brain size, is 482 cubic centimeters. This is close to the average capacity of the present-day gorilla. The similar appearances of the Mrs. Ples skull and that of an adult, present-day, female orangutan is shown in figures 125–132. As expected, the bases of the two skulls are almost identical with respect to the basicranial line and the wide separation of the vomer bone from the spheno-occipital synostosis, which allows the sphenoid bone to be seen (Figures 131 and 132). Therefore, the upper part of their respiratory systems had to be just as similar. The famous Taung australopithecine child skull shows that the australopithecines went through the skull development of a present-day ape (Figures 134 and 135). At birth the Taung skull must have been very similar to that of a human or chimpanzee newborn infant (Figures 114 and 116). By the time the full set of deciduous teeth had erupted, the Taung skull had the beginnings of a brow ridge and a sloping forehead, similar to that of a chimpanzee at an equivalent stage of development but quite unlike that of a modern human skull with a full set of erupted deciduous teeth (Figures 117, 119, 134, 135).

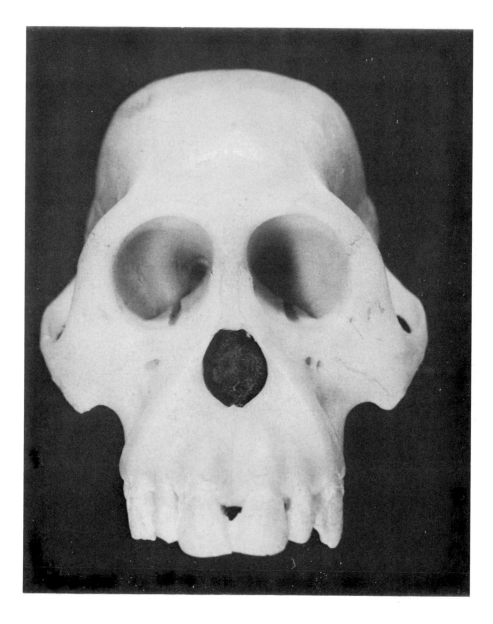

Figure 126. Anterior view of a plastic cast of a present-day adult female orangutan skull minus a mandible. *Gift of Dr. Ian Tattersall.*

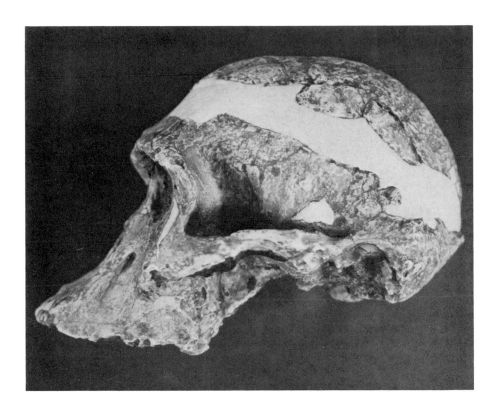

Figure 127. Left lateral view of the cast of the *Australopithecus africanus* skull shown in figure 125. *Photographs of casts used courtesy of the Wenner-Gren Foundation for Anthropological Research, Inc., New York, and with permission of the owners of the original specimens. Permission granted by the Transvaal Museum.*

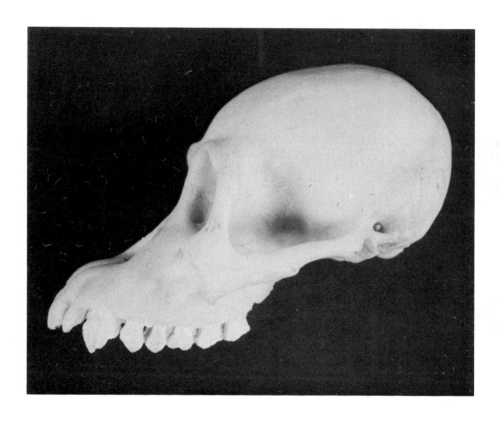

Figure 128. Left lateral view of the cast of the orangutan skull shown in Figure 126.

Figure 129. A view of the top of the cast of the *Australopithecus africanus* skull shown in Figures 125 and 127. *Photographs of casts used courtesy of the Wenner-Gren Foundation for Anthropological Research, Inc., New York, and with permission of the owners of the original specimens. Permission granted by the Transvaal Museum.*

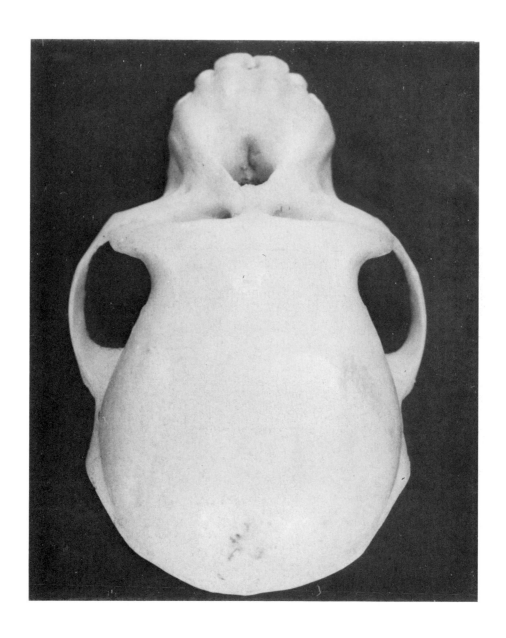

Figure 130. A view of the top of the cast of the orangutan skull shown in Figures 126 and 128.

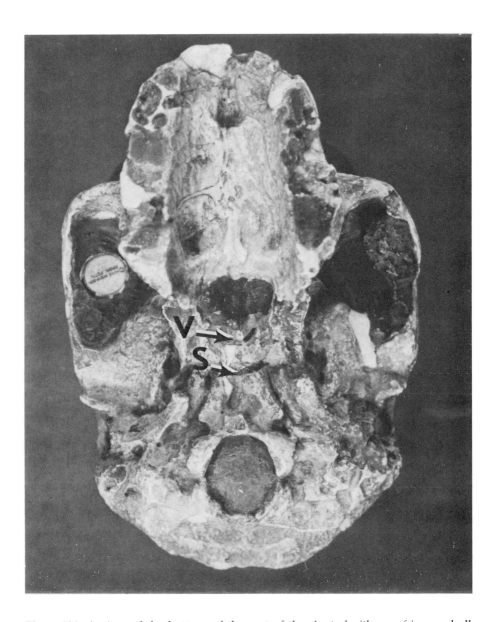

Figure 131. A view of the bottom of the cast of the *Australopithecus africanus* skull shown in Figures 125, 127, and 129. The posterior border of the vomer bone (V) and the spheno-occipital synostosis (S) are demarcated with a black line. *Photographs of casts used courtesy of the Wenner-Gren Foundation for Anthropological Research, Inc., New York, and with permission of the owners of the original specimens. Permission granted by the Transvaal Museum.*

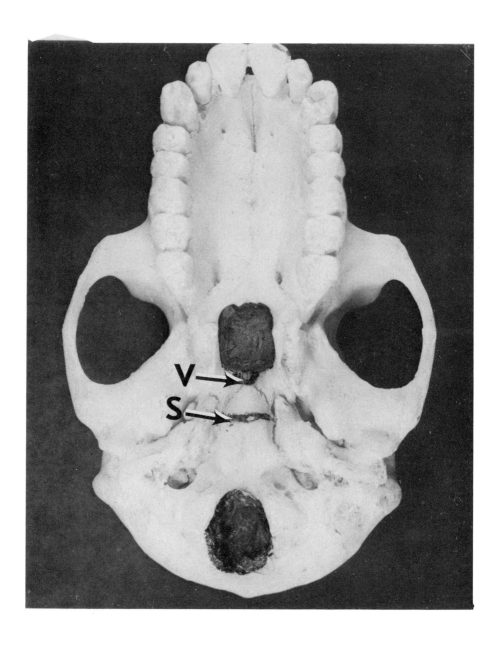

Figure 132. A view of the bottom of the cast of the orangutan skull shown in Figures 126, 128, and 130. The posterior border of the vomer bone (V) and the spheno-occipital synostosis (S) are demarcated with a black line.

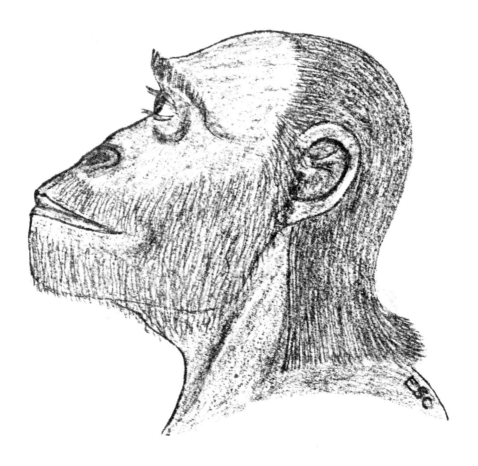

Figure 133. The author's determination of what the *Australopithecus africanus* "Mrs. Ples" looked like when she was alive.

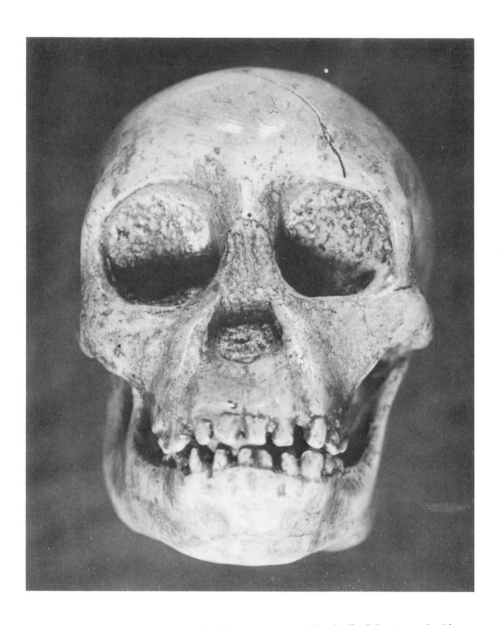

Figure 134. Anterior view of the PA Museum cast of the skull of the *Australopithecus africanus* infant skull known as the "Taung child." The milk or deciduous teeth are present.

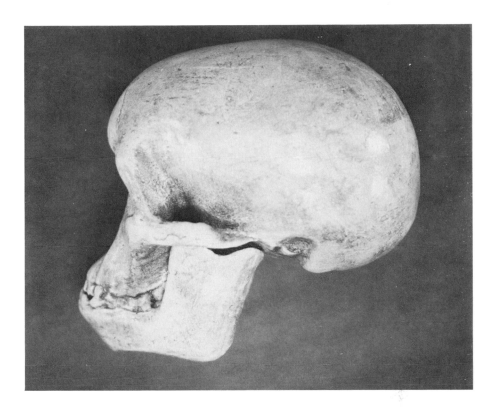

Figure 135. Left lateral view of the cast of the *Australopithecus africanus* infant shown in Figure in 134.

All present-day animals are the surviving members of families consisting of many closely related forms, some of which are now extinct. Since human beings are animals, there is no scientific reason why they should be any different. It is only natural to assume that there were several hominid species evolving on this earth at the same time. In fact, there were probably a number of australopithecine species. Some species died off as australopithecines and other hominids evolved into other forms. Surely, the robust *Australopithecus boisei* line must have died off by one million years ago (Figures 141 and 142). It is not only difficult but illogical to imagine that a creature with such a small brain and massive masticatory apparatus as late as one million years ago could have evolved into any of the later hominids.

Actually, some of the gracile australopithecine forms may have died

141

out between one and two million years ago, and this could include the species represented by Mrs. Ples. Even so, all of the australopithecine skulls are essentially apelike. Therefore, I didn't hesitate to reconstruct the upper part of the respiratory system of Mrs. Ples to serve as an example of the typical australopithecine type. It was obvious what the form of the reconstructed respiratory system would be, since the crucial skull base anatomy is so similar to that of a present-day orangutan. The tongue of Mrs. Ples was located entirely within her oral cavity, and she could lock her larynx into her nasopharynx. She could swallow liquid and breathe air simultaneously. Using modeling clay, I sculpted the two sides of Mrs. Ples's vocal tract (Figures 136 and 137). I then filled the spaces of both sides of her vocal tract with silicone rubber paste (Figure 138). When the rubber set, I fused the two sides together with rubber paste to represent the total space of the australopithecine vocal tract. Using key landmarks on the skull of Mrs. Ples, I was able to estimate topographically the size and shape of the nasal cavities and nasopharynx. I made a cast of these as well with silicone rubber and attached it to the cast of the vocal tract (Figure 139). Naturally, the casts were almost exactly the same shape as the vocal tract, nasal cavities, and nasopharynx of an adult chimpanzee (Figure 53). I also made a clay cast of the vocal tract and coated it with latex rubber to make a hollow rubber copy of the tract in the same manner that I described for making a copy of the adult tract in Chapter 2 (Figure 140). Using the same plastic larynx described in Chapter 2, I tested the ability of the australopithecine tract to produce vowel sounds. Of course, the results were identical to those obtained when the chimpanzee rubber tract was tested. Although the simian shelf was a hindrance to modifying the shape of the oral cavity, I could have improved the production of the vowel sounds by pulling down the pharynx and larynx to elongate the pharynx and create somewhat of a right angle bend at the junction of the oral cavity and oropharynx, as I did when testing the two-year–old human rubber tract. After all, the australopithecines had the neck of an erect biped. This is easily deduced from the fact that the foramen magnum of *Australopithecus* is more horizontal and set further forward than that of an ape (Figures 131 and 132). However, australopithecines may have held their necks in an apelike manner, tilted forward at an angle especially when walking, because their fossil hip joints show that they had a waddling gait. Also, pulling down the pharynx and larynx was not justified, because there is no positive evidence that an australopithecine used its vocal tract for communicating to a greater degree than present-day apes do. Moreover, as pointed out before, the brain of a two-year–old human is genetically programmed for the child to acquire fully articulate speech, whereas the brain of an australopithecine hominid was not.

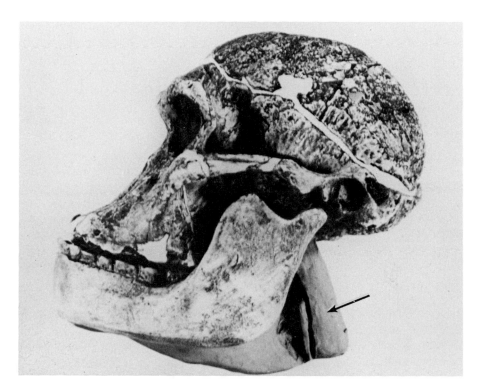

Figure 136. Left lateral view of the cast of the "Mrs. Ples" skull to which a PA Museum cast of an *Australopithecus africanus* mandible has been articulated. Modeling clay (arrow) is attached to the base of the skull. *Photographs of casts used courtesy of the Wenner-Gren Foundation for Anthropological Research, Inc., New York, and with permission of the owners of the original specimens. Permission granted by the Transvaal Museum.*

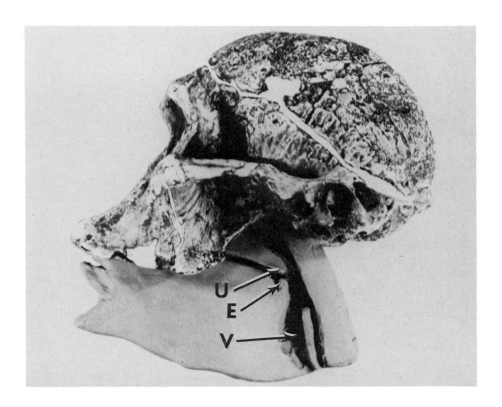

Figure 137. Left lateral view of the cast of the "Mrs. Ples" skull to which modeling clay is attached. The space of the right half of the vocal tract has been sculpted out of the clay. U: uvula of the soft palate. E: epiglottis. V: vestibule of the larynx. *Photographs of casts used courtesy of the Wenner-Gren Foundation for Anthropological Research, Inc., New York, and with permission of the owners of the original specimens. Permission granted by the Transvaal Museum.*

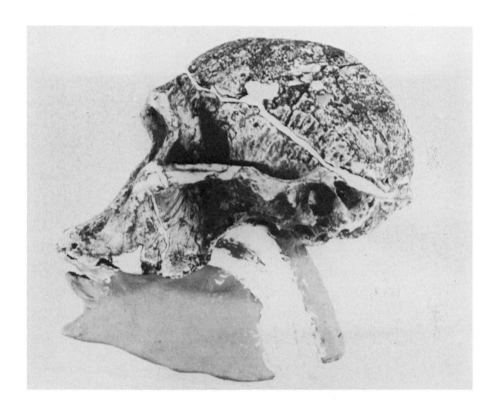

Figure 138. Left lateral view of the cast of the "Mrs. Ples" skull. Silicone rubber fills the space of the right half of the vocal tract sculpted out of the clay attached to the base of the skull and shown in Figure 137. *Photographs of casts used courtesy of the Wenner-Gren Foundation for Anthropological Research, Inc., New York, and with permission of the owners of the original specimens. Permission granted by the Transvaal Museum.*

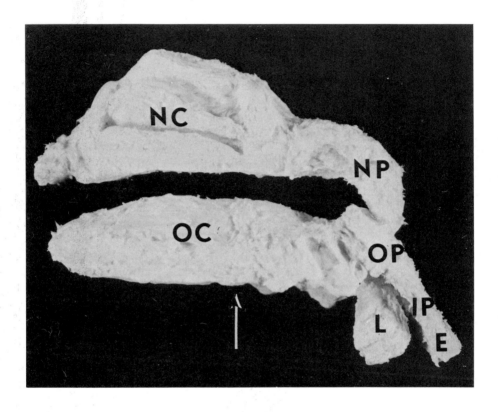

Figure 139. Left lateral view of the solid silicone rubber cast representing the space of the reconstructed upper respiratory system of the *Australopithecus africanus* hominid, "Mrs. Ples." The arrow points toward the foramen cecum located at the junction between the anterior two-thirds and the posterior one-third of the tongue. NC: nasal cavities. NP: nasopharynx. OC: oral cavity. OP: oropharynx. IP: infra-laryngeal pharynx. E: esophagus. L: larynx.

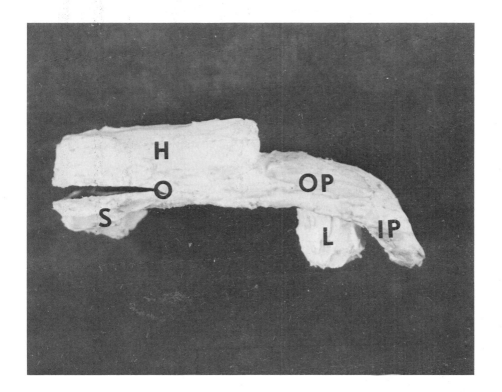

Figure 140. Left lateral view of the hollow rubber copy of the reconstructed vocal tract of the *Australopithecus africanus* hominid, "Mrs. Ples." H: hard palate. S: simian shelf. O: oral cavity. OP: oropharynx. IP: intralaryngeal pharynx. L: larynx.

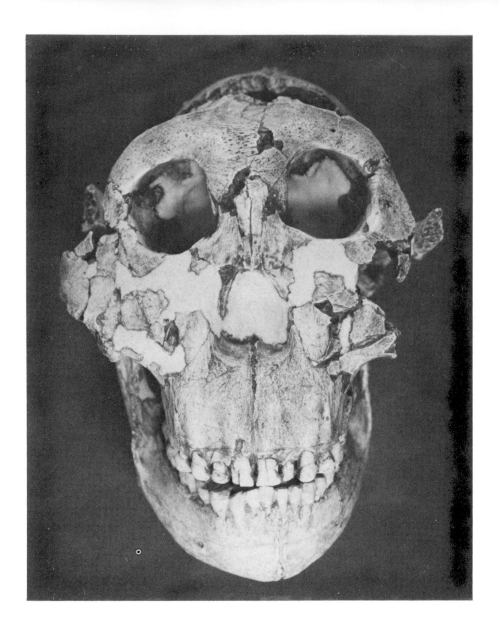

Figure 141. Anterior view of the W-G foundation cast of the fossil skull of the adult *Australopithecus boisei* known as "Zing" and dated at around 1 3/4 million years old. The mandible is dated at around 500,000 years old and was found at Peninj in Tanzania, Africa, which is close to Olduvai in Tanzania, where the face and brain case constituting "Zing" were found. *Photographs of casts used courtesy of the Wenner-Gren Foundation for Anthropological Research, Inc., New York, and with permission of the owners of the original specimens. Permission granted by Dr. Mary Leakey.*

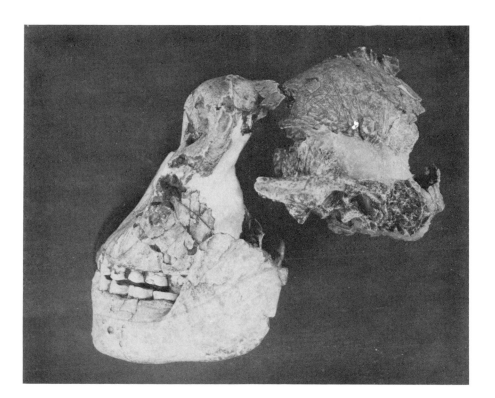

Figure 142. Left lateral view of the casts of the fossil skull parts constituting the *Australopithecus boisei* "Zing" and the Peninj mandible shown in figure 141. *Photographs of casts used courtesy of the Wenner-Gren Foundation for Anthropological Research, Inc., New York, and with permission of the owners of the original specimens. Permission granted by Dr. Mary Leakey.*

As we shall see, increased mental ability was reflected by an enlargement of the evolving hominid brain. *Australopithecus afarensis, africanus,* and *robustus* had been walking erect with freed hands for a few million years, and yet their brains were about the same size as those of present-day apes. These little bipedal hominids, no more than 4½ feet tall, probably were just as reluctant as present-day mammals to make meaningful variations of vowel sounds that required a significant resistance to the flow of air in their vocal tracts (Figure 133).

Homo Habilis Skulls

Recently a few fossil skulls have been found in Africa that are the same as those of *Australopithecus* hominids, except that the cranial capacity averages 700 cubic centimeters (Pilbeam 1981; Walker and Leakey 1978). These skulls, which encased a significantly larger brain, are classified as *Homo habilis* (Figure 143). Unfortunately, much of the base is missing from these skulls. Since the larger brain case causes only a slight modification in the overall size and shape of the *Homo habilis* skulls compared to the typical australopithecine skull, it is most likely that the vocal tract was completely apelike. The dating of *Homo habilis* skulls to around two million years ago causes a problem, because they could then predate some *Australopithecus africanus* skulls. This would indicate that *afarensis* may have evolved into *habilis.* My skull studies indicate that *habilis* could have evolved from either *africanus* or *afarensis.* Also, it is possible that *Homo habilis* evolved directly into early archaic *Homo sapiens.* However, this would mean that *Homo erectus,* who existed from 1½ million to possibly 500,000 years ago, was not in the direct lineage of *Homo sapiens.* The most recent date for *Homo erectus* is blurred by the fact that some of the *Homo erectus* forms probably gradually evolved into the so-called early archaic *Homo sapiens* hominids. Excluding *Homo erectus* from the direct *Homo sapiens* lineage is not such an audacious act, because it only involves a small number of fossil skulls classified as *Homo erectus.* The majority of these are only skullcaps. This is due to the fact that the decay of the mass of soft tissue attached to the skull base often caused the base to undergo partial or complete dissolution following death. However, on the basis of the known hominid fossil skulls, I favor the view that *Homo habilis* hominids evolved into *Homo erectus* hominids in Africa and then dispersed into Asia and Europe. They subsequently evolved into archaic *Homo sapiens* hominids on all three continents. I feel this way because I determined that some *Homo erectus* hominids had a vocal tract intermediate in form between australopithecines and archaic *Homo sapiens.*

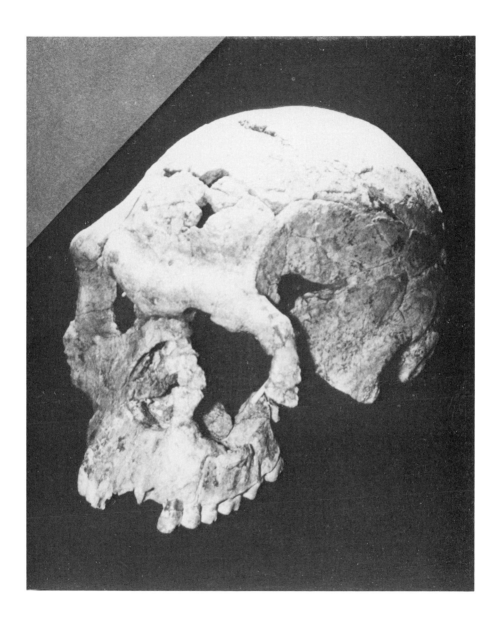

Figure 143. Left anterior view of the fossil skull of an australopithecine *Homo habilis* hominid found in Kenya, Africa. It is dated at around two million years old. *Photo by Margo Crabtree from Rensberger (1984).*

Homo Erectus Skulls

Fortunately, the most complete fossil skull classified as *Homo erectus* (KNM-ER 3733) is the oldest found (Figures 144). It is dated at 1½ million years old and was found in Kenya, Africa (Pilbeam 1984; Rensberger 1984; Walker and Leakey 1978). The mandible is missing but the skull base is complete. Dr. Laitman examined the original fossil skull and made a craniometric analysis of the base. He found it had marked similarities to the skull base of living apes and probably had a larynx and pharynx positioned high in the neck (Laitman and Heimbuch 1984). Although his measurements indicated a slight degree of flexion in the skull base, a photograph of the base shows a relatively long distance between the bony palate and the foramen magnum (Figure 145). The sphenoid bone would be exposed between the vomer bone and the spheno-occipital synostosis. Therefore, I judge that the vocal tract was basically apelike.

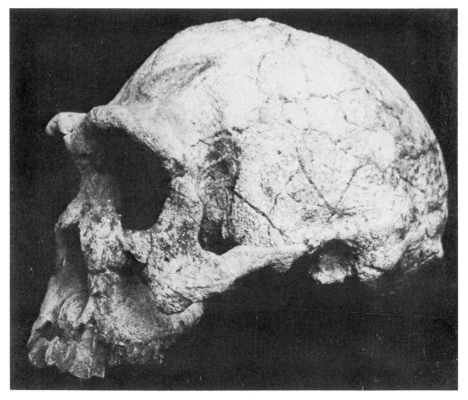

Figure 144. Left lateral view of the oldest known *Homo erectus* fossil skull. It is dated at 1.6 million years old and was found in Kenya, Africa. *Photo by Margo Crabtree from Rensberger (1984).*

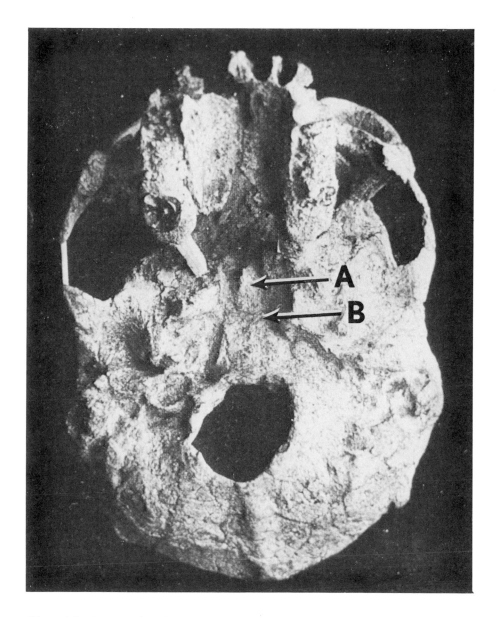

Figure 145. A view of the base of the *Homo erectus* fossil skull shown in Figure 144. A: position of the posterior border of the vomer bone. B: site of the spheno-occipital synostosis. *Photo by Margo Crabtree from Rensberger (1984).*

If there had been an *Australopithecus* species not in the direct lineage of *Homo sapiens*, some of them could have evolved into *Homo erectus* hominids and then become extinct. Or some of the *Homo erectus* hominids could have evolved into classic Neanderthal hominids before becoming extinct. Be that as it may, *Homo erectus* appears to have originated in Africa around 1½ million years ago and then migrated into southeastern and eastern Asia by 1 million years ago (Pilbeam 1984). The *Homo erectus* Heidelberg or Maver mandible found in West Germany is dated at 500,000 years old (Figures 146 and 147). *Homo erectus* hominids were larger than the aus-

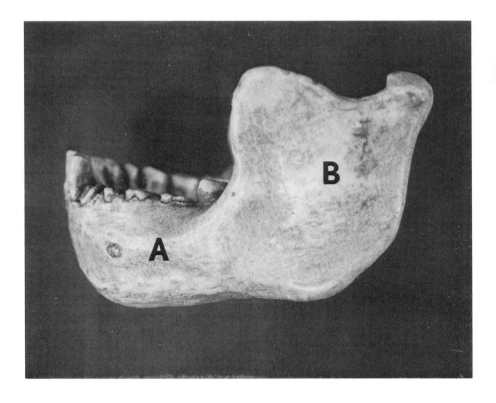

Figure 146. Left lateral view of the PA Museum cast of the *Homo erectus* Heidelberg or Mauer mandible found in the Mauer sands near Heidelberg, West Germany. It is dated at about 500,000 years old. A: body. B: ramus.

tralopithecines and *Homo habilis,* averaging 5½ feet tall (Pilbeam 1984). A recent find in Africa indicates that a 1½ million-year–old *Homo erectus* skeleton of a possible twelve-year–old male child could have grown to six feet in height. There was an increase in brain size from 600 cubic centimeters in the 1½ million-year–old African *Homo erectus* adult skull to over 1,000 cubic centimeters in both the African and Asian *erectus* skulls dated at 500,000 years old (Figures 150 and 151). The increase in brain size is related not only to an increase in overall body size, but also to evidence that there was big game hunting, the use of tools such as hand axes, and the use of

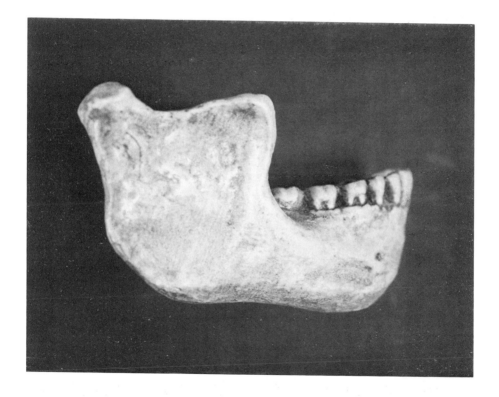

Figure 147. Right lateral view of the PA Museum cast of the *Homo erectus* Heidelberg or Mauer mandible shown in Figure 146.

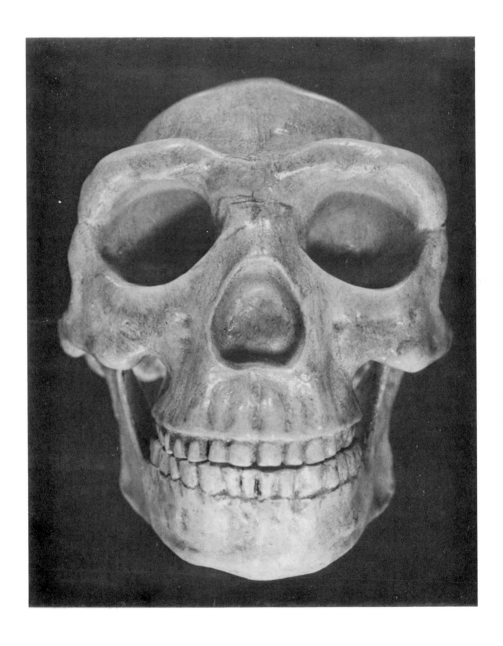

Figure 148. Anterior view of a PA museum cast of a reconstructed *Homo erectus* fossil skull found in the lower cave near Peking, China. Although referred to as Peking man, it is probably from an adult female and is dated at between 400,000 and 500,000 years old.

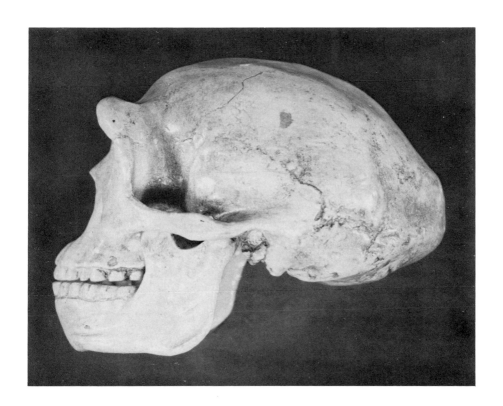

Figure 149. Left lateral view of the cast of the *Homo erectus* fossil skull shown in Figure 148.

fire. It must be pointed out that increased brain size is not necessarily related to increased intelligence. Brain function is at the level of the invisible nerve cells. For example, the human brain before birth, when it is the size of a hen's egg, has more than the ten billion nerve cells of the cerebral cortex found in a 1,500 cubic centimeter adult brain. The brain of the Peking woman *Homo erectus* hominid was 1,000 cubic centimeters which equals the size of the brain of many present-day human adults. The range of present-day adult human beings is 1,000 to 2,000 cubic centimeters with the average being 1,300 cubic centimeters. Even so, it would be absurd to equate the mental ability of the *erectus* brain with that of present-day human beings. Also, as the brain increased in size from birth to adulthood in the *Australopithecus, Homo habilis,* and *Homo erectus* hominids, the frontal lobes underwent a relative decrease in size (Figure 220). As this occurred, protruding brow ridges developed and the originally high vertical forehead became sloped. This is evident in the immature australopithecine, *erectus,* and present-day ape skulls (Figures 119, 134, 135, 160).

In order to reconstruct the vocal tract in *Homo erectus,* I had to use parts of different skulls. Other than the oldest *Homo erectus* fossil skull, none has a completely intact base. For the face and mandible, I used the well-known PA Museum cast of the Franz Weidenreich reconstruction of a complete adult female from parts found in the Choukoutien lower cave near Peking, China (Figures 148 and 149). The reconstructed base lacks details. For the front of the brain case, I used a W-G Foundation cast of a *Homo erectus* skull from Sangiran, Indonesia, which is the same size as the Peking cast (Figure 151). For the back of the brain case and the skull base I used a W-G Foundation cast of a *Homo erectus* skull also from Sangiran and the same size as the other casts (Figures 153–158). A cast of maxillae that are thought to be part of this latter fossil and part of a mandible also found at Sangiran were also included (Figures 152 and 153). The incline of the basilar part of the occipital bone demonstrated that the skull base between the bony palate and foramen magnum was relatively short and formed a fairly deep concavity. However, the snout, related to relatively large maxillae, coupled with a relatively short robust mandibular ramus indicated that only a part of the posterior third of the tongue was located low enough in the neck to serve as a short anterior wall to the oropharynx (Figures 149 and 205). My calculations on the length of the hominid tongue during evolution shows that it maintained just about the same length from the australopithecines to present-day human beings (Figure 205). Therefore, the larger-than-present-day-human maxillae of the *Homo erectus* reconstructed skull did not allow the tongue to be lowered into the neck to the full extent found in a present-day human being without making the tongue unduly long.

Figure 150. Left lateral view of a W-G Foundation cast of an adult *Homo erectus* fossil skull (Olduvai hominid 9) lacking a face and mandible. It was found at Olduvai Gorge, Tanzania, Africa, and is dated at about 500,000 years old. *Photographs of casts used courtesy of the Wenner-Gren Foundation for Anthropological Research, Inc., New York, and with permission of the owners of the original specimens. Permission granted by Dr. Mary Leakey.*

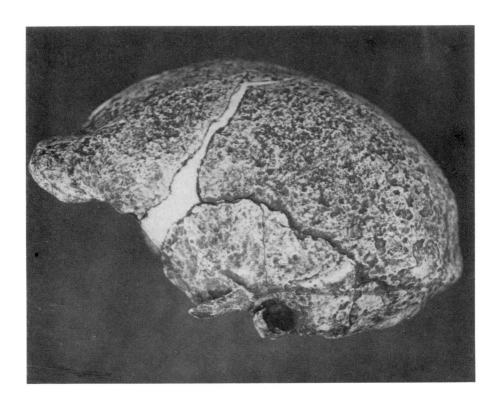

Figure 151. Left lateral view of a W-G Foundation cast of an adult *Homo erectus* fossil skull lacking a face, base, and mandible. It was found at Sangiran, Indonesia, and is dated at between 500,000 and 700,000 thousand years old. *Photographs of casts used courtesy of the Wenner-Gren Foundation for Anthropological Research, Inc., New York, and with permission of the owners of the original specimens. Permission granted by the Natur-Museum, Senckenberg, West Germany.*

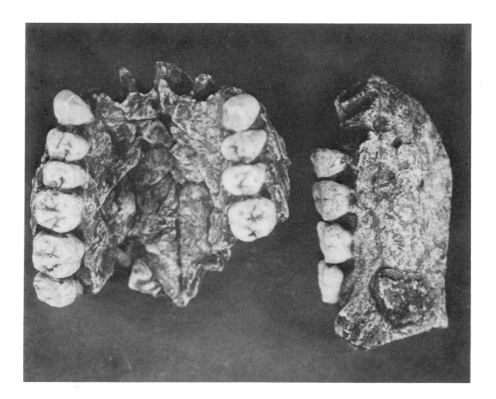

Figure 152. On the left is a ventral view of a W-G Foundation cast of a fossil maxilla, and on the right a lateral view of a W-G Foundation cast of a fossil right mandibular ramus. They were found at the same site at Sangiran, Indonesia, along with the *Homo erectus* fossil skull shown in Figure 153. *Photographs of casts used courtesy of the Wenner-Gren Foundation for Anthropological Research, Inc., New York, and with permission of the owners of the original specimens. Permission granted by the Natur-Museum, Senckenberg, West Germany.*

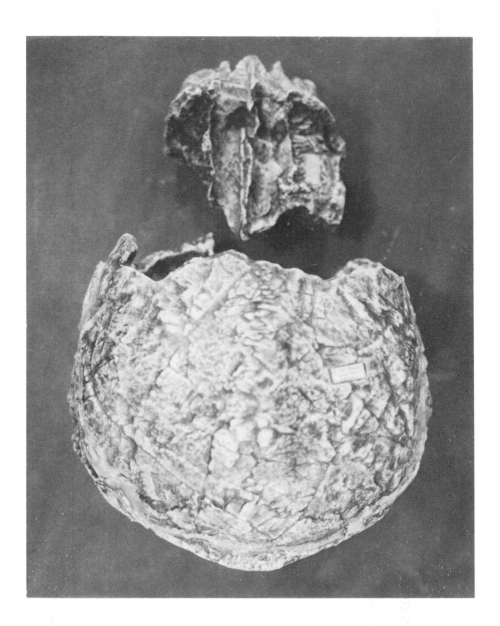

Figure 153. A view of the top of the maxilla shown in Figure 152 and the top of a W-G Foundation cast of a fossil *Homo erectus* skull lacking the face and the anterior part of the brain case. They were found at the same site at Sangiran, Indonesia, and are dated at between 500,000 and 700,000 years old. *Photographs of casts used courtesy of the Wenner-Gren Foundation for Anthropological Research, Inc., New York, and with permission of the owners of the original specimens. Permission granted by the Natur-Museum, Senckenberg, West Germany.*

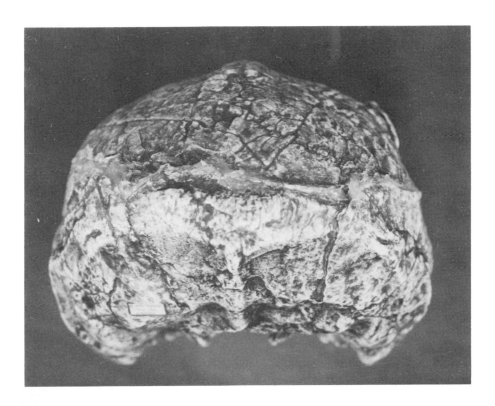

Figure 154. A posterior view of the cast of the fossil *Homo erectus* skull shown in Figure 153. *Photographs of casts used courtesy of the Wenner-Gren Foundation for Anthropological Research, Inc., New York, and with permission of the owners of the original specimens. Permission granted by the Natur-Museum, Senckenberg, West Germany.*

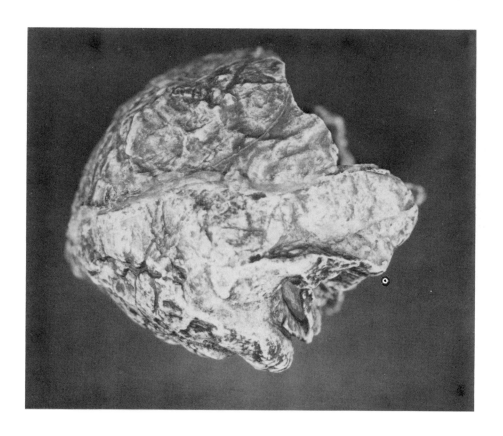

Figure 155. A right lateral view of the cast of the fossil *Homo erectus* skull shown in Figures 153 and 154. *Photographs of casts used courtesy of the Wenner-Gren Foundation for Anthropological Research, Inc., New York, and with permission of the owners of the original specimens. Permission granted by the Natur-Museum, Senckenberg, West Germany.*

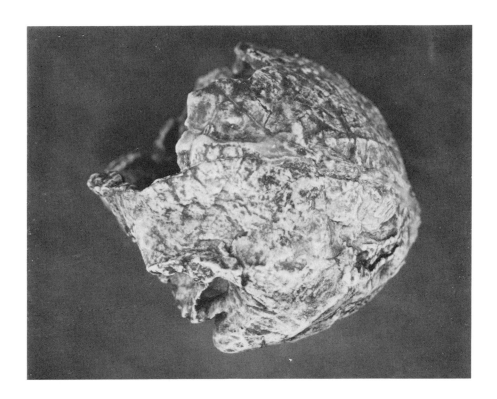

Figure 156. A left lateral view of the cast of the fossil *Homo erectus* skull shown in Figures 153–155. *Photographs of casts used courtesy of the Wenner-Gren Foundation for Anthropological Research, Inc., New York, and with permission of the owners of the original specimens. Permission granted by the Natur-Museum, Senckenberg, West Germany.*

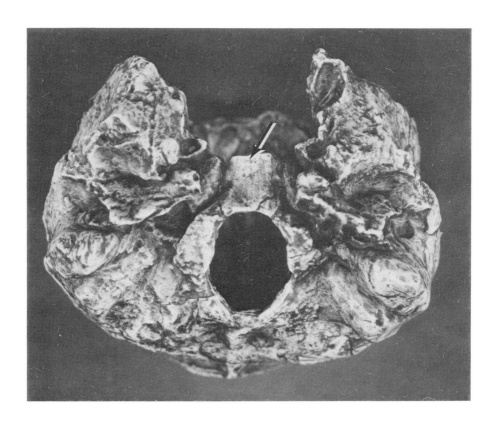

Figure 157. A view of the base of the cast of the fossil *Homo erectus* skull shown in Figures 153–156. The arrow points to the basilar part of the occipital bone. *Photographs of casts used courtesy of the Wenner-Gren Foundation for Anthropological Research, Inc., New York, and with permission of the owners of the original specimens. Permission granted by the Natur-Museum, Senckenberg, West Germany.*

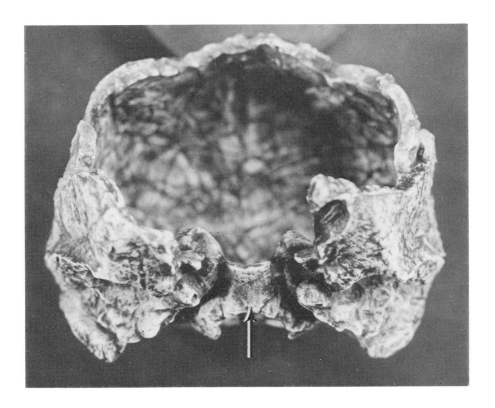

Figure 158. An anterior view of the cast of the fossil *Homo erectus* skull shown in Figures 153–157. The arrow points to the basilar part of the occipital bone that is inclined more toward the vertical than the horizontal plane. *Photographs of casts used courtesy of the Wenner-Gren Foundation for Anthropological Research, Inc., New York, and with permission of the owners of the original specimens. Permission granted by the Natur-Museum, Senkenberg, West Germany.*

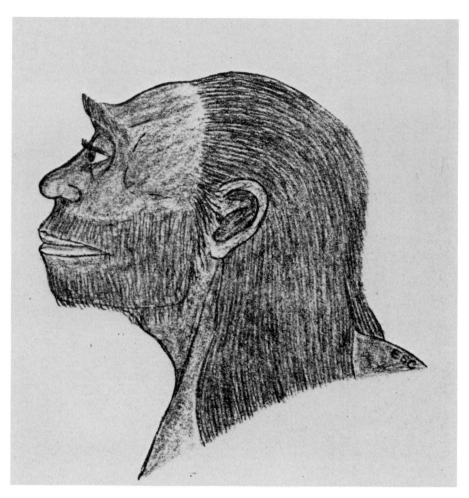

Figure 159. The author's determination of what a "typical" *Homo erectus* adult female looked like when she was alive.

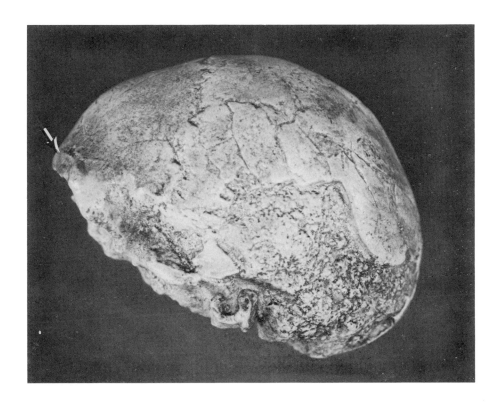

Figure 160. Left lateral view of a PA museum cast of a fossil *Homo erectus* skull of a child found at Modjokerto, Indonesia. It is dated between 500,000 and 700,000 years old. The author estimates the child was about three years old when it died. The arrow points to an early forming brow ridge.

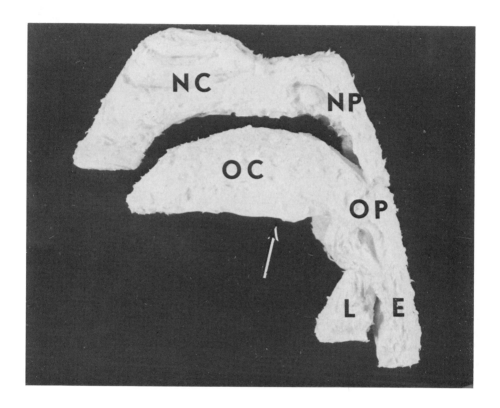

Figure 161. Left lateral view of a solid silicone rubber cast representing the space of the reconstructed upper respiratory system of an adult *Homo erectus* hominid. The arrows point toward the foramen cecum located at the junction between the anterior two-thirds and the posterior one-third of the tongue. NC: nasal cavities. NP: nasopharynx. OC: oral cavity. OP: oropharynx. E: esophagus. L: larynx.

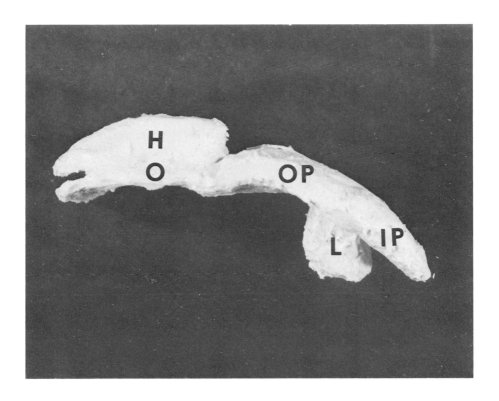

Figure 162. Left lateral view of a hollow rubber copy of the reconstructed vocal tract of an adult *Homo erectus* hominid. H: hard palate. O: oral cavity. OP: oropharynx. IP: infralaryngeal pharynx. L: larynx.

Using clay and silicone rubber, I made a cast of the upper part of the respiratory system of this reconstructed skull (Figure 161). The cast of the vocal tract resembles that of a 3½-year–old present-day child, the posterior part of whose tongue and larynx is partially descended into a lower position in the neck (Figure 226). I made a hollow rubber copy of the reconstructed *Homo erectus* vocal tract and tested its ability to make vowel sounds using the same plastic larynx that produced the glottal wave for all of the other rubber tracts tested (Figure 162). Although there is no projecting chin, the *Homo erectus* mandible has a very slight simian shelf (Figures 149 and 159). Even though the partial descent of the larynx resulted in part of the pharynx being able to modify the glottal wave, there wasn't a sufficient length to make much of an improvement in function compared to the chimpanzee and australopithecine rubber vocal tracts. The bulk of the tongue would still be within the oral cavity and cause the same difficulties in producing consonant sounds as it does in a 3½-year–old child. That *Homo erectus* could have lowered his larynx to create a right angle bend at the junction of the oral cavity and pharynx and thus increase the length of the oro-pharynx to more efficiently produce vowel sounds, just as a 3½-year–old child does when vocalizing, doesn't mean he did. Again, the brain of the present day 3½-year–old child is genetically programmed for the acquisi-tion of fully articulate speech, whereas the brain of *Homo erectus* was not. The relatively small size of the frontal lobes of the cerebral hemispheres of the *Homo erectus* brain are also negative evidence of a significant level of vocal communication, as will be pointed out later in the chapter (Figures 220 and 222). Why then was the skull base and upper part of the respiratory system undergoing a change in form, if it was not due to the natural selection pressures related to the acquisition of a vocal tract that ultimately allowed the production of the articulate speech sounds with facility? Du Brul (1958), speaking about the evolution of the speech apparatus, con-cludes, "With the shift to the upright posture, changes of the skull, jaws, mouth muscles and pharyngeal relations made the oral channel available for sounds blown out of the larynx." This statement is incorrect for two reasons. One, I have already pointed out that present-day children stand erect long before the changes occur, and hominids were standing erect millions of years before the changes began in *Homo erectus*. Two, the apelike vocal tract made the oral channel directly available for sounds blown out of the larynx, whereas the vocal tract changes result in the larynx being situated at a greater distance from the oral cavity, separated by a length of pharynx.

I am at a loss to attribute the skull base and vocal tract changes to anything other than the use of the tract for improved vocal communication.

If the changes were the result of something completely unrelated to vocal communication, they would be considered an exaptation for speech and not a natural selection adaption (Lewin 1982). They may have been merely the result of molecular drive (Dover 1982). If so, accidental mutations in genes could have been copied and multiplied to the point where they produced the skull base and vocal tract changes in *Homo erectus* hominids. Whatever the initial cause or causes were, the changes didn't begin to occur in all *Homo erectus* hominids. Some must have retained the apelike skull base and vocal tract similar to that of the *Homo erectus* skull shown in Figures 144 and 145. These hominids could either have become extinct or have evolved into classic Neanderthal hominids and then become extinct.

Early Archaic Homo Sapiens Skulls

The latest concensus on hominid evolution is that the *Homo erectus* species survived in southeastern and eastern Asia at least until 300,000 years ago (Pilbeam 1984). Between 40,000 and 45,000 years ago, modern *Homo sapiens* appeared. For the time period between 300,000 and 100,000 years ago, two skulls have been found that are sufficiently intact for their vocal tracts to be reconstructed scientifically. They are classified as archaic *Homo sapiens* and are closely similar. One was found in a gravel pit at Steinheim, West Germany, in 1933. It is reasonably intact, but the left side of the face is distorted (Figures 163–167). The other was found at Swanscombe, Kent, England, and consists of three bones (Figures 168–173). The occipital bone was found in 1935, the left parietal in 1936, and the right parietal in 1955. All three bones are almost complete and undistorted and clearly fit together (Day 1965). The Steinheim and Swanscombe skulls are believed to be from young adult females and are dated at between 200,000 and 250,000 years old. I observed the actual Steinheim fossil and found the PA Museum cast to be an accurate duplicate of the original. There are a number of plastic reconstructed Steinheim skull copies commercially available, but all are inaccurate in size and form. There has been only one serious attempt that I know of to reconstruct the Steinheim skull accurately. This was by H. Weinert in 1936 (Weinert 1936). The reconstructed skull is bilaterally symmetrical, which, of course, no skull ever is, and Weinert failed to restore the missing part of the base to the right side and rear of the foramen magnum. However, he did accurately rearrange the out-of-position parts of the base between the bony palate and foramen magnum so that they form a deep concavity, just as they do in present-day adult human skulls.

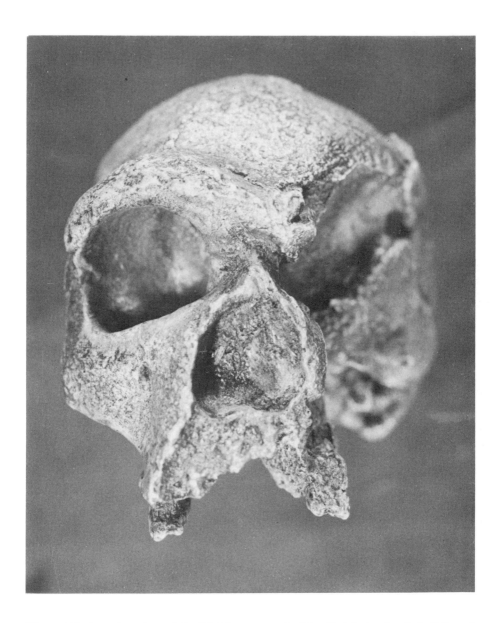

Figure 163. Anterior view of the PA Museum cast of the Steinheim fossil skull found at Steinheim, West Germany. It is dated at 200,000 years old and judged to be female. The mandible was not found.

Figure 164. A view of the top of the cast of the Steinheim fossil skull shown in Figure 163.

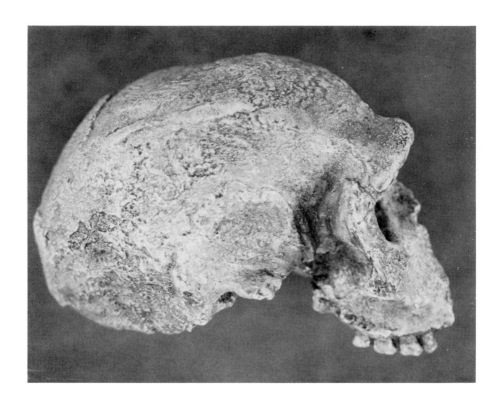

Figure 165. A right lateral view of the cast of the Steinheim fossil skull shown in Figures 163 and 164.

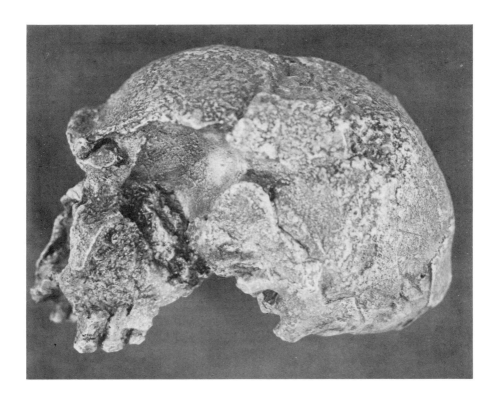

Figure 166. A left lateral view of the cast of the Steinheim fossil skull shown in Figures 163–165.

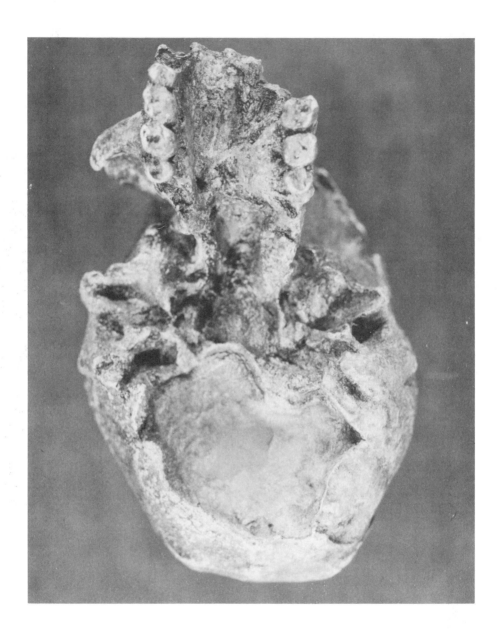

Figure 167. A view of the base of the cast of the Steinheim fossil skull shown in **Figures 163–166.**

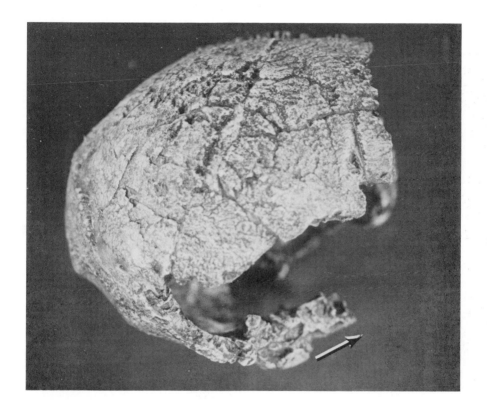

Figure 168. Right lateral view of the W-G Foundation cast of the Swanscombe fossil skull found at Swanscombe, Kent, England. It consists of the occipital and two parietal bones, which are dated as being around 200,000 years old. The arrow indicates that the basilar part of the occipital bone is inclined midway between the vertical and horizontal planes. *Photographs of casts used courtesy of the Wenner-Gren Foundation for Anthropological Research, Inc., New York, and with permission of the owners of the original specimens. Permission granted by the British Museum (Natural History).*

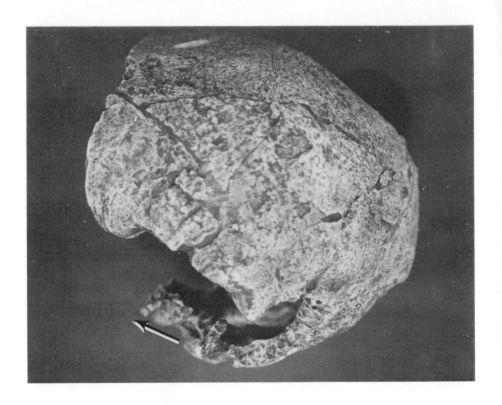

Figure 169. Left lateral view of the cast of the Swanscombe fossil skull shown in Figure 168. The arrow indicates that the basilar part of the occipital bone is inclined midway between the vertical and horizontal planes. *Photographs of casts used courtesy of the Wenner-Gren Foundation for Anthropological Research, Inc., New York, and with permission of the owners of the original specimens. Permission granted by the British Museum (Natural History).*

I decided to make my own restoration of the Steinheim skull so I could accurately reconstruct the vocal tract (Crelin 1973b). I took a PA Museum cast of the original fossil, and, using a dental drill, I carefully freed the parts of the skull that were displaced by some unknown force occurring either to cause the death of the individual or at some time after death. Using modeling clay, I properly repositioned the excised parts. I also used the clay to restore parts that were missing. My former graduate student, Dr. Ian Tattersall, took this reconstructed cast to the American Museum of Natural History in New York City, where he was a curator in anthropology, and made a beautiful plastic duplicate with his own hands (Figures

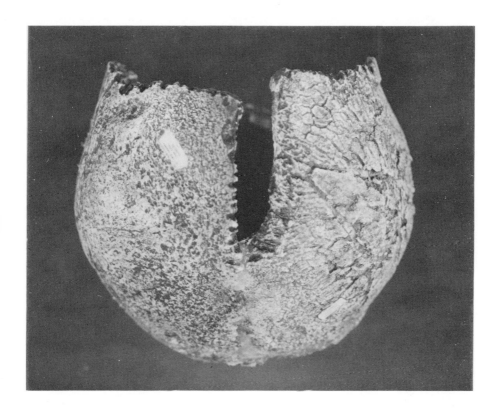

Figure 170. A view of the top of the cast of the Swanscombe fossil skull shown in Figures 168 and 169. *Photographs of casts used courtesy of the Wenner-Gren Foundation for Anthropological Research, Inc., New York, and with permission of the owners of the original specimens. Permission granted by the British Museum (Natural History).*

174–178). The cast is not only accurate but complete, because every depression, projection, and foramen that were present in the skull during life were restored. The cast was asymmetrical, with the left side being slightly larger overall. The part of the skull base to the right and rear of the foramen magnum that is missing from the original fossil was accurately restored using as a guide the Swanscombe skull, where that part of the base is present. The restored skull base is identical to that of a present-day *Homo sapiens* skull (Figure 178). Therefore, it was obvious that the reconstruction I made of the vocal tract cast using modeling clay and silicone rubber would be identical in size and shape to that of a present-day human adult (Figure 16 and 179).

Figure 171. A posterior view of the cast of the Swanscombe fossil skull shown in Figures 168–170. *Photographs of casts used courtesy of the Wenner-Gren Foundation for Anthropological Research, Inc., New York, and with permission of the owners of the original specimens. Permission granted by the British Museum (Natural History).*

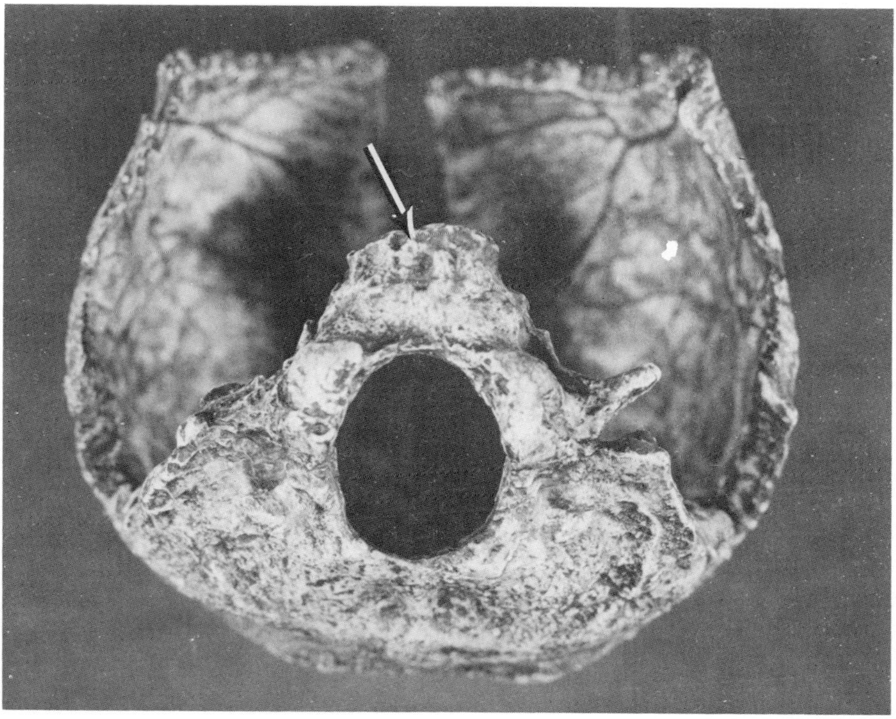

Figure 172. A view of the base of the cast of the Swanscombe fossil skull shown in Figures 168–171. The arrow points to the basilar part of the occipital bone. *Photographs of casts used courtesy of the Wenner-Gren Foundation for Anthropological Research, Inc., New York, and with permission of the owners of the original specimens. Permission granted by the British Museum (Natural History).*

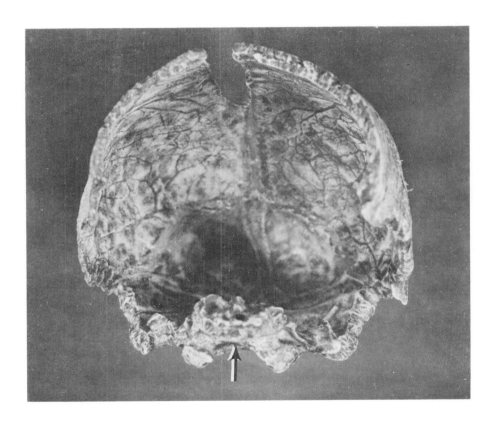

Figure 173. An anterior view of the cast of the Swanscombe fossil skull shown in Figure 168–172. The arrow points to the inclined basilar part of the occipital bone. *Photographs of casts used courtesy of the Wenner-Gren Foundation for Anthropological Research, Inc., New York, and with permission of the owners of the original specimens. Permission granted by the British Museum (Natural History).*

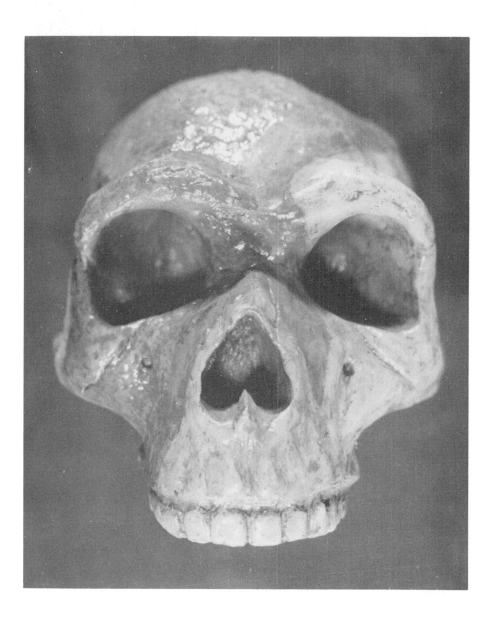

Figure 174. Anterior view of the plastic duplicate cast of the reconstructed Steinheim fossil skull made by the author. The plastic duplicate was made by Dr. Ian Tattersall.

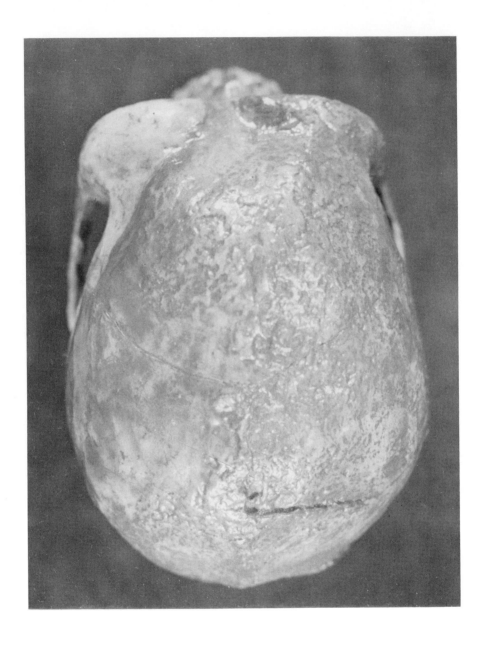

Figure 175. A view of the top of the plastic cast of the reconstructed Steinheim fossil skull shown in Figure 174.

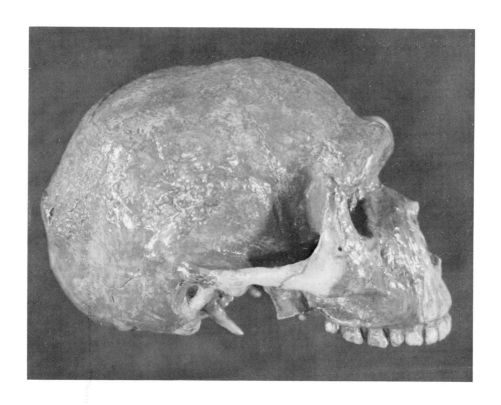

Figure 176. Right lateral view of the plastic cast of the reconstructed Steinheim fossil skull shown in Figures 174 and 175.

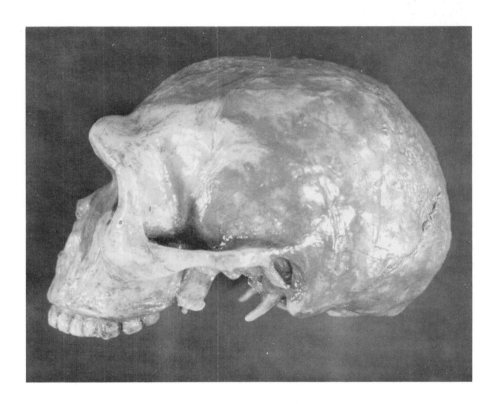

Figure 177. Left lateral view of the plastic cast of the reconstructed Steinheim fossil skull shown in Figures 174–176.

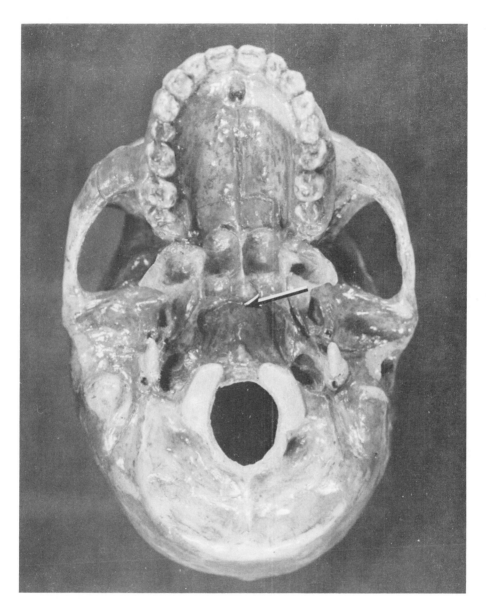

Figure 178. A view of the base of the plastic cast of the reconstructed Steinheim fossil skull shown in Figures 174–177. The arrow points to where the vomer bone abuts the basilar part of the occipital bone.

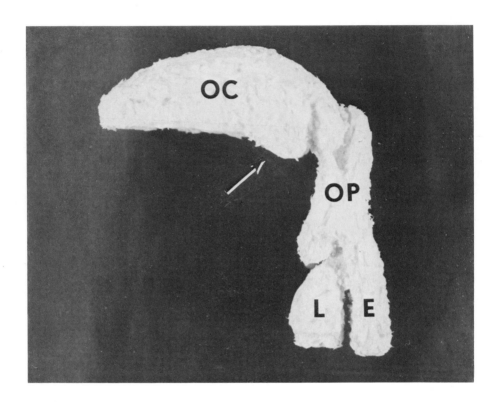

Figure 179. Left lateral view of the solid silicone rubber cast representing the space of the reconstructed vocal tract of the Steinheim archaic *Homo sapiens*. The arrow points toward the foramen cecum located at the junction between the anterior two-thirds and the posterior one-third of the tongue. OC: oral cavity. OP: oropharynx. E: esophagus. L: larynx.

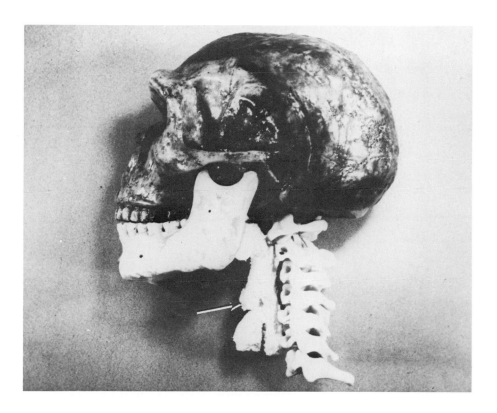

Figure 180. Left lateral view of the plastic cast of the reconstructed fossil Steinheim skull shown in Figures 174–178. A mandible and cervical vertebral column from a present-day female adult *Homo sapiens* has been articulated with the skull. The silicone rubber cast (arrow) of the Steinheim reconstructed vocal tract shown in Figure 179 is in its proper position.

I was able to articulate a mandible and cervical vertebral column from a present-day human being correctly to the Steinheim reconstructed skull (Figure 180). Thus, the masticatory structures, neck structures, and the posterior part of the skull were the same as those of present-day human beings. However, the brow ridges and the sloping forehead that are present are so primitive that they alone warrant classifying the Steinheim adult female as an archaic *Homo sapiens* (Figures 177 and 181). The fact that the Steinheim female had a completely modern vocal tract that allowed her to make all of the sounds of articulate speech with facility raises the question, "Did she?" There is no doubt that she did. In fact, there is little doubt that the direct lineage of hominids from either *Homo habilis* or *Homo erectus* began to make the sounds of articulate speech as more and more of the pharynx was incorporated into the vocal tract so that it was better able to modify the glottic waves emitted from the larynx. Note that I said "the sounds of articulate speech" and not "language." An increased repertoire of speech sounds must have enhanced vocal communication sufficiently to consider it an important natural selection pressure for the attainment of the fully modern vocal tract found in Steinheim woman. Once the vocal tract was fully modern, the use of the tract for more complex vocal communication undoubtedly occurred, even though there is little evidence of it. I hesitate to describe the more complex vocal communication as primitive language, even though that is probably a good way to do it. The acoustic input to the nervous system surely must have encoded the adaptable, or plastic, brain, leading to the establishment of new nerve cells, or neurons, and new connections, or synapses, between nerve cells already present in the association areas of the cerebral cortex. The association areas of the parietal, temporal, and frontal lobes are the analytical centers of all forms of sensory input (Figure 219). The integration, coordination, analysis, and storage of all forms of sensory information that is received from the environment is known as thought. Ultimately, language became an integral part of abstract or conceptual thought where a thought could be entirely conceived within the mind, entirely dissociated from any specific instance. My studies indicate that it took a long time to develop a high level of conceptual thought. This is discussed later in this chapter. In the meantime, archaic *Homo sapiens* began a long, slow improvement in vocal communication and thinking ability. The cranial capacity of the Steinheim skull is 1,325 cubic centimeters, and the Swanscombe skull is 1,070 cubic centimeters (Day 1965). This shows that the brain sizes were within the lower limits of present-day adults. A possible indication that archaic *Homo sapiens* may have begun to use his modern vocal tract as an aid to thinking conceptually is an unusual engraved ox rib dated as over 200,000 years old. It was found in 1969 by F. Bordes in a cave in France. A. Marshack (1975)

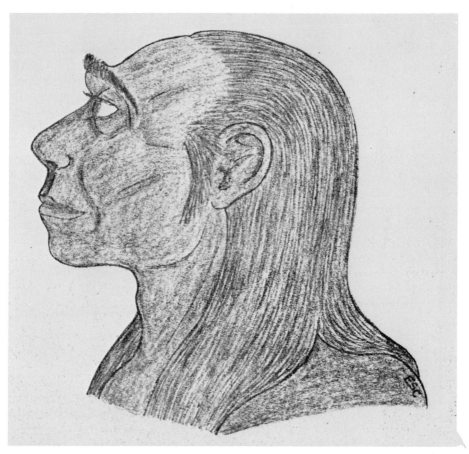

Figure 181. The author's determination of what the adult Steinheim archaic *Homo sapiens* female looked like when she was alive.

studied the engraving and concluded that it was made by a human being, that it was intentional, cumulative, and sequential, and that the bone had apparently been kept for some time.

Broken Hill (Rhodesian) Skull

Passing from the time of archaic *Homo sapiens* 200,000 years ago down to 50,000 years ago, we come to a skull that has been an enigma to most anthropologists. It was found in 1921 in a cave at Broken Hill, Zambia, which was then Northern Rhodesia. Therefore, it was known as *Homo*

193

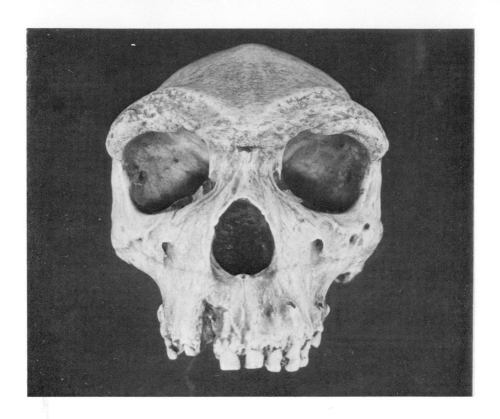

Figure 182. Anterior view of the W-G Foundation cast of the Rhodesian, or Broken Hill, fossil skull found in Zambia, Africa. It is tentatively dated at 40,000 to 100,000 years old. The mandible was not found. *Photographs of casts used courtesy of the Wenner-Gren Foundation for Anthropological Research, Inc., New York, and with permission of the owners of the original specimens. Permission granted by the British Museum (Natural History).*

sapiens rhodesiensis, Rhodesian man, or simply Broken Hill Man (Figures 182–184). Broken Hill hominids are believed to be " neanderthaloids" (recent archaic *Homo sapiens*) and to have evolved into Bushman or Negroes, or to have become extinct, either after some hybridizing with modern populations or without issue (Pilbeam 1984). My studies don't show Broken Hill man to be or have done any of these things. The dating of the skull is not definite. Day (1965) states, "Thus, on faunal, archaeological and chemical grounds, it seems that Rhodesian man lived during the Upper Pleistocene." The Upper Pleistocene ranges from 10,000 to 200,000 years ago. However, the skull is usually dated at between 40,000 and 50,000 years ago (Clark 1969; Pilbeam 1970). My findings indicate the skull is much older than that. If it is close to 100,000 years old, then it can simply be

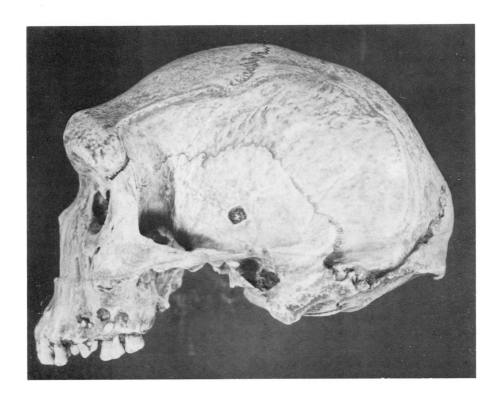

Figure 183. Lateral view of the cast of the fossil Broken Hill skull shown in Figure 182. *Photographs of casts used courtesy of the Wenner-Gren Foundation for Anthropological Research, Inc., New York, and with permission of the owners of the original specimens. Permission granted by the British Museum (Natural History).*

regarded as an adult male, early archaic *Homo sapiens*. The almost complete skull, lacking a mandible, is large compared to a large, present-day, human adult skull. The brow ridges are the largest of any known fossil hominid skull. The palate and teeth are a little larger than the largest present-day adult male skull in my collection. The back of the skull base shows that the massive posterior neck musculature of the *Homo erectus* hominids was still present. However, even though the bony palate is large, there is no snout, because the distance between the bony palate and the foramen magnum is relatively short. Also, the skull base in this interval is a deep concavity, indicating that the vocal tract was similar in shape to that of present-day human beings (Figure 184). A craniometric analysis of the skull base confirms this (Laitman, Heimbuch, and Crelin 1978, 1979). The cranial capacity is 1,289 cubic centimeters, indicating the brain was close to the average size of present-day adults. However, as with the Steinheim skull, the frontal lobes of the cerebral hemispheres of the brain are relatively

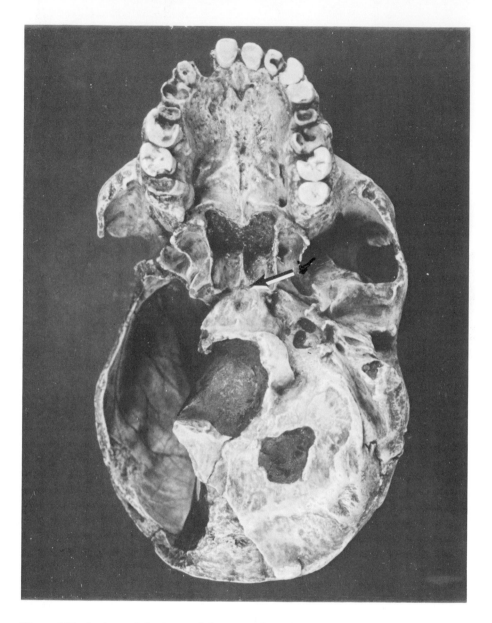

Figure 184. A view of the base of the cast of the fossil Broken Hill skull shown in Figures 182 and 183. The arrow points to where the vomer bone abuts the basilar part of the occipital bone. *Photographs of casts used courtesy of the Wenner-Gren Foundation for Anthropological Research, Inc., New York, and with permission of the owners of the original specimens. Permission granted by the British Museum (Natural History).*

small compared to a present-day human adult brain. If the very thick, projecting brow ridges are not a universal, male, sexual dimorphic feature of early archaic *Homo sapiens* then they could merely be a characteristic of an isolated, inbred group of such hominids. After all, the Broken Hill skull was found in Africa, whereas the Steinheim skull was found in Germany. Thus, Broken Hill man could have descended from a type of *Homo erectus* found in Olduvai (Upper Bed II), South Africa, and dated as 500,000 years old (Figure 150). This skull consists of a brain case and has larger brow ridges than the Asian *Homo erectus* skulls. Broken Hill man, as an early archaic *Homo sapiens*, could then have been ancestral to the so-called "neanderthaloid," recent archaic *Homo sapiens* types which evolved into modern *Homo sapiens*.

Brow (Supraorbital) Ridges

Brow ridges are bony struts forming the superior margins of the orbits that connect with the part of the zygomatic bones that forms the outer edges or margins of the orbits. The zygomatic bones have a broad articulation with the maxillae, or upper jaw bones, which contain the upper teeth. This inverted U–shaped arch of compact bone is subjected to a considerable force when the jaws are tightly closed together, by virtue of the very powerful masticatory muscles attaching the mandible to the remainder of the skull. The amount of compact bone in the inverted U–shaped arch is related to the robustness of the masticatory apparatus. The larger the jaws and teeth, the greater the amount of solid compact bone. The amount of compact bone tends to increase along with the overall increase in the size of the bony arch. However, a certain amount of the overall size is due to the frontal sinuses. In present-day apes and human beings, the frontal sinuses begin at puberty to invade the brow ridges. The sinuses are extensions of the mucous lining of the nasal cavities that pneumatize the skull bones. They do not warm or moisten inspired air, do not affect the resonance of the voice, and do not affect a significant lightening of the weight of the skull. The brow ridges form a buttress in both apes and hominids. (Figures 121, 127, 128, 142, 144, 150, 165, 183, 199, 209.) In the hominids, the projecting brow ridges become reduced, so that they seem to have completely disappeared in present-day human beings (Figures 116, 117, 123). This is an illusion, because the bony struts are masked by the retention of the vertical parts of the frontal bones of the forehead during development. Slight bulges related to anteriorly situated frontal sinuses may be present above the superior margins of the orbits, especially in adult males. If so, they are known as the superciliary ridges or bulges (Figure 216). The masked supraorbital bony buttress in present-day adult human skulls is still quite strong, because it is subjected to great force during mastication. When all of the jaw muscles are working, they can close the teeth together with a force of as much as fifty-five pounds on the incisors and two hundred pounds on the molars. When this is applied to a small object, such as a small seed between the molars, the actual force per square inch may be several thousand pounds (Guyton 1976).

Solo (Ngandong) Skulls

The brow ridges are less prominent in a number of skulls found at Ngandong, Indonesia. Skulls lacking a face and a mandible from eleven individuals were found at the same site between 1931 and 1933. Of these, six adult skulls are fairly intact. However, only one, number 11, has a fairly intact base. It is complete, except that the bony palate and nasal cavities are absent. I judge from a photograph of its base (Day 1965) that the interval between the foramen magnum and what would have been the posterior border of the bony palate was the same as that of a present-day *Homo sapiens* adult skull. I would place the posterior border of the vomer bone in contact with the spheno-occipital synostosis or very close to it, indicating that the larynx had descended to a low position in the neck. Therefore, the vocal tract had a configuration identical to or nearly the same as that of present day adult human beings. The W-G casting program includes casts of skulls number 4, 5, 8, and 9 (Figure 185). Since the site where they were found is the valley of the river Solo, they are called the Solo skulls. In 1949, von Koenigswald dated them to the Upper Pleistocene, which could be anywhere between 10,000 to 200,000 years ago (Day 1965). Campbell (1970) lists them as 30,000 years old and Pilbeam (1970) states, "The beds have a late Pleistocene fauna known as the Ngandong; the absolute age is unknown. A fair estimate would place it within the last 250,000 years, possibly around 150,000 years ago, although even this is a guess." My skull studies make me classify them as archaic *Homo sapiens*. Although the posterior part of the skull is still prominent, it is not the typical occipital "bun" found in the *Homo erectus* skulls. Likewise, the projecting brow ridges are not so prominent. The average brain size was a little over 1,000 cubic centimeters. Since these skull differences are small compared to those of the *Homo erectus* skulls from Indonesia, the form of the skull base is a most crucial definitive characteristic. However, I only had a photograph of the number 6 skull base to judge that the vocal tract was modern. Overall, the Solo skulls appear to be a step toward evolving into modern *Homo sapiens*. Therefore, I would estimate that Solo skulls are from 100,000 to 200,000 years old and classify them as early archaic *Homo sapiens*. They would be the Asian equivalent of the early African archaic *Homo sapiens* represented by the Broken Hill skull.

198

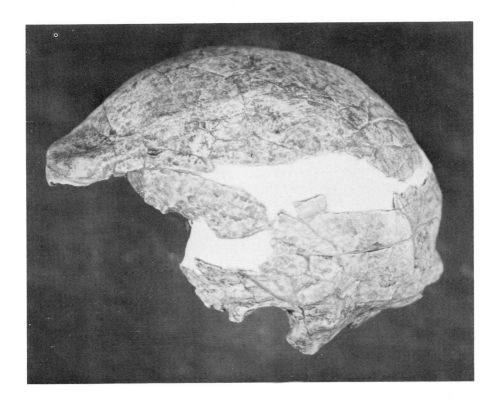

Figure 185. Left lateral view of a W-G Foundation cast of an adult early archaic *Homo sapiens* skullcap (Solo 4). It was found at Ngandong, Indonesia, and dated at about 150,000 years old. *Photographs of casts used courtesy of the Wenner-Gren Foundation for Anthropological Research, Inc., New York, and with permission of the owners of the original specimens. Permission granted by Gadjah Meda University, Yogyakarta, Indonesia.*

Recent Archaic Homo Sapiens "Neanderthaloid" Skulls

Relying on front and side view photographs and a written description (Day 1965), I classify the reconstructed Tabun skull found in Israel and dated at 40,000 to 45,000 years old as a recent archaic *Homo sapiens*, just one step from modern *Homo sapiens* that could quite reasonably have evolved directly into modern *Homo sapiens*. I classify it as a recent archaic *Homo sapiens* because the brow ridges are prominent and the forehead is low. However, no protuberance, or occipital bun, is present, and there is no snout. Unfortunately, most of the skull base is missing. On this same

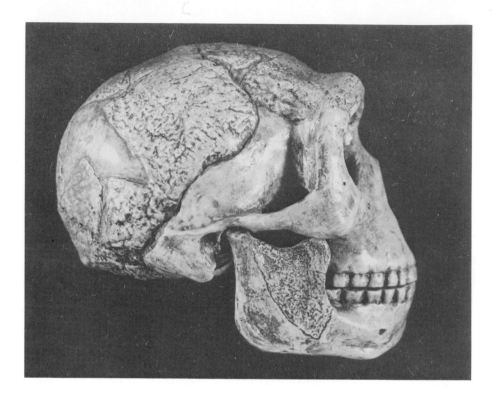

Figure 186. Right lateral view of the PA Museum cast of the skull of Saldanha (Hopefield) man reconstructed by R. Singer. It was found near Saldanha Bay, Hopefield, Republic of South Africa, and is dated at 55,000 years old.

basis, I would also include the following as recent archaic *Homo sapiens*: the Gibraltar I PA Museum cast of a skull found at Forbes' Quarry, Gibraltar, and dated at 35,000 to 70,000 years old; the PA Museum casts of two skullcaps found at Spy, Belgium, and dated at 35,000 to 70,000 years old; the PA Museum cast of the Saldanha reconstructed skull found at Hopefield, South Africa, and dated at 55,000 years old (Figure 186). In addition, I include four Shanidar fossil skulls found in the Shanidar Cave in Iraqi Kurdistan. Their photographs and descriptions are in the book *The Shanidar Neandertals*, by E. Trinkaus (1983). Skull number one is reconstructed, but its base is largely intact (Figure 187). I judge the base to be such that the vocal tract was modern in configuration. The palate is present, but the vomer bone is missing. Even so, the vomer would have been in direct contact with or very close to the synostosis of the basilar part of the occipital bone, which is significantly inclined toward the vertical plane.

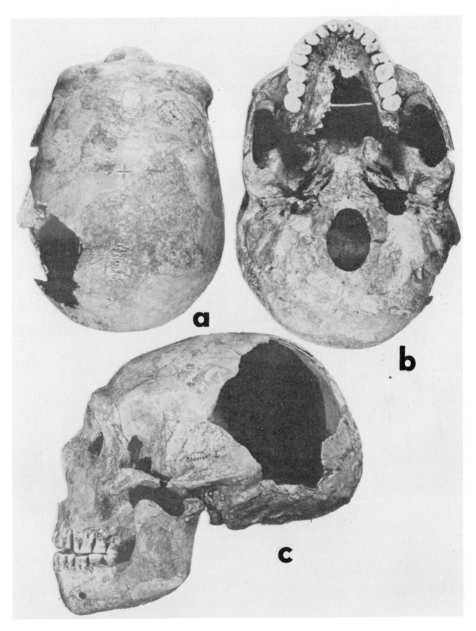

Figure 187. The Shanidar 1 skull. It has the size and shape of a typical archaic *Homo sapiens* skull. The top view (a) is similar to that of the Steinheim skull shown in Figure 175. The base (b) and the left side and mandible (c) are similar to those of the La Ferrassie skull shown in Figures 188, 189, and 190. *From Trinkaus (1983). Courtesy of Dr. E. Trinkaus.*

The mandible of the number one skull is almost complete. The mandibular rami of skulls number one, two, and four are vertical and equal to the mandibular body in length, similar to that of modern *Homo sapiens*. The cranial capacity of the number one skull is 1,600 cubic centimeters, and its cranial index (maximum cranial breadth/glabello-occipital length) is within the range of variation of modern *Homo sapiens* skulls. Only a small occipital protuberance and snout are present. However, the brow ridges are prominent and the forehead is markedly slanted. Therefore, the Shanidar skulls are recent archaic *Homo sapiens*, around 50,000 to 70,000 years old, and not classic Neanderthals. I would add one more skull to this recent archaic *Homo sapiens* group: the La Ferrassie 1 skull found at La Ferrassie, France, and dated at 50,000 to 70,000 years old (Figure 188). An intact mandible was found (Figure 189). A sufficient amount of the base of this skull is

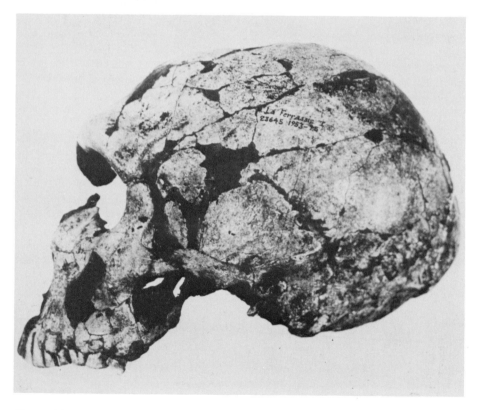

Figure 188. Left lateral view of the La Ferrassie recent archaic *Homo sapiens* skull located at the Musée de l'Homme, Paris, France. It is dated at 50,000 to 70,000 years old. Its mandible (not shown) is intact. *Photograph courtesy of Dr. J. T. Laitman.*

present so that, from photographs and descriptions, I may classify it as a recent archaic *Homo sapiens* with a modern vocal tract configuration (Figure 190). It is unfortunate that all of these more recent archaic hominids came to be referred to as "neanderthaloid," because they have no direct relationship to the classic, or traditional, Neanderthals, although they may have coexisted with some of them. They should more properly be regarded as being recent archaic *Homo sapiens*, between 50,000 to 100,000 years old, with modern vocal tracts. I use the word "archaic" to mean primitive. The confusing and incorrect label "neanderthaloid" should be discarded.

So, the early archaic *Homo sapiens* of 100,000 to 300,000 years ago, represented by the Steinheim, Swanscombe, Broken Hill, and Solo skulls, evolved into the recent archaic *Homo sapiens* of 35,000 to 100,000 years ago, represented by the Tabun, Spy, Saldanha, Shanidar, Gibraltar, and La Ferrassie skulls. The most notable changes in the hominid skull from *Homo habilis* through *Homo erectus* were (1) those related to a larger brain that maintained relatively small cerebral frontal lobes and (2) those in the skull bases of at least some of the *Homo erectus* hominids, which were related to modifications in the configuration of the vocal tract leading to the modern form. The masticatory structures also changed in form but remained fairly robust. Thus, prominent brow ridges and a sloping forehead were retained

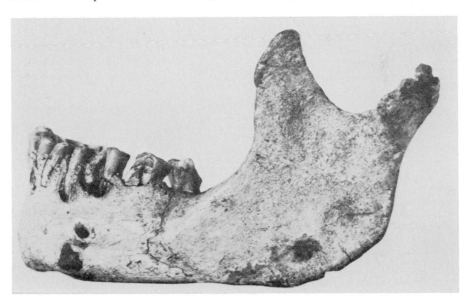

Figure 189. Left lateral view of the mandible of the La Ferrassie recent archaic *Homo sapiens* skull shown in Figure 188. *Photograph courtesy of Dr. J. T. Laitman.*

203

along with robust posterior neck muscles. In the archaic *Homo sapiens*, the skull base changes were related to a vocal tract that had a modern configuration, and the masticatory structures and posterior neck muscles became less robust. Although the brain stayed pretty much the same size with relatively small cerebral frontal lobes, the skull rounded a little. The brow ridges remained prominent. Thus, the transition from the early to the recent archaic *Homo sapiens* was a very gradual one in regard to skull changes. Also, there is no doubt that archaic *Homo sapiens* gradually over a 250,000 year period became smarter. They were on the verge of beginning to make quantum leaps in their intelligence around 50,000 years ago. But before I take this up, I must first deal with the classic Neanderthals.

Classic Neanderthal Skulls

According to my studies, there are only three skulls I can classify as traditional, or classic, Neanderthals. I should refer to them merely as Neanderthals, because any other known fossil skulls referred to as Neanderthals or "neanderthaloid" hominids I have judged to be recent archaic *Homo sapiens*. One of these classic Neanderthal skulls is the first hominid fossil skull ever found (Figures 191–193). It was discovered in a cave in Neander Valley, West Germany, by a workman in 1856. It is a skullcap, most likely that of an adult male. Other bones found with it were upper and lower limb bones, some ribs, and part of the pelvis. It was not possible to date the skull because no artifacts or fossil mammalian bones were found with it (Day 1965). However, it is likely that the man died between 50,000 and 70,000 years ago. Darwin knew about it. A local science teacher, J. K. Fuhlrott, theorized that the skullcap came from an ancient man, some poor mortal who had been washed into the cave by Noah's flood (Constable 1973). R. Virchow (1872) believed the skullcap was pathological, and T. H. Huxley (1863) recognized the primitive features of the skeleton but could not accept that it was an intermediate form between man and apes. The second classic Neanderthal skull is the PA Museum cast of the Circeo I skull, which is a reconstruction of a brain case with an attached face. The mandible is missing. The skull was found at Monte Circeo, Italy, and is dated at between 50,000 and 70,000 years old (Figures 194 and 195). The part of the base surrounding the foramen magnum is missing. The size and shape of the reconstructed skull is very similar to that of the La Chapelle skull, which is the third skull that I classify as a classic Neanderthal.

TABLE I

TENTATIVE SCHEME OF THE DESCENT OF THE HOMINIDS BASED ON THE
EVOLUTION OF THE VOCAL TRACT AND RELATED SKULL CHANGES

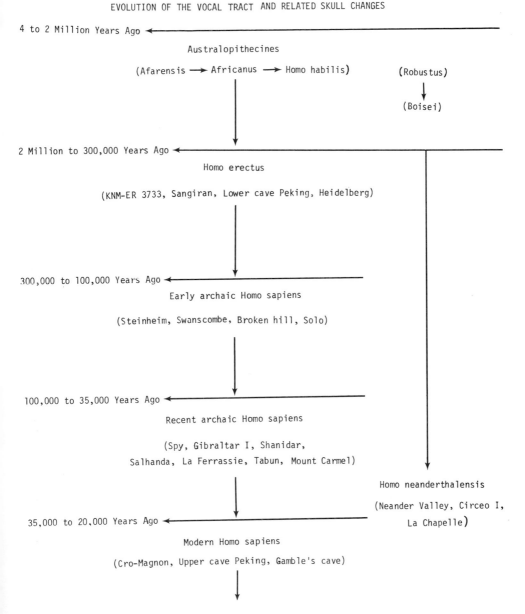

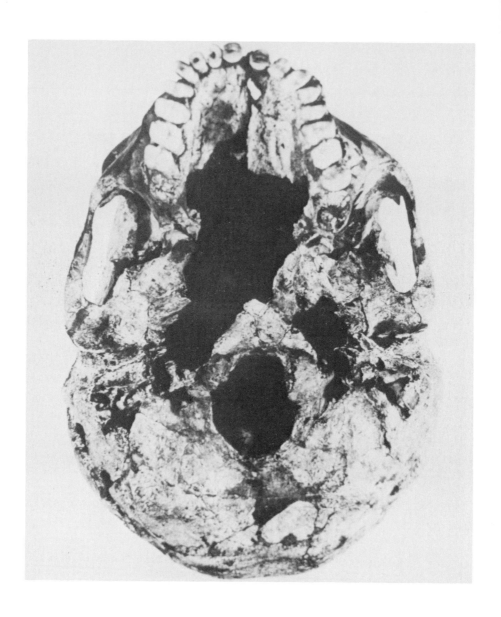

Figure 190. A view of the base of the La Ferrassie recent archaic Homo sapiens skull shown in Figure 188. *Photograph courtesy of Dr. J. T. Laitman.*

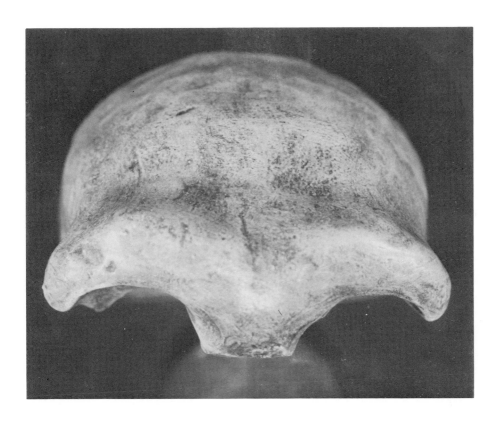

Figure 191. Anterior view of the PA Museum cast of the Neanderthal fossil skullcap found in Neander Valley, West Germany, in 1856. It was the first hominid fossil skull ever found and is dated at between 35,000 and 70,000 years old.

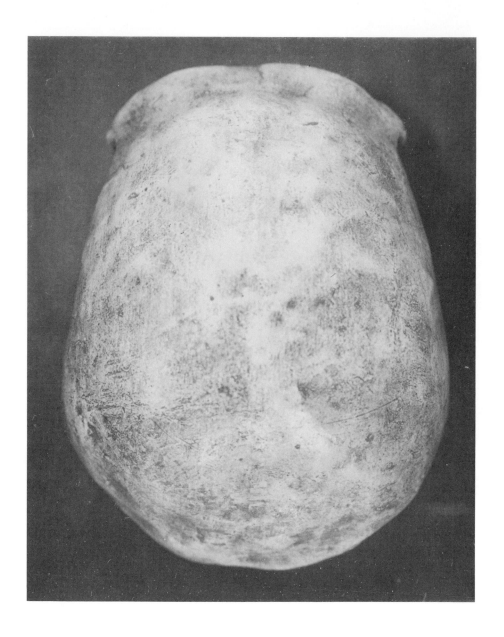

Figure 192. A view of the top of the cast of the fossil Neanderthal skullcap shown in Figure 191.

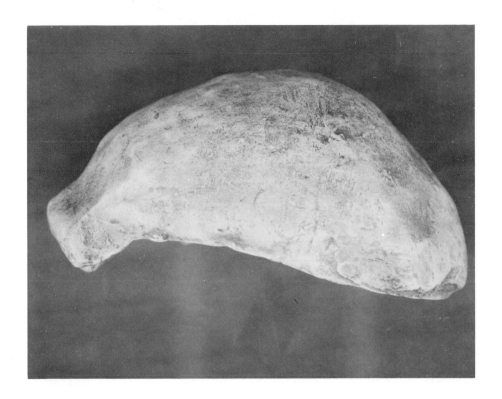

Figure 193. Left lateral view of the cast of the fossil Neanderthal skullcap shown in Figures 191 and 192.

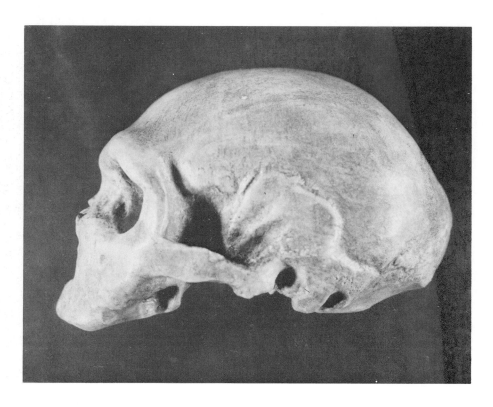

Figure 194. Left lateral view of the PA Museum cast of the Circeo I Neanderthal skull reconstruction. It was found at Monte Circeo, Italy, and is dated at between 50,000 and 70,000 years old.

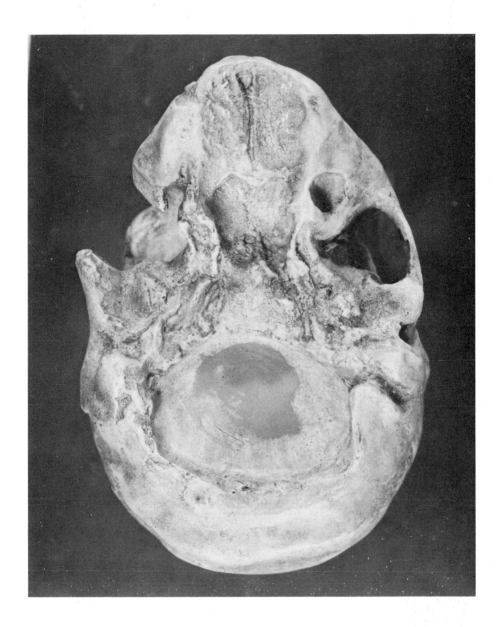

Figure 195. A view of the base of the cast of the Circeo I Neanderthal skull shown in Figure 194.

La Chapelle Skull

The La Chapelle skull was found as part of an almost complete skeleton, buried in the floor of a small cave near the village of La Chapelle-aux-Saints, France, in 1908 (Day 1965) (Figures 196 and 197). The mandible is nearly complete, but it contains only one tooth. Although some anterior midline skull base is missing, there is sufficient surrounding bone present to allow an accurate restoration of the missing part. The PA Museum restoration of the skull was made by J. H. McGregor (Figures 198–200). This was the first cast of a fossil hominid skull I ever saw. Without any preconceived notions, I studied the cast and compared it with an adult

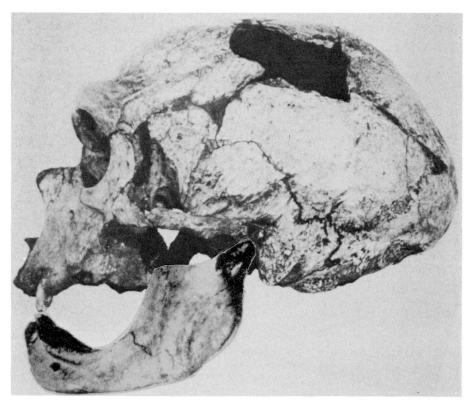

Figure 196. Left lateral view of the La Chapelle-aux-Saints Neanderthal fossil skull located at the Musée de l'Homme, Paris, France. It is dated at 35,000 to 45,000 years old. *Photograph courtesy of Dr. J. T. Laitman.*

212

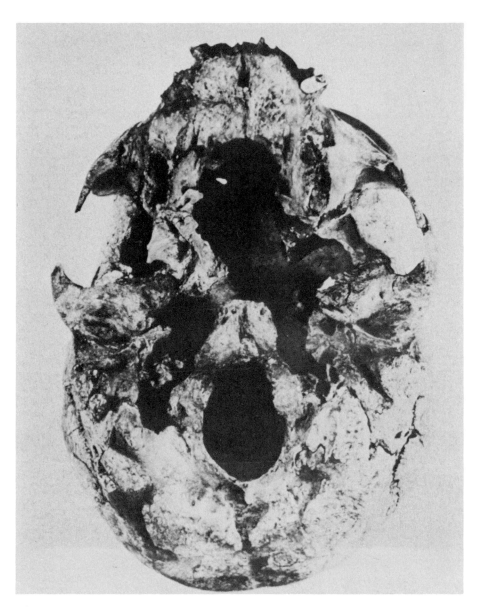

Figure 197. A view of the base of the La Chapelle-aux-Saints Neanderthal fossil skull shown in Figure 196. *Photograph courtesy of Dr. J. T. Laitman.*

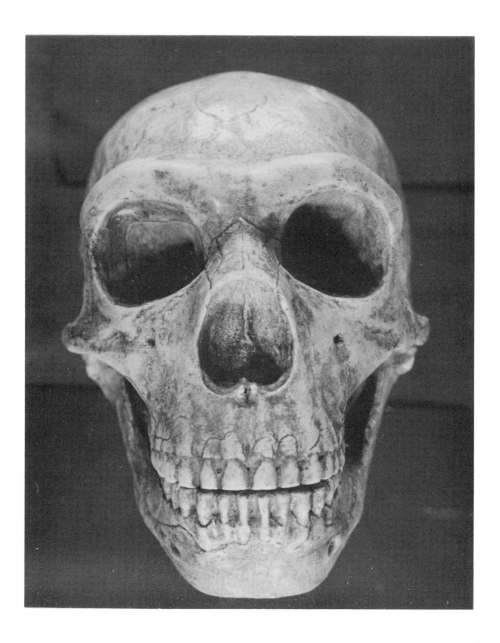

Figure 198. Anterior view of the PA Museum cast of the reconstruction of the La Chapelle-aux-Saints Neanderthal fossil skull shown in Figures 196 and 197.

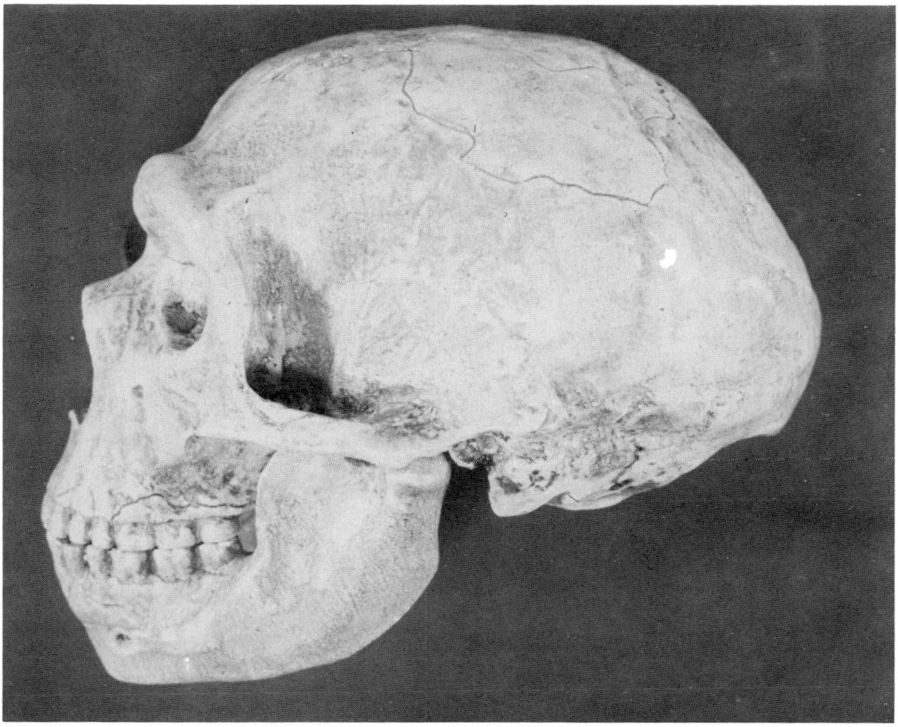

Figure 199. Left lateral view of the cast of the reconstructed La Chapelle-aux-Saints Neanderthal fossil skull shown in Figure 198.

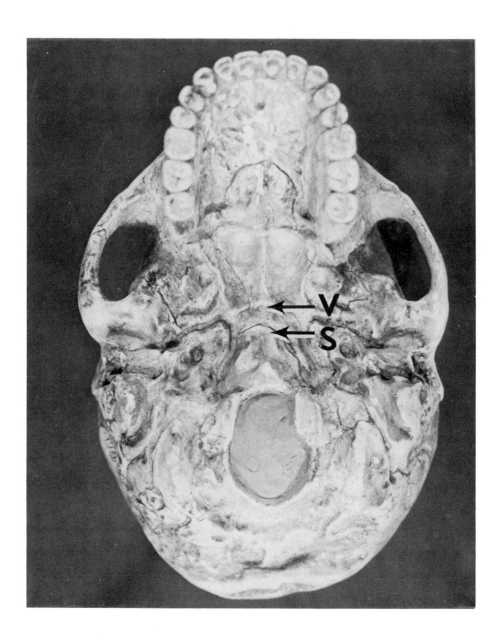

Figure 200. A view of the base of the cast of the reconstructed La Chapelle-aux-Saints Neanderthal fossil skull shown in Figures 198 and 199. V: posterior border of the vomer bone. S: site of the spheno-occipital synostosis.

chimpanzee, an adult present-day male human, and a present-day newborn human skull. I found that the base of the skull resembles more closely that of the chimpanzee and newborn human skulls than it does that of the adult human male, in that there is a relatively long distance between the bony palate and the foramen magnum (Lieberman and Crelin 1971; Lieberman, Crelin, and Klatt 1972). In this interval, the skull base forms only a shallow concavity. The vomer bone is some distance from the spheno-occipital synostosis, exposing the body of the sphenoid bone (Figure 200). When I reconstructed the La Chapelle vocal tract with modeling clay and silicone rubber, I placed all of the tongue within the oral cavity and the larynx high in the neck. I placed it so high that it is conceivable that the larynx could be locked into the nasopharynx, just as it can in the human newborn, and in adult australopithecine hominids. I naively let Dr. Lieberman use my data to hypothesize about La Chapelle's speaking abilities before I knew how controversial the La Chapelle Neanderthal hominid was. Lieberman calculated that my vocal tract reconstruction prevented Neanderthal man from making quick shifts in pronunciation, as modern humans can, and that he would have been incapable of using the key vowels "ah" as in "top", "ē" as in "teem", and "ü" as in "tool" in rapid combinations (White and Brown 1973). Soon there appeared in the literature the Lieberman-Crelin hypothesis of linguistic deficiency (Constable 1973), for which I give Dr. Lieberman full credit. To infer that Neanderthal man was less human than archaic *Homo sapiens* is blasphemous to his devotees, whom I judge to include nearly all anthropologists and a number of others from different disciplines. During the ten years since Lieberman and Crelin (1971) and Lieberman, Crelin, and Klatt (1972), while I was developing a scientific basis to be able to hypothesize about the evolution of the vocal tract, a number of reports critical of my anatomical findings appeared in the literature. Though tempted, I never took time to respond in a publication. Le May (1975) states that modern human beings who have normal speech have a long, flattened skull base, comparable to that of La Chapelle Neanderthal man. To illustrate this, the author produces one radiograph of a person with a normal skull and scribblings representing tracings made on two radiographs. I have yet to see a modern adult human skull that has an elongation and flattening that comes anywhere near that of the La Chapelle skull.

Du Brul (1976) states that, with the high positioning of the hyoid bone, as I first depicted it with the jaws approximated (Lieberman and Crelin 1971), "it is difficult to see how the creature could even open his jaw!" (Figure 201.) Any mammal, in any position, except when hanging upside down or with the side of his head resting against a horizontal surface, merely has to relax his jaw-closing muscles and let his mouth fall open

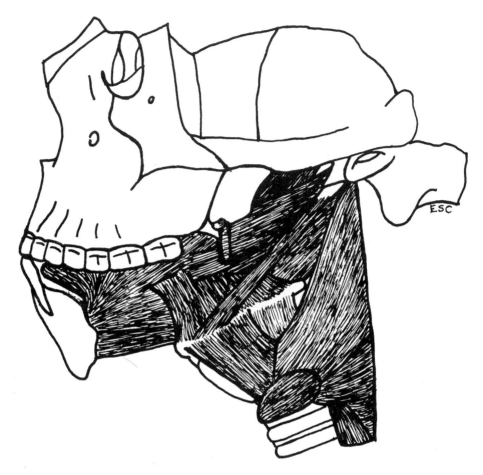

Figure 201. A drawing of a left lateral view of the reconstructed La Chapelle-aux-Saints Neanderthal fossil skull lacking the upper part. The left half of the mandible was excluded to expose the extrinsic laryngeal muscles and the pharyngeal constrictor muscles.

under the pull of gravity. The mouth is kept closed by continuous contractile activity in the jaw-closing muscles, even during sleep. Thus, the lower jaw drops open in an unconscious or anesthetized person. It did this in the La Chapelle man. Once the lower jaw drops under the pull of gravity, it can pivot at the points where the strong sphenomandibular ligaments suspending the jaw attach to it, due to the contraction of the lateral pterygoid muscles. This action would open the mouth wide. If La Chapelle man had to open his lower jaw against resistance, which would be rare,

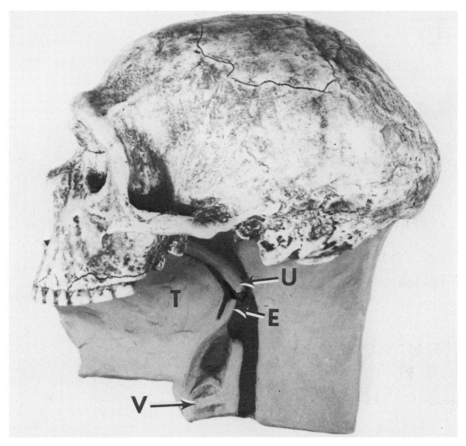

Figure 202. Left lateral view of the cast of the reconstructed La Chapelle-aux-Saints Neanderthal fossil skull shown in Figures 198–200. Modeling clay is attached to the skull from which the space of the right half of the vocal tract has been sculpted out. T: tongue. U: uvula of soft palate. E: epiglottis. V: vocal folds (cords).

the infrahyoid strap muscles attaching the hyoid bone to the sternum, clavicles, first ribs, and scapulas would be very effective in pulling down the mandible along with the suprahyoid muscles attaching the hyoid bone to the mandible (Figure 13). As I look back on my early report (Lieberman and Crelin 1971) of La Chapelle's anatomy, I would keep the reconstructions of the vocal tract and associated neck structures just about the way I originally described them. In fact, I feel obliged to do so because of a subsequent study I made of the evolution of the tongue.

Hominid Tongues

Determining what the length and width of the tongue was in an extinct hominid by measuring its skull is a straightforward process. Even if the skull base is not completely intact and the mandible is missing, it is still possible to make a close estimate of the size and shape of the tongue. The distance from the front of the bony palate to the foramen magnum allows an estimate of the length of the oral cavity. The midline distance between the teeth or their alveolar sockets in the bony palate shows the limit in width of the tongue when the mouth was closed. In the present-day apes, I found that the tongue occupies the entire oral cavity with the jaws closed, and its length is directly related to the length of the oral cavity. Thus, the length of the adult tongue is shortest in the gibbon, longer in the chimpanzee, even longer in the orangutan, and longest in the gorilla. The length of the oral cavity becomes smaller as one passes from an australopithecine the size of Mrs. Ples to *Homo erectus* to early and recent archaic *Home sapiens* to present-day *Homo sapiens*. But, because the posterior part of the tongue descended into the neck as the oral cavity became shorter, the tongue maintained its original length (Figure 205). It did become a little wider, at least the part within the oral cavity. The one exception to the gradual shift in position of the tongue and the maintenance of its size during hominid evolution was La Chapelle's tongue (Figure 205). Even keeping the La Chapelle tongue entirely within the oral cavity with the jaws closed, the tongue was still longer and wider than it ever was during hominid evolution. The length of the tongue in Mrs. Ples was between ten to eleven centimeters, just as it is in a present-day adult male human being. In La Chapelle, it was at least 13 centimeters long with the tongue entirely within the oral cavity. Of course, keeping the tongue entirely within the oral cavity makes La Chapelle Neanderthal man ape-like in this regard. Therefore, I have been chastized by his devotees for not lowering his larynx to between the fifth and sixth cervical vertebrae, as it is in present-day adult male human beings. To appease them, I have done so in Figure 206. However, this makes his tongue about 15 centimeters long, or as long as that of an adult male orangutan!

La Chapelle Man's Vocalizations

Using modeling clay and silicone rubber, I made a cast of the space of the upper respiratory system of La Chapelle Neanderthal man (Figures 202–204). I then made a hollow rubber copy of the reconstructed vocal tract and tested its ability to make vowel sounds using the plastic larynx described in Chapter 2 (Figure 207). Even though La Chapelle had only a slight simian shelf, I had the same difficulties making the vowel sounds,

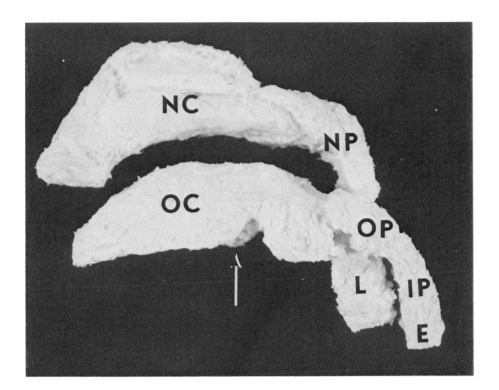

Figure 203. Left lateral view of the solid silicone rubber cast representing the space of the reconstructed upper respiratory system of the La Chapelle-aux-Saints Neanderthal hominid. The arrow points toward the foramen cecum located at the junction between the anterior two-thirds and the posterior one-third of the tongue. NC: nasal cavities. NP: nasopharynx. OC: oral cavity. OP: oropharynx. IP: infralaryngeal pharynx. E: esophagus. L: larynx.

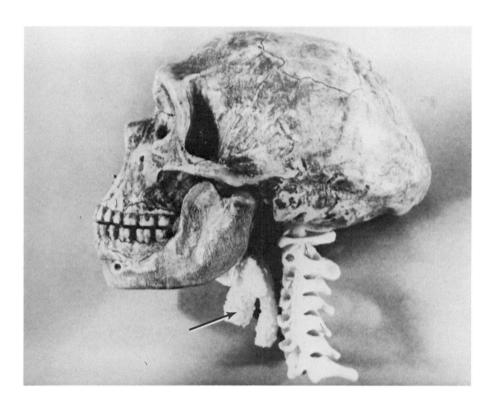

Figure 204. Left lateral view of the cast of the reconstructed La Chapelle-aux-Saints Neanderthal fossil skull shown in Figures 198–200. A cervical vertebral column from present-day *Homo sapiens* has been articulated with the skull. The silicone rubber cast (arrow) of the La Chapelle-aux-Saints Neanderthal reconstructed vocal tract shown in Figure 203 is in its proper position.

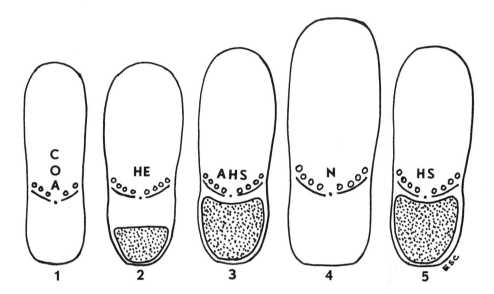

Figure 205. An illustration depicting the relative sizes and shapes of the adult hominid tongue during evolution. Each tongue is shown to be completely flat. The stippled areas represent the vertical part of the tongue when it forms the anterior wall of the oropharynx. The circles are the vallate papillae located along the junction of the anterior two-thirds and the posterior one-third of the tongue. The tongue labeled C, O, and A represents one from an adult male chimpanzee, an adult female orangutan, or a man-ape australopithecine hominid, such as Mrs. Ples. The tongue labeled HE represents one of a *Homo erectus* hominid such as Peking woman. The tongue labeled AHS represents one of an archaic *Homo sapiens* hominid such as Steinheim woman. The tongue labeled N represents one of a classic Neanderthal hominid such as La Chapelle-aux-Saints. The tongue labeled HS represents one of a present-day *Homo sapiens* male.

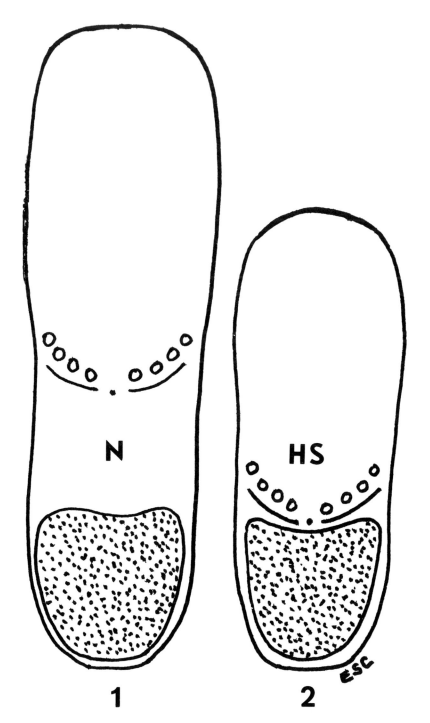

Figure 206. An illustration depicting on the left an adult classic Neanderthal hominid tongue (N) that not only occupies the entire oral cavity, but also extends to the same low level in the neck as that of an archaic or a present-day *Homo sapiens* adult (HS) shown on the right.

that required a restriction of the air flow through the tract as I did with the chimpanzee tract. Lieberman hypothesized that my reconstruction of the vocal tract wouldn't allow La Chapelle man to make the "ah" sound in "top", "ē" as in "teem", and "ü" as in "tool" (Lieberman, Crelin, and Klatt 1972). In actuality, the rubber tract didn't do too badly in producing the "ah" sound, but, as with the chimpanzee tract, "ē" and "ü" vowels were so raspy and had to be of such a low volume that they were difficult to make out. Even pulling down the larynx, which greatly improved the vowel productions by the two-year old child rubber tract, didn't make too much difference. The long, wide tract of La Chapelle man offered too much resistance to the flow of air when the vowel sounds requiring restrictions in the tract lumen were tried. This leads me to conclude that, even if La Chapelle man was able to make passable vowel sounds, he would have found it difficult to switch from one to another very rapidly. When making consonant sounds, he would have had even more trouble manipulating such a large tongue, located entirely within the oral cavity.

His cranial capacity was 1,620 cubic centimeters (Day 1965), which puts his brain size midway in the present-day human brain range of 1,000 to 2,000 cubic centimeters. Although his brain was large, its cerebral frontal lobes were relatively small (Figure 220). He lived during a fairly restricted time period—the early part of the last glaciation, between 50,000 and 70,000 years ago—and in a very restricted region—Western Europe (Pilbeam 1970). Where did he come from? A good supposition is that La Chapelle man is from a lineage of *Homo erectus* that did not evolve changes in the vocal tract configuration as they evolved into classic Neanderthals. These hominids also maintained the occipital bun, massive posterior neck muscles, and a snout that are related to robust masticatory structures. What were the capabilities of La Chapelle man? To be able to survive for so long a time he must have been quite capable in many ways, although much that he has been given credit for must surely have been accomplished by the coexisting "neanderthaloid" recent archaic *Homo sapiens.* Where did he go? I would like to attribute his demise to an infectious virus or bacterium, or to cold weather. However, while the smarter recent archaic *Homo sapiens* were becoming modern *Homo sapiens,* they had become the most efficient killers of big game that ever existed. I'm sure they had become just as efficient at killing each other. The classic Neanderthal was no match for them. The classic Neanderthal was the last of the hominid lines outside of the lineage that ultimately gave rise to modern *Homo sapiens.* Those late great anatomists, Sir Arthur Keith and Sir Wilfred Le Gros Clark (Brace 1968; Clark 1969), on the basis of elements of La Chapelle's anatomy other than the base of the skull and the vocal tract, concluded that he was not a direct ancestor of *Homo sapiens* and became extinct. Therefore, they classified the classic Neanderthals as *Homo neanderthalensis.*

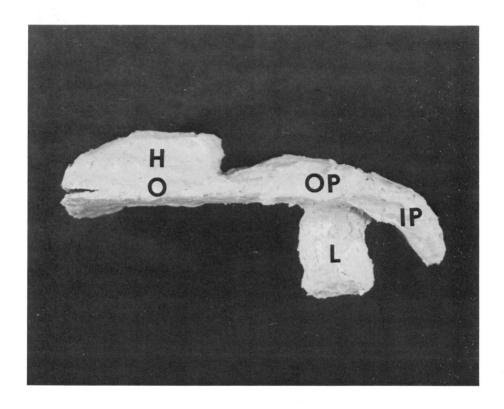

Figure 207. Left lateral view of the hollow rubber vocal tract of the La Chapelle-aux-Saints Neanderthal hominid. H hard palate. O: oral cavity. OP: oropharynx. IP: infralaryngeal pharynx. L: larynx.

Can it be that La Chapelle man was actually an archaic *Homo sapiens* who had a long skull base due to a form of the developmental abnormality known as platybasia? Too many factors argue against it. Platybasia usually includes a malformed upper cervical vertebral column and is most often lethal. The La Chapelle skull base and cervical vertebral column are not grossly abnormal. The long base of the La Chapelle skull results in the exposure of the body of the sphenoid bone, a primitive feature normally present in the ape, australopithecine, *Homo habilis,* and early *Homo erectus* fossil skulls. Other primitive features are the *Homo erectus*–type occipital bun and a snout. The La Chapelle mandible more closely resembles that of *Homo erectus* in regards to the shape and robustness of the ramus than those of archaic and modern *Homo sapiens* (Figures 146, 147, 149, 180, 187, 189, 196, 199, 204, 209, 212, 214, 216). Even so, it is essential that additional Neanderthal skulls with these primitive features be discovered before it is established on the basis of the single La Chapelle skull that there was such a unique group of hominids extant with archaic *Homo sapiens.*

Over the years, the La Chapelle Neanderthal man has often been represented in portraits and sculpted busts (Constable 1973). He was at one time depicted as a subhuman brute, incapable of standing completely erect. Since he has been shown to have had this posture because of arthritis (Strauss and Cave), he has often been depicted as very similar to a present-day human being. I might add that his arthritis did not alter his skull base anatomy or the form and function of his vocal tract. Brace (1968) states, "From what we actually know, it is probable that if a properly clothed and shaved Neanderthal were to appear in a crowd of modern urban shoppers or commuters, he would strike the viewer as somewhat unusual in appearance—short, stocky, large of face—but nothing more than that. Certainly few would suspect he was their 'caveman' ancestor." I agree, because, if a mastodon were shaved and put in an enclosure at a zoo, he would strike the viewer as somewhat unusual in appearance—stocky and large—but nothing more than an elephant. Certainly, few would suspect it to be an extinct form. Of all of the head and neck reconstructions of La Chapelle, I favor Boule's (Constable 1973), where the musculature is the most anatomically accurate (Figure 208).

Mount Carmel (es-Skūhl V) Skull

While the classic Neanderthal hominid in Western Europe was hypothetically becoming extinct, the recent archaic *Homo sapiens* were undergoing the last anatomical changes to become modern *Homo sapiens* in Europe, Asia, and Africa between 50,000 and 70,000 years ago. These

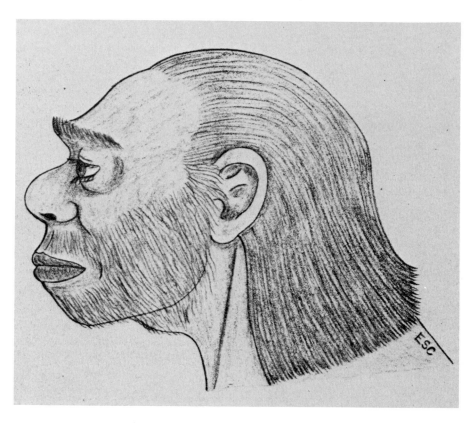

Figure 208. The author's determination of what the adult La Chapelle-aux-Saints Neanderthal man looked like when he was alive.

changes consisted in the loss of the protruding brow ridges and the acquisition of a vertical forehead, directly related to the relative enlargement of the cerebral frontal lobes of the brain. Only one fossil skull has been found that has the last vestiges of the primitive brow ridges. This is the best-preserved adult skull of about five incomplete ones found in a rock shelter at Mugharet es-Skūhl, Mount Carmel, Israel (Figures 209 and 210). The fairly complete skull is dated at around 45,000 years old. Except for the brow ridges, the skull is identical to that of a present-day *Homo sapiens* (Figure 211).

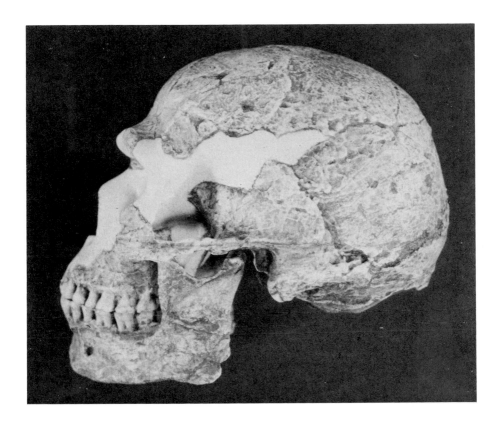

Figure 209. Left lateral view of the W-G Foundation cast of the Mount Carmel (es-Skūhl V) fossil skull found at Mount Carmel, Israel, and dated at between 35,000 and 45,000 years old. *Photographs of casts used courtesy of the Wenner-Gren Foundation for Anthropological Research, Inc., New York, and with permission of the owners of the original specimens. Permission granted by the Peabody Museum of Archeology and Ethnology, Cambridge, Massachusetts.*

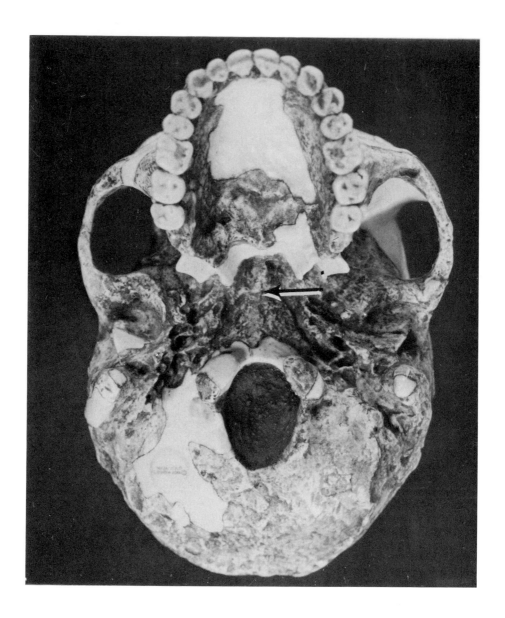

Figure 210. A view of the base of the cast of the Mount Carmel fossil skull shown in Figure 209. The arrow points to where the vomer bone abuts the basilar part of the occipital bone. *Photographs of casts used courtesy of the Wenner-Gren Foundation for Anthropological Research, Inc., New York, and with permission of the owners of the original specimens. Permission granted by the Peabody Museum of Archeology and Ethnology, Cambridge, Massachusetts.*

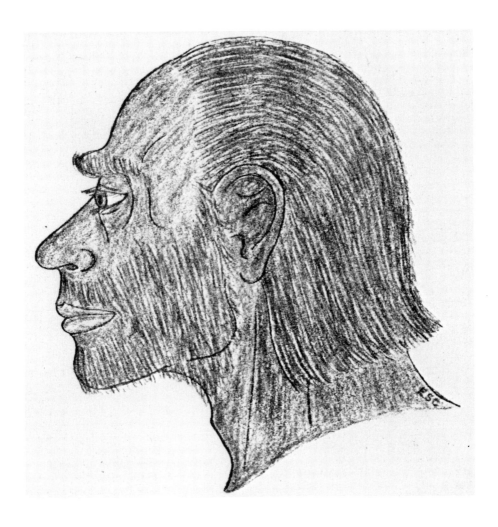

Figure 211. The author's determination of what the adult Mount Carmel man looked like when he was alive.

Stone Tool Industries

About 50,000 to 70,000 years ago in Europe, a complex stone tool industry flourished. It is known as Mousterian after an archeological excavation at Le Moustier, France. It lasted in Western Europe until around 35,000 to 40,000 years ago, when it was suddenly replaced by the Upper Palaeolithic stone tool industries (Pilbeam 1970). Fossil men associated with Upper Palaeolithic industries are similar to modern types. Thus, the changeover in stone tool industries can be associated with the last phase of the evolutionary transition from recent archaic *Homo sapiens* to completely modern *Homo sapiens*. It is quite likely that this association can be made in Asia and Africa, where the changeover may have been more gradual. Examples of early modern *Homo sapiens* skulls found in Asia and Africa are the Upper Cave Peking and the Gamble's Cave skulls (Figures 212 and 213).

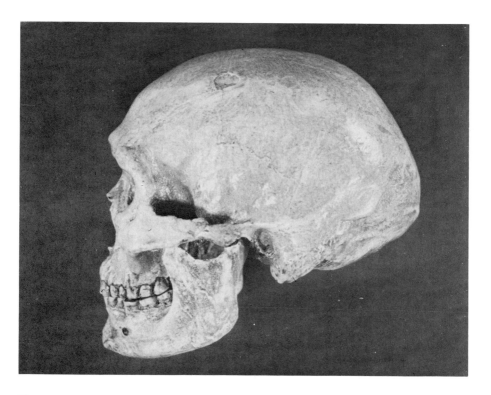

Figure 212. Left lateral view of the PA Museum cast of a reconstructed skull of Upper Cave Peking man found near Peking, China. It is a modern *Homo sapiens*–type, dated at around 35,000 years old.

232

Early Modern Homo Sapiens Skulls

The most famous early modern *Homo sapiens* skull was the best preserved of five adult skeletons found at Cro-Magnon, France (Figure 214). The skull belonged to an adult male, known as the "Old Man of Cro-Magnon" although he was probably less than fifty years old at the time of his death, which was about 20,000 to 30,000 years ago (Day 1965). The skull is identical to that of present-day human beings. It has a vertical forehead and, since it is from an adult male, a slight bulge produced by the frontal sinuses masks what would be a protruding bony brow ridge if the forehead were more slanted. The equivalent compact bone of the prominent brow ridges in the skulls of australopithecines, *Homo erectus*, archaic *Homo sapiens*, and Neanderthals are the supraorbital margins of the modern *Homo sapiens* skull. Adult male Australian aborigines are mistakenly considered to have primitive brow ridges. They tend to have bushy eyebrows

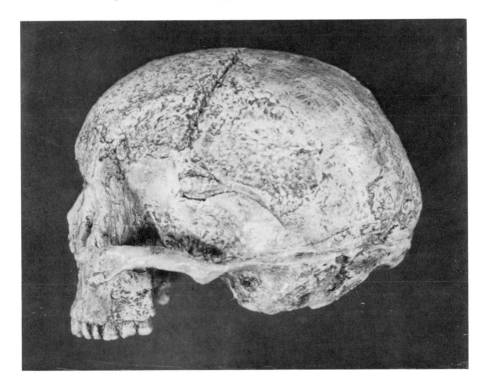

Figure 213. Left lateral view of the PA Museum cast of the reconstructed skull discovered in Gamble's Cave, Kenya, Africa, and dated at around 35,000 years old.

233

over well-developed frontal sinuses, which gives them a somewhat frowning expression (Figure 215). Their skulls are completely modern, especially the base (Figures 216 and 217). This is to be expected since they are descendants of human beings who entered Australia between 20,000 and 45,000 years ago.

Brain and Speech Evolution

As I examined the fossil skulls of the last one million years of hominid evolution, I found that I had a scientific basis for determining when all of the sounds of speech could be produced with facility. This was when the modern configuration of the vocal tract appeared in the early archaic *Homo sapiens* of between 300,000 and 500,000 years ago. However, I could not find any anatomical evidence indicating when the archaic *Homo sapiens* first used their modern vocal tracts to utter sounds which could be regarded

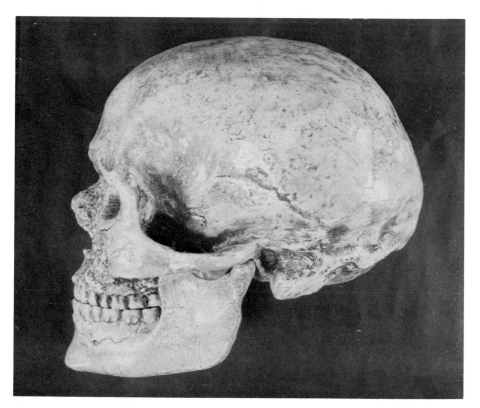

Figure 214. Left lateral view of the PA Museum cast of the Cro-Magnon fossil skull found at Cro-Magnon, France, and dated at between 20,000 and 30,000 years old.

Figure 215. A drawing of an adult male present-day Australian aborigine.

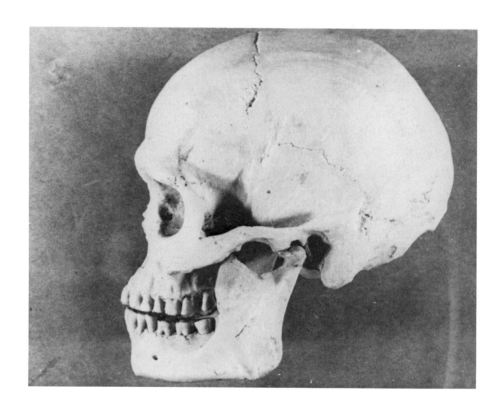

Figure 216. Left lateral view of the skull of a present-day adult male Australian aborigine. *Courtesy of my former graduate student Dr. David Roberts.*

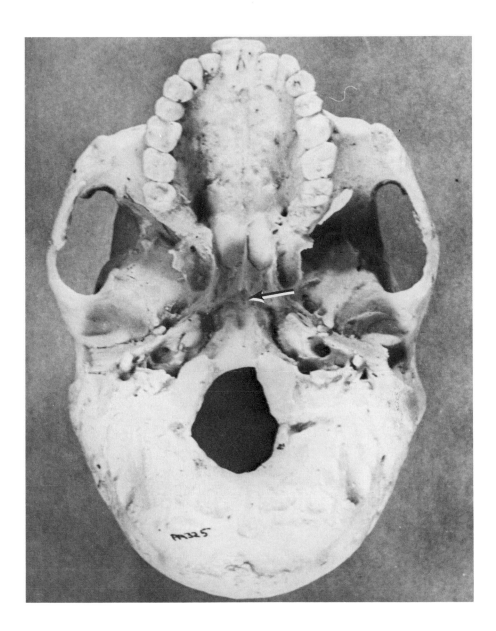

Figure 217. A view of the base of the present-day adult male Australian aborigine skull shown in Figure 216. The arrow points to where the vomer bone abuts the basilar part of the occipital bone.

as a language. Surely one would suspect that *Homo erectus* hominids communicated vocally and gesturally at a level well above that of present-day apes, and, presumably, the australopithecine hominids. Anatomically, I find that the brain became significantly larger in *Homo habilis* and then, in *Homo erectus* reached the size found in modern *Homo sapiens*. I recognize that this correlates with the overall increase in body size that occurred then. So, one must rely on the evidence of big game hunting, more complex stone tool making, and the use of fire as indications of what level of vocal and gestural communication *Homo erectus* had while the modern vocal tract was evolving and whether or not vocal communication served as the primary natural selection pressure for the vocal tract's evolution. It is basic that the peripheral structures, such as the hands and vocal tract, evolved by a series of accidents or mutations. The nervous system did not direct their evolution. Even so, it aided and abetted the evolution of the peripheral structures through neural feedback. This encoded the modifiable, or plastic, nervous system to maximize the function of the peripheral structures that enhanced the survival or competitive attributes of an individual or group. I had hoped that the responsive nervous system could give me an anatomical clue to the evolution of language by modifying the skeleton, in this instance the brain modifying the skull.

Planum Temporale of Brain

The concept of cerebral dominance was accepted after Broca's demonstration in 1861 that lesions producing language disorders were nearly always located in the left cerebral hemisphere of the brain (Galaburda, Le May, Kemper, and Geschwind 1978). Geschwind and Levitsky (1968) confirmed the presence of asymmetries in the gross configuration of the human cerebral cortex on the upper surface of the temporal lobe, known as the planum temporale (Figure 218). They tabulated the frequency of the different asymmetries of the planum, which are readily visible to the naked eye, in 100 adult brains. The planum was larger on the left side in 65 percent of the brains, approximately equal in 24 percent, and larger on the right in 11 percent. The planum is only one of the interconnected centers of the cerebral cortex related to language. It is not known how much of the bulk of the planum is due to the role it plays in language. Language disorders are related to handedness, migraine headaches, autoimmune diseases, and a host of other phenomena yet to be discovered (Marx 1983a). It is all part of a long evolutionary history of brain asymmetry, which is supported by the finding of behavioral and anatomical asymmetries in the brains of birds, rats, and great apes (Fromkin and Rodman 1978; Marx 1983b). Even with all of the negative aspects of trying to relate the planum temporale to the acquisition of speech during evolution, I still made an

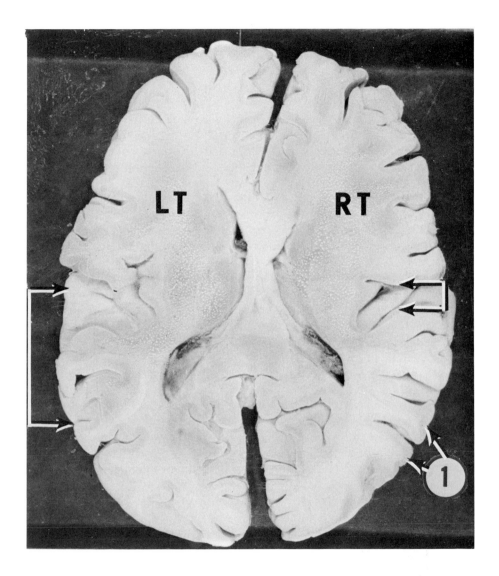

Figure 218. A slice of a human adult brain. The planum temporale of each cerebral hemisphere is demarcated by brackets. There is the usual asymmetry where the speech area is located in the larger planum temporale on the left side. LT: left. RT: right. (1): cerebral cortex. *Specimen prepared by the author.*

attempt. At the onset, I knew full well that a normal human brain cannot affect in any detail the bony configuration of the inner surface of the normal skull. The brain is in essence a bag of fluid, bathed within and without with fluid inside the skull. When I open the skull of a recently deceased adult and remove the brain, I must handle it very gently so as not to tear its intimate, transparent covering, the *pia mater*. If I do that, the brain substance oozes out through the torn area with the consistency of warm yogurt. If the brain is placed on a hard, flat surface, it flattens out to a marked degree. If the brain is left in an unembalmed cadaver at a warm room temperature, within a matter of hours the brain substance becomes watery in consistency due to digestive enzymes released in the dead cells. The process is known as autolysis. I describe all of this to show how the living or dead brain cannot produce an imprint of itself on the inner surface of the bony skull. An additional factor negating this occurrence is the intervening tough, smooth-walled *dura mater*, which forms an outer sheath, or meninx, to the brain and a periosteal sheath to the inner surface of the skull bone.

I have looked at the interior of hundreds of modern human skulls for evidence of the presence of the planum temporale of the brain during life, to no avail. Therefore, it was ludicrous for me to expect to find any evidence of it in the W-R Foundation and PA Museum fossil skull casts, and I didn't. Holloway (1974), an authority on endocranial casts, states, "The skull interiors of apes and men, both living and fossil, are notable for bearing only a minimal impression on the brain surface. In virtually all cases the only detailed features that can be traced on the endocranial cast of a higher primate are the paths of the meningeal blood vessels. Depending on the fossil's state of preservation, however, even a relatively featureless cast will reveal at least the general proportions and shape of the brain" (Figure 222). And yet, Ashpole (1984) reports that "The owner of skull KNM-1470, a very primitive man *(Homo habilis)* who lived two million years ago, had a well-developed capacity to talk." This fossil skull has no base, and the top and sides of the brain case were restored from numerous small pieces. A number of the pieces are missing (Walker and Leakey 1978). Ashpole (1984) goes on to state, "This important discovery by Dean Falk of the University of Puerto Rico is just one more item of information that shows the uniqueness of man's brain and its evolution. . . . But on the cast from skull KNM-1470 Dr. Falk found marks of convolutions and fissures like those of a human brain. Most importantly, the cast showed the area in the brain's left hemisphere which in man is responsible for language and speech. We know that the part of the brain which gives us our human awareness is closely associated with this language area."*

*The quote from Ashpole (1984) is reprinted by permission of the Gemini News Service, London, England.

Cerebral Cortex

Although I failed in my attempt to derive a clue from the fossil skulls as to when a uniquely human language came into being, I did find that they could give me a clue as to the evolution of human abstract or conceptual thought. The brains of mammals are unique in that the cerebral hemispheres contain a complicated outer layer of nerve or neuron cell bodies known as the cerebral cortex (Figure 218). There are over ten billion nerve cell bodies in the adult human cortex, which is only 1.5 to 4.5 millimeters in thickness. In all of the submammalian vertebrates, the cerebral hemispheres either do not contain a cortex or only a very rudimentary one, and their primary sensory input is concerned with olfaction or smell. During evolution, the cerebral hemispheric input was probably exclusively olfaction. The remainder of the brain, known as the stem, in these submammalian vertebrate forms (fishes, amphibians, reptiles, and birds) receives both general (touch, pressure, temperature, pain, and so on) and special sensory (vision, hearing, taste) input. All of the sensory input signals to the brainstem end on, or synapse with, groups of neuron cell bodies known as nuclei. The cells constituting these nuclei relay the signals to other neurons forming circuits in the brainstem that analyze and integrate the signals so that a proper reflex response for survival can result. Out of the olfactory cerebral hemispheres, or *archipallium,* the cerebral hemispheres with a cortex, or *neopallium,* evolved (Crelin 1974). As the mammals gradually evolved from the reptiles, there was a progressive cranial shift of sensory input connections and functions from the brainstem to the cerebral cortex, known as telencephalization. Thus, in all living mammals, the group of neuron cell bodies, or nuclei, constituting the two thalami of the brainstem are the major relay stations for the transmission of all of the sensory input to the cerebral cortex, both general and special, except olfaction or smell. There are specific regions in the cortex where thalamic projectional neurons transmit the sensory information. In a primitive mammal, the bulk of the cerebral cortex receives direct olfactory input from the olfactory bulb (Figure 219). The remainder of the cortex receives the other sensory information (general somatic, visual, acoustic or auditory, and taste). The nerve cells that interconnect the regions receiving the different types of sensory input information are known as association neurons. The nerve cells that cross from the cortex of one cerebral hemisphere to that of the other are known as commissural neurons. After the sensory input information is analyzed, integrated, and/or stored, a response or reaction may or may not follow. If there is to be response, association neurons that end on the neuron cell bodies that constitute the motor cortex transmit a signal to specific neurons there. These neurons of the motor cortex, known as upper motor neurons, in turn transmit signals to certain neurons at

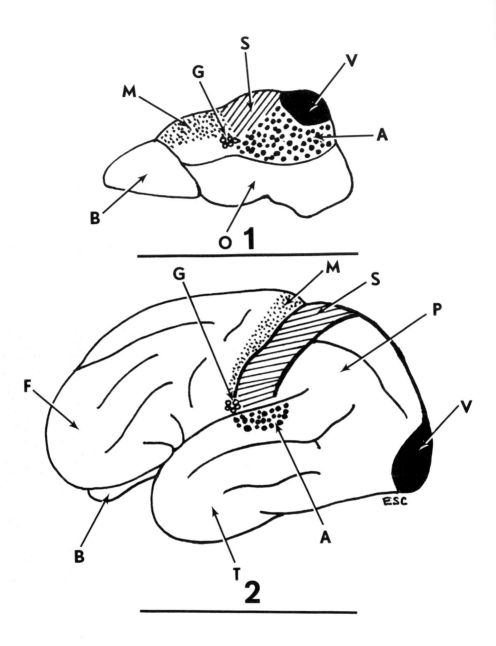

Figure 219. Diagrams of a left lateral view of the left cerebral hemisphere of (1) a primitive mammal and (2) an adult modern human being. A: acoustic or auditory cortex. B: olfactory bulb. F: frontal lobe. G: gustatory or taste cortex. M: motor cortex. O: olfactory lobe. P: parietal lobe. S: somatic general sensory cortex. T: temporal lobe. V: visual cortex.

specific levels of the brainstem and spinal cord. These latter neurons, known as lower motor neurons, transmit signals via their cell extensions, known as axons, to specific striated, skeletal, or voluntary muscles. The muscles that then contract may cause a finger to point to something, the face to change its expression, or the tongue to move and cause a specific speech sound to be made.

The human newborn mentality is a clean slate. There are present only a few instinctive abilities, too few to allow independent survival for a number of years. There is only a genetic potential to develop a mentality. The basic cortical neural connections are there at birth, but the many new and diverse neural connections and the necessary stimulus for many of them to become insulated, or myelinated, so they can function properly only come about by the inducement of sensory input signals to the cortex both from inside and outside of the body. The sensory input, whether it originates as light, sound, or pressure on the skin, ends up at the cortex via the thalamic neurons, which transmit signals to specific cortical neurons. If the stimulus was originally sound, the receptor neurons would be located in the acoustic cortex (Figure 219). Since a neuron is, in essence, a modified gland cell, the signal transmitted to a neuron in the acoustic cortex is the release of a neurohormone, or neurotransmitter, by a neuron in the thalamus. The neurotransmitter in turn stimulates the acoustic cortical neuron to release its neurohormone. All of the neuronal signals are the same. A neuron does not conduct electricity to cause another neuron to act; it releases an activating hormone at the interneuronal connection or synapse. The signals at neuron endings on voluntary muscle fibers, involuntary smooth muscles, or gland cells, causing a muscle to contract or not, or a gland to secrete or not, are also the release of neurohormones. Likewise, a sensory signal whether it be light, sound, or pressure on the skin, ultimately is reduced to the secretion of a hormone by a neuron. The increased intensity of any sensory input signal, be it a brighter light, a louder sound, or a stronger pressure, results in a more frequent sequence of secretion and removal of a neurohormone during a given period of time. It is a universal property of the nervous system that signaling is coded by information like this. It is like a Morse code with dots only (Eccles 1977).

The cerebral cortex develops through encoding into a unique human personality. It is the human being. Loss of just the cerebral cortex reduces what was a person to a vegetating organism incapable of having any thought or surviving on its own. Although the neural connections of the brainstem that are found in the submammalian vertebrates normally lacking a cerebral cortex may survive in a human being who has lost his or her cortical neurons, they do not function to allow the individual to survive on his or her own. Such a person is, in essence, permanently dead, since the cortical neurons are not replaced. In regards to the cortex, human beings are not all created equal. There is a genetic potential that is inherited. However, that potential can never be realized without the input of all forms of sensory information necessary to program the cortex during specific times during development from birth to maturity. This includes the complex form of sensory input known as education along with the good nutrition needed for the growth and myelination of the neurons.

Originally, the cerebral cortex of the primitive mammals was more of a supra-brainstem analyzer and integrator of sensory input information (Figure 219). This made for a less stereotyped (more intelligent?) response compared to the submammalian vertebrates with their more instinctive, predictable, inherent, reflex responses. As the mammalian brain evolved, more and more association neurons with more connections with other neurons were added. This, along with the increase in blood vessels and glial cells with the myelin sheaths they form, added to the bulk of the brain. More and more association neurons formed memory circuits. As association centers enlarged, the receptive areas for the various sensory inputs from the thalami maintained their close spatial relationship, except for the visual area (Figure 219). The association centers gave rise to the parietal, temporal, and frontal lobes, which enlarged to envelop the original olfactory region (Figure 219). In the primates, the originally dominant olfactory sense region of the primitive mammalian brain became reduced in relative size and importance. Those individual mammals with a genetic propensity to have the most modifiable or plastic cerebral cortical neurons, in regards to being programmed to respond to all forms of sensory input by establishing more complex interconnections, were most adaptable for competition and survival. As the association centers increased in size and function, more specific subcenters of the association centers became established, many of them predominantly in one hemisphere. This led to an increase in brain asymmetry. Vocal communication input always played a role in the development of the mammalian association centers. However, it wasn't until the modern type of vocal tract had evolved in early archaic *Homo sapiens* that all of the sounds of speech could be articulated with facility. Thus, whatever progress in vocal communication occurred in *Homo erectus* could now be advanced rapidly to develop a spoken language. This was a step in brain development beyond that which the modern apes ever achieved. So, it is reasonable to assume that the unique, dominant, cortical human language center began to be established by 500,000 years ago, usually in the left cerebral hemisphere. Language allows one to think conceptually or abstractly; it is quite plausible that a primitive ability to think this way is reflected in the engravings made by an early archaic *Homo sapiens* on an ox rib 200,000 years ago (Marshack 1975).

Cerebral Frontal Lobes

I assume that the planum temporale as a language center in one or the other cerebral hemisphere did not become a region of the brain large enough to be visible to the naked eye until conceptual thought had become quite highly sophisticated. Can the skull give an indication as to when that occurred? Yes, it can. Of the three association areas of each adult cerebral hemisphere—the parietal, temporal, and frontal—it is the relatively large size of the frontal lobe that is uniquely human. The frontal lobe is also the last to evolve to its maximum relative size. In adult, present-day apes and the australopithecine hominids, the frontal lobes are and were relatively small (Figures 220 and 221). The forehead is quite flat; therefore, the anterior cranial fossae of the skull that house the frontal lobes are relatively small. The anterior cranial fossae are further reduced in size by the elevation of the roof of the orbits that form the floors of the fossae (Figure 220). This creates a deep depression on the underside of each frontal lobe (Figure 221). In the *Homo erectus* skull, the frontal lobes, though absolutely larger compared to those of australopithecine hominids, were still relatively small compared to the rest of the *Homo erectus* brain (Figures 220 and 222). There was also a deep depression on the under surface of each frontal lobe. Again, in the early and recent archaic *Homo sapiens* and the Neanderthal skulls, the frontal lobes, though absolutely a little larger than those of *Homo erectus*, were still relatively small compared to the rest of the brain (Figure 220). Likewise, there was a deep depression on the underside of each frontal lobe due to the elevation of the floor of the anterior cranial fossae.

The fully modern *Homo sapiens* brain was present in Mount Carmel man between 35,000 to 45,000 years ago (Figures 209, 220). The frontal lobes are relatively large compared to the rest of the brain (Figures 223 and 224). According to Crosby, Humphrey, and Lauer (1962), "From developmental and phylogenetic standpoints, it is the differences in the frontal lobe that distinguish most especially the human from the subhuman brain. Its high degree of development in man is possible only through its rich and intricate interrelations with other association and projection areas, which are likewise elaborated through the ascending mammalian scale. The complicated projection and commissural connections of the prefrontal cortex lay the anatomical basis for the most complicated intellectual and emotional responses of which the individual is capable." A unified concept of frontal lobe function has yet to be established, except to say that its associative functions play a key role with associative areas of the cortex of the other parts of the brain (Adams and Victor 1977). The loss of the frontal lobe function in a human adult results in a multitude of permanent per-

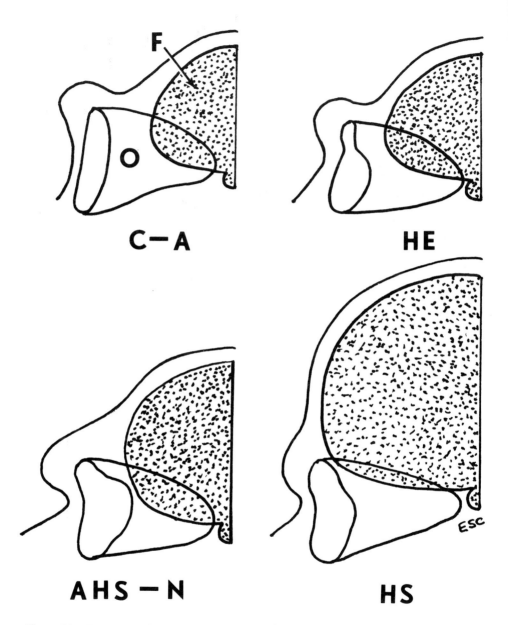

Figure 220. Diagrams showing the relative differences in the relationships and size of the frontal lobe of the left cerebral hemisphere of the brains (F) and the left orbit of the skulls (O) of an adult male chimpanzee (C) and an australopithecine adult hominid (A); a male adult *Homo erectus* hominid (HE); an archaic *Homo sapiens* (AHS) and a classic Neanderthal man (N); and a male adult modern *Homo sapiens* (HS).

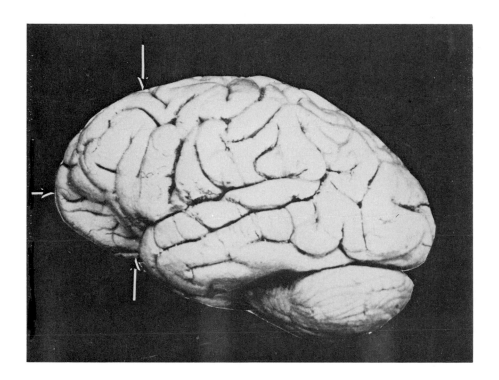

Figure 221. Left lateral view of an adult male chimpanzee brain. Arrows demarcate the extent of the frontal lobe of the left cerebral hemisphere.

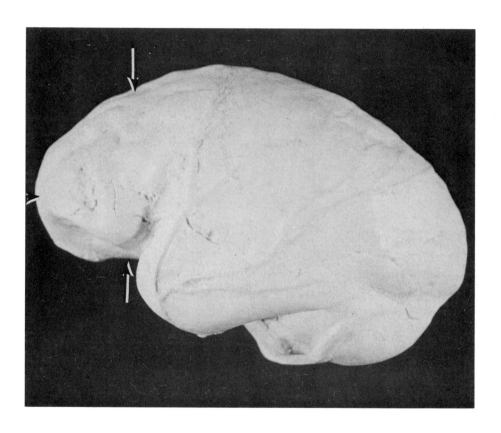

Figure 222. Left lateral view of the PA Museum endocranial cast of a reconstructed *Homo erectus* skull found at Trinil, Indonesia. Arrows demarcate the extent of the frontal lobe of the left cerebral hemisphere of the brain.

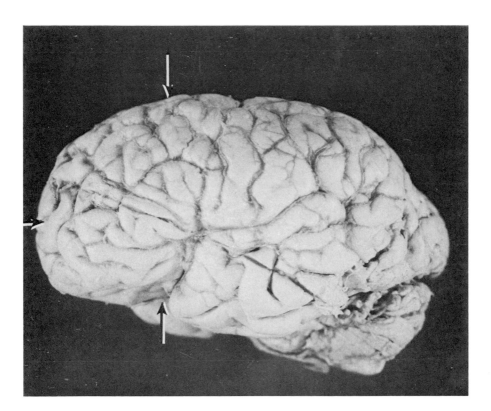

Figure 223. Left lateral view of the brain of a present day adult male human being. Arrows demarcate the extent of the frontal lobe of the left cerebral hemisphere. *Specimen prepared by the author.*

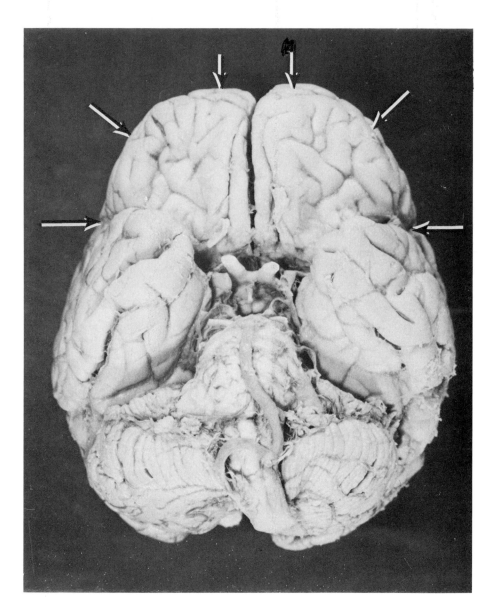

Figure 224. A view of the bottom of the brain of a present-day adult male human being shown in Figure 223. Arrows demarcate the extent of the frontal lobes of the cerebral hemispheres.

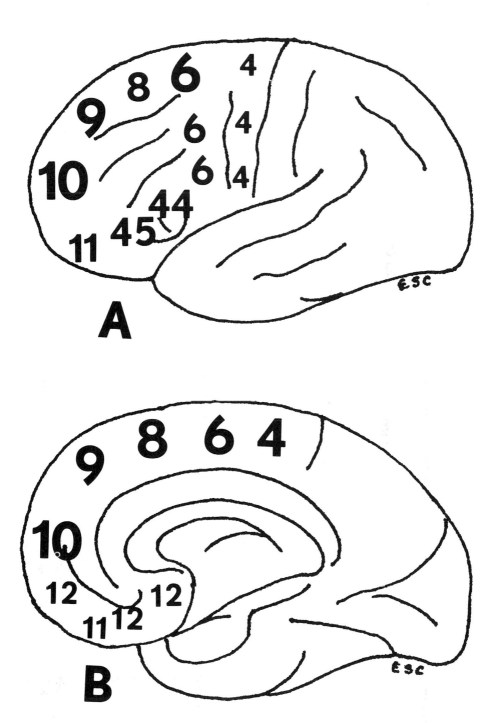

Figure 225. Cytoarchitectural map of the frontal lobes of the adult human cerebral cortex. A represents the lateral surface of each cerebral hemisphere. B represents the medial surface of each cerebral hemisphere. The numbers indicate the areas of Brodmann.

sonality changes, including an inability to plan ahead for future goals, a rigidity and concreteness of response, and deficits in abstract reasoning (Curtis, Jacobson, and Marcus 1972).

The frontal lobes have been mapped out into numbered areas according to the cytoarchitecture of the cortex (Curtis, Jacobson, and Marcus 1972). (See Figure 225.) Areas 9, 10, 11, and 12 are prefrontal areas concerned with emotional control and other aspects of cognitive functions. Area 6 is anterior to the area 4 motor cortex; therefore it is known as the premotor cortex. It functions as a motor association or elaboration area. Area 8 is often grouped with area 6. It functions in relation to head and eye turning. Areas 44 and 45 in the dominant hemisphere constitute Broca's center of motor speech and related functions of the lips, tongue, and so on. If areas 44 and 45 of both frontal lobes are affected, there is paralysis of articulation, phonation, and swallowing (Adams and Victor 1977). From the foregoing data on the evolution of the frontal lobes and the functional knowledge we now have of them, I think it is quite reasonable to assume that the increase in the size of the frontal lobes of the hominid brain during evolution reflected an increase in the ability to have a highly sophisticated language and conceptual or abstract thought. Although the modern vocal tract was present in early archaic *Homo sapiens* of 200,000 to 500,000 years ago, it was not until 50,000 years ago that recent archaic *Homo sapiens* lost their last vestiges of prominent brow ridges when a high vertical forehead appeared as a result of the enlargement of the frontal lobes of the cerebral hemispheres. The enlarged frontal lobes, in turn, reflected the ability to have a complex language and conceptual or abstract thought. When did the modern *Homo sapiens* begin to use a language and to think conceptually at a uniquely human, high level? The evidence points to the period of the fully modern *Homo sapiens* skulls that reflect the presence of relatively large-sized, cerebral frontal lobes about 50,000 years ago. These *Homo sapiens* tell us this was so—that they were thinkers, solvers of problems, and symbol makers—with their cave paintings in France and Spain, which date to about 40,000 years ago. These works of symbolic art were a human activity that required intelligence and a use of a language (Marshack 1975).

Summary of Vocal Tract Evolution

In summary, the hominid skulls tell us that, between 500,000 and one million years ago, the modern type of vocal tract evolved, allowing the hominids to make all of the sounds of articulate speech with facility. This phylogenetic event is recapitulated in the development of every present-day human being between birth and six years of age (Figure 226). Between 50,000 and 500,000 years ago, there was a gradual acquisition of a complex

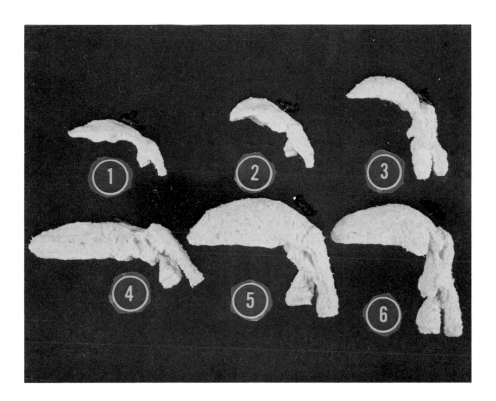

Figure 226. Silicone rubber casts of vocal tracts are arranged to show that the development or ontogeny of a present-day human individual's tract from birth to six years of age is a résumé of the evolution or phylogeny of the hominid tract, from 500,000 to one million years ago. (1): 2-year–old child. (2) 31/2-year–old child. (3) 6-year–old child. (4) australopithecine hominid. (5) *Homo erectus* hominid. (6) archaic *Homo sapiens* hominid.

spoken language that led to the development in the hominids of uniquely human conceptual thought. It was not until around 5,000 years ago that the first written language appeared, and it is associated with the rise of agriculture. The Sumerians, who lived in southern Mesopotamia, were the first people to reach a stage of primitive word writing, about 3,100 B.C. (Gelb 1963) (Figure 227). The Egyptians developed another important system of word-syllabic writing, known as hieroglyphic, about 3000 B.C. Egypt was one of the "cradlelands" of civilization, where the oldest civilizations arose (Coon 1963). The others were the Middle East, Indus Valley of India, and the Hwang Ho Valley of China. In my personal osteology collection, I have a skull from an adult female human being found 580 miles south of Cairo, Egypt, that is dated at between 4,500 and 5,500 years old (Figure 228). She was present when Egypt first developed as a nation and had acquired a written language. One thousand years later, her descendants were part of the beginning of a 500-year period known as the "age of pyramids," when the Egyptians achieved their greatest accomplishments in art and architecture (Wilson 1963).

Simpson (1968) states, "Above the individual level, language and related powers of symbolization make possible the acquisition, sharing, and preserving of knowledge far beyond what would be possible for any single individual. That is an indispensable element in all forms of human social organization and cultural accomplishment, even the most primitive." Dr. Simpson (1966) also states:

Language has become far more than a means of communication in man. It is also one of the principal (although far from the only) means of thought, memory, introspection, problem-solving and all other mental activities. The uniqueness and generality of human symbolization have given our mental activities not only a scope but also a quality far outside the range of other animals. It keeps us aware, to a greater extent than can otherwise be, of past and future, of the continuity of existence and its extension beyond what is immediately sensed. Along with other peculiarly human capacities, it is involved in what I consider the most important human characteristic from an ethical point of view: foresight. It is the capacity to predict the outcome of our own actions that makes us responsible for them and that therefore makes ethical judgment of them both possible and necessary.

Figure 227. Duplicate of a Sumerian clay tablet. It is a medical prescription that reads, "Pulverize pears and the roots of the manna plant: put in beer and let the man drink." *Presented to the author by the Branford, Connecticut, Intermediate school class, Team 5, March 1973.*

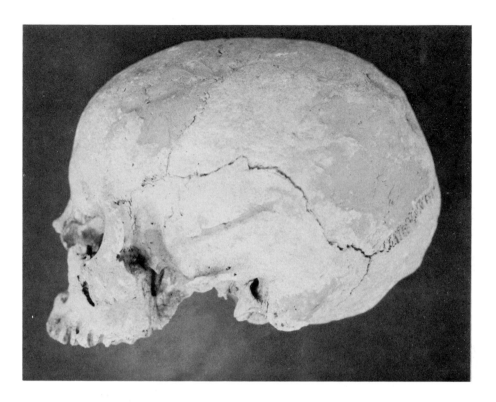

Figure 228. Left lateral view of the skull of an Egyptian female adult dated at 4,500 to 5,500 years old. *From the author's osteology collection.*

In conclusion, I find it fascinating to realize that, less than one million years ago, the first of the pure accidents, known as genetic mutations, began to occur in the human ancestors, resulting in the upper respiratory tract being able to produce a wide variety of sounds with rapidity and ease. These sounds became a spoken language, which led to a unique form of thinking. The human mind acquired the ability to reason, to know right from wrong. Yet when it is so critical to be reasonable, human beings have not only been unreasonable, but destructive to the extreme. The conceptual human mind has made astounding discoveries in pure science. The applications of these discoveries have no limits in their benefits to humankind. However, the applications to destroy have succeeded to the point where they can erase all of the beneficial ones in a moment. I purposely chose medical science to be my life's work because I wanted to dedicate myself to the benefit of humankind. However, the mental achievements of my parents' generation bequeathed to my generation a weapon capable of destroying all of humankind. My generation, in turn, bequeathed to the generation of my two sons and two daughters an arsenal of these destructive weapons, all set in readiness, by purposeful intent or by accident, to destroy all of the human beings on earth many times over. This precarious, insane condition can no longer be tolerated. If human beings don't act soon to defuse these destructive weapons completely and permanently, the marvelous, unique, conceptually thinking human brain will destroy itself in a moment—after existing for only a few hundred thousand years compared to the 150 million years the dinosaurs existed—by a device of its own creation! (Figure 229).

Figure 229. Nuclear bomb explosion. *Defense Department.*

Bibliography

Adams, R. D. and M. Victor. 1977. *Principles of neurology.* New York: McGraw-Hill Book Co.

Andrew, R. J. 1963. The origins and evolution of calls and facial expression of the primates. *Behavior* 20:1–109.

Ashpole, E. 1984. The thinking man's ape. Skull KNM-1470 reveals new evidence. Gemini News Service in *New Haven Advocate* (April 25): 9.

Basmajian, J. V. 1978. *Muscles alive.* 4th ed. Baltimore: Williams and Wilkins.

Bauer, H. R. 1984. A comparative study of common chimpanzee and human infant sounds. In *Selected papers of the ninth congress of the International Primatological Society, 1982.* Vol. 2; *Current perspectives in primate social dynamics.* New York: Van Nostrand-Rheingold.

Beckwith, J. B., J. S. Drage, and R. Naeye. 1978. When an infant dies "without cause." *Patient Care* 12:216–232.

Brace, L. 1968. Neanderthal. *Natural History* 77:38–46.

Brown, D. B. B., J. E. J. John, H. L. Owrid, and I. B. Taylor. 1974. Linguistic development. In *Scientific foundations of paediatrics*, eds. J. A. Davis and J. Dobbing. Philadelphia: W. B. Saunders Co.

Buhr, R. D. 1980. The emergence of vowels in an infant. *J. of Speech and Hearing Res.* 23: 73–94.

Campbell, B. G. 1970. *Human evolution.* Chicago: Aldine Publishing Co.

Clark, W. E. 1969. *The fossil evidence for human evolution.* Chicago: Univ. of Chicago Press.

Constable, G. 1973. *The Neanderthals.* Emergence of Man Series. New York: Time-Life Books.

Coon, C. S. 1963. Civilization. In *The world book encyclopedia.* Chicago: Field Enterprises Educational Corp.

Crelin, E. S. 1969. *Anatomy of the newborn: An atlas.* Philadelphia: Lea and Febiger.

Crelin, E. S. 1973a. *Functional anatomy of the newborn.* New Haven: Yale Univ. Press.

Crelin, E. S. 1973b. The Steinheim skull: A linguistic link. *Yale Scientific* 48: 10–14.

Crelin, E. S. 1974. Development of the nervous system. *Clinical Symposia, Ciba Pharmaceutical Co.* 26: 1–32.

Crelin, E. S. 1975. Development of the lower respiratory system. *Clinical Symposia, Ciba Pharmaceutical Co.* 27: 1–28.

Crelin, E. S. 1976. Development of the upper respiratory system. *Clinical Symposia, Ciba Pharmaceutical Co.* 28: 1–30.

Crelin, E. S. 1981. Development of the musculoskeletal system. *Clinical Symposia, Ciba Pharmaceutical Co.* 33: 1–36.

Crelin, E. S. and R. G. Sherz. 1978. Can the cause of SIDS be this simple? *Patient Care* 12:234-240.

Crosby, E. C., T. Humphrey, and E. W. Lauer. 1962. *Correlative anatomy of the nervous system.* New York: The Macmillan Co.

Curtis, B. A., S. Jacobson, and E. M. Marcus. 1972. *An introduction to the neurosciences.* Philadelphia: W. B. Saunders Co.

Darwin, E. 1803. *Temple of nature.* London: J. Johnson.

Day, M. H. 1965. *Guide to fossil man.* Cleveland: The World Publishing Co.

Day, R. L., E. S. Crelin, and A. B. Dubois. 1982. Choking: The Heimlich abdominal thrust vs back blows: An approach to measurement of inertial and aerodynamic forces. *Pediatrics* 70: 113–119.

Dover, G. 1982. Molecular drive: A cohesive mode of species evolution. *Nature* 299: 111–117.

Du Brul, E. L. 1958. *Evolution of the speech apparatus.* Springfield: C. C. Thomas.

Du Brul, E. L. 1976. Biomechanics of speech sounds. *Annals N.Y. Acad. Sci.* 280: 631–642.

Eccles, J. C. 1977. *The understanding of the brain.* New York: McGraw-Hill Book Co.

Fromkin, V. and R. Rodman. 1978. *Introduction to language.* New York: Holt, Rinehardt and Winston.

Galaburda, A. M., M. Le May, T. L. Kemper, and N. Geschwind. 1978. Right-left asymmetries in the brain. *Science* 199: 852–856.

Gelb, I. J. 1963. Writing. In *The world book encyclopedia.* Chicago: Field Enterprises Educational Corp.

Geschwind, N. and W. Levitsky. 1968. Human brain: Left-right asymmetries in temporal speech region. *Science* 161: 186–187.

Goodrich, E. S. 1958. *Studies on the structure and development of vertebrates.* New York: Dover Publications, Inc.

Gould, S. J. 1977. *Ontogeny and phylogeny.* Cambridge, Massachusetts: Harvard Univ. Press.

Guyton, A. C. 1976. *Textbook of medical physiology.* Philadelphia: W. B. Saunders Co.

Holloway, R. L. 1974. The casts of fossil hominid brains. *Sci. Amer.* 231: 106–115.

Howell, F. C., 1972. *Wenner-Gren Foundation/Casting Program.* New York: Wenner-Gren Foundation for Anthropological Research, Inc.

Huxley, T. H. 1863. *Evidence as to man's place in nature.* London: Williams and Norgate.

Hyman, L. H. 1946. *Comparative vertebrate anatomy.* Chicago: Univ. of Chicago Press.

Johanson, D. C. and A. E. Maitland. 1981. *The beginnings of mankind.* New York: Simon and Schuster.

Laitman, J. T., E. S. Crelin, and G. J. Conlogue. 1977. The function of the epiglottis in monkey and man. *Yale J. Biol. and Med.* 50: 43–48.

Laitman, J. T. and R. C. Heimbuch, 1984. The basicranium and upper respiratory system of African Homo erectus and early Homo sapiens. *Amer. J. Phy. Anthro.* 63: 180.

Laitman, J. T., R. C. Heimbuch, and E. S. Crelin. 1978. Developmental change in a basicranial line and its relationship to the upper respiratory system in living primates. *Amer. J. Anat.* 152: 467–482.

Laitman, J. T., R. C. Heimbuch, and E. S. Crelin. 1979. The basicranium of fossil hominids as an indicator of their upper respiratory systems. *Amer. J. Phy. Anthro.* 51: 15–34.

Le May, M. 1975. The language capability of Neanderthal man. *Amer. J. Phys. Anthrop.* 42:9–14.

Lewin, R. 1982. Adaptation can be a problem for evolutionists. *Science* 216: 1212–1213.

Lieberman, P. and E. S. Crelin. 1971. On the speech of Neanderthal man. *Linguistic Inquiry* 2: 203–222.

Lieberman, P., E. S. Crelin, and D. H. Klatt. 1972. Phonetic ability and related anatomy of the newborn and adult human, Neanderthal man, and the chimpanzee. *Amer. Anthropologist* 74: 287–307.

Marshack, A. 1975. Exploring the mind of Ice Age man. *Nat. Geographic* 147: 62–89.

Marx, J. L. 1983a. Autoimmunity in left-handers. *Science* 217: 141–144.

Marx, J. L. 1983b. The two sides of the brain. *Science* 220: 488–490.

Menyuk, P. 1972. *The development of speech.* New York: Bobbs-Merrill.

Negus, V. E. 1949. *The comparative anatomy and physiology of the larynx.* London: William Heinemann Medical Books Ltd.

Parker, T. J. and W. A. Haswell. 1921. *A text-book of zoology.* London: Macmillan and Co.

Perkell, J. A. 1969. *Physiology of speech production: Results and implications of a quantitative cineradiographic study.* Cambridge, Massachusetts: MIT Press.

Peterson, G. E. and H. L. Barney. 1952. Control methods used in a study of the vowels. *Acoust. Soc. Am.* 24: 175–184.

Pilbeam, D. 1970. *The evolution of man.* London: Thames and Hudson.

Pilbeam, D. 1984. The descent of hominoids and hominids. *Sci. Amer.* 250: 84–96.

Polgar, G. and G. P. Kong. 1965. The nasal resistance of newborn infants. *J. of Pediatrics* 67: 557–567.

Polgar G. and T. R. Weng. 1979. The functional development of the respiratory system. *Amer. Rev. of Respiratory Disease* 120: 625–695.

Potter, E. L. and J. M. Craig. 1976. *Pathology of the fetus and the infant.* Chicago: Year Book Medical Publishers, Inc.

Rensberger, B. 1984. Bones of our ancestors. *Science 84* 5: 28–39.

Russell, G. O. 1928. *The vowel.* Columbus, Ohio: Ohio State U. Press.

Sasaki, C. T., P. A. Levine, J. T. Laitman, and E. S. Crelin. 1977. Postnatal descent of the epiglottis in man. *Arch. Otolaryngol.* 103: 169–171.

Sicher, H. and E. L. Du Brul. 1975. *Oral anatomy.* St. Louis: C. V. Mosby Co.

Simpson, G. G. 1966. Naturalist ethics and the social sciences. *Amer. Psychologist* 21: 27–36.

Simpson, G. G. 1968. The biological nature of man. In *Perspective on human evolution 1*, eds. S. L. Washburn and P. C. Jay. New York: Holt, Rinehart and Winston.

Storer, T. I. 1943. *General zoology.* New York: McGraw-Hill Book Co.

Straus, W. L. and A. J. E. Cave. 1957. Pathology and posture of Neanderthal man. *Quart. Rev. Biol.* 32: 348–363.

Terrace, H. S., L. A. Petitto, R. L. Sanders, and T. G. Bever. 1979. Can an ape create a sentence? *Science* 206: 891–902.

Trinkaus, E. 1983. *The Shanidar Neandertals.* New York: Academic Press.

Virchow, R. 1872. Untersuchung des Neanderthal-Schädels. *Z. Ethn.,* 4: 157–165.

von Frisch, K. 1964. *Biology.* New York: Harper and Row.

Walker, A. and R. E. F. Leakey. 1978. The hominids of East Turkana. *Sci. Amer.* 239: 54–66.

Weinert, H. 1936. Der Urmenschenschäde von Steinheim. *Z. Morph. Anthr.* 35: 463–518.

White, E. and D. Brown. 1973. *The first men.* Emergence of Man Series. New York: Time-Life Books.

Williams, P. L. and R. Warwick. 1980. *Gray's anatomy.* Philadelphia: W. B. Saunders Co.

Wilson, J. A. 1963. *Ancient Egypt.* In *The world book encyclopedia.* Chicago: Field Enterprises Educational Corp.

Winther, L. K. 1978. Congenital choanal atresia. *Arch. Otolaryngol.* 104: 72–78.

Yerkes, R. M. and A. W. Yerkes. 1929. *The great apes.* New Haven: Yale Univ. Press.

Index

263